D1061734

THE POEMS OF ALEXANDER POPE
VOLUME III i
AN ESSAY ON MAN

I Sepia drawing by Pope, probably the original
of the frontispiece to the ESSAY ON MAN

See note on page XC

ALEXANDER POPE

AN ESSAY ON MAN

*

Edited by
MAYNARD MACK

METHUEN & CO. LTD. LONDON
YALE UNIVERSITY PRESS, NEW HAVEN

FIRST PUBLISHED IN THIS EDITION 1950
REPRINTED TWICE
REPRINTED 1970
PRINTED IN GREAT BRITAIN BY
JOHN DICKENS AND CO LTD, NORTHAMPTON
SBN 416 47730 5
1.4

PREFACE

IN its demands on the modern reader, the *Essay on Man* is both less difficult and more difficult than most of Pope's other works. It is less difficult because it requires almost no acquaintance with Augustan social backgrounds; more difficult because it presupposes sympathy with a tradition of thought and feeling that is not congenial to our day. Though it has increasingly been recognized that re-examinations of this tradition illuminate the structure and meaning of earlier works like *Paradise Lost*, it has not been recognized that they can illuminate as well the structure and meaning of the *Essay on Man*. On the contrary: such is the power of one bad custom to corrupt the world that criticism of the twentieth century has in the main accepted blandly from the nineteenth the notion that in this poem Pope was incapable of structure and could have had no meaning beyond the snapping up of trifles from the table of his philosopher and friend. The persistence of this opinion in face of the rising reputation of Pope's other works invites us now to apply the advice that Wordsworth gave his readers on a parallel occasion: "If an Author, by any single composition, has impressed us with respect for his talents, it is useful to consider this as affording a presumption that on other occasions where we have been displeased, he, nevertheless, may not have written ill or absurdly; and further, to give him so much credit for this one composition as may induce us to review what has displeased us with more care than we should otherwise have bestowed upon it."

This edition seeks to supply the materials for that review. The introduction is directed primarily toward interpretation of the *Essay on Man* as an artistic whole; the notes to the poem, primarily toward such questions as the meaning, provenience, and prevalence of the ideas out of which the poetic whole was made. In the notes I have therefore been liberal of analogues. Singly, these help to define more precisely than any amount of editorial summary can, the emotional shading, weight, and texture of individual ideas and their connections with each other; collectively, they supply a context within which the modern reader will find it helpful to read the poem, and by testifying to the wide acceptance of the

ideas Pope manipulates, both in his own and earlier times, point
our attention to fundamental aspects of the work: its strong tra-
ditionalism and its equally strong Augustan contemporaneity. As
for phrasal analogues, it has become the custom of Pope's editors to
preserve and augment them on the same grounds as those on which
the connoisseur of honey is said to refine his sense of flavour by
striving to detect the flower. Though I am not sure that this reasoning will justify indefinitely a procedure that is bound at last to bury
the poet's text, I have elected in this edition to follow established
practice. With few exceptions the analogues, both of phrase and
idea, come from writings Pope could have known while writing the
Essay on Man; they are not, however, presented here as sources but
as aids to explication.

In the preparation of this edition, I have had generous assistance
of many sorts. Among institutions, I wish to thank my own university for having, at an early period, helped me to carry on
investigations far from home through the Blanche Elizabeth
MacLeish Billings Memorial Award, and for having steadily supplied me clerical assistance (particularly that of R. L. Conway,
D. M. Knight, and H. K. Thompson), through the Committee on
Bursary Appointments, at the kindly instigation of that committee's administrative assistant, Mrs Ruth M. Rowe. The John Simon
Guggenheim Memorial Foundation for having permitted me to
spend a year as Fellow, free from academic duties. The Morgan,
Harvard, and New York Public Libraries for giving me access to
important manuscripts. And the staffs of the Yale, Harvard,
Huntington, University of Texas, Bodleian, and British Museum
libraries for all those little nameless unremembered acts that form
a portion of the good librarian's life. Among individuals, though
some are specified in the notes, I wish to thank also Mr K. A. Con-
nelly, Mr William Frost, Miss Katharine Hornbeak, Mr Helge
Kökeritz, Mr John Pope, Mr F. A. Pottle, Mr George Sherburn,
Mr René Wellek, and Mr W. K. Wimsatt, Jr, each of whom has
read the manuscript of this edition in whole or part and made it less
imperfect than it would otherwise have been; Mr R. H. Griffith,
who has helped me with encouragement and advice as well as the
hospitality of his Grotto; Mr J. T. Babb, Mr D. H. Clift, Mr J. G.
Kenefick, and Mr D. G. Wing, who have between them accorded
me more privileges in the Yale library than I should dare record;

Mr John Butt, who has been, as always, editorially heroic beyond
the call of duty; Mr C. B. Tinker, who directed my dissertation on
the intellectual background of Pope's *Essay* and to whom I have
other obligations that no acknowledgement can define; and my
wife, whose assistance I shall not specify, for Phaedrus' reason:
κοινὰ γὰρ τὰ τῶν φίλων.

Pope would have understood, and been able to express, the
nature of my debt to the two persons to whom this book is dedicated: my father and mother.

M. M.

1314 Davenport College,
   Yale University.
   1 *October* 1947.

CONTENTS

PLATES

INTRODUCTION

I: THE PLAN, COMPOSITION, AND EARLY HISTORY OF THE *ESSAY*

I

THE *Essay on Man* was originally designed as the introduction to a much larger work, in which Pope intended to include his four *Moral Essays* as well as some materials subsequently incorporated in other poems. According to a description given to Spence toward the close of Pope's life, the work as a whole would have been comprehended in four books. The first book was to contain the *Essay on Man* as we now have it; the second was to treat of "Knowledge and its limits"; the third, of "Government; both ecclesiastical and civil"; and the fourth, of "Morality; in eight or nine of the most concerning branches of it; four of which would have been the two extremes to each of the Cardinal Virtues".[1]

This extensive programme was not so well-defined in Pope's mind during the years when he was actually composing. We know from earlier entries in Spence that the plan changed rapidly on his hands. In May 1730, for example, he was still able to conceive of the introductory matter on man as complete in one epistle, whereas Spence's next entry, in November 1730, reveals that this matter was to occupy "four or five epistles", followed by "the rest . . . on moderation, or 'The Use of Things' ". "In the latter part", Spence adds, "each class may take up three epistles: one, for instance, against Avarice; another against Prodigality; and the third on the moderate use of Riches; and so of the rest."[2] By 1734 this scheme, or possibly another even more ambitious, is reported to be "drawn in . . . much narrower than it was at first". Pope's sketch of it, sent at this time to several friends, limits the design to the four published epistles of the *Essay on Man*, labelled Book I, together with nine miscellaneous titles labelled Book II. Three of the nine titles in Book II evidently cover the four *Moral*

---

1. Spence, p. 315. 2. *Ibid.*, pp. 16, 48.

Essays,[1] all of which had been completed by the beginning of 1734 and all but one published. The remaining six pieces are entitled "Of the Limits of Human Reason", "Of the Use of Wit", "Of the Principles and Use of Civil and Ecclesiastical Polity", "Of the Use of Education", and "A View of the Equality of Happiness in the several Conditions of Men".[2] Elements of the fifth of these (and probably of the first and second) found their way eventually into the fourth book of the *Dunciad*, as did elements of the fourth into the plan of the unwritten epic, *Brutus*,[3] and a few passages perhaps (e.g. the portrait of Vice that concludes the first dialogue of the *Epilogue to the Satires*) into the Horatian poems. For a time, in the collected editions of his *Works*, Pope kept alive a suggestion of his larger plan by describing the *Essay on Man* and the *Moral Essays* as the first and second books of *Ethic Epistles*. But this title was dropped from the *Moral Essays* after 1736, and the alteration may have been a tacit recognition that the *Essay on Man* formed a species of its own. Beyond this, the whole matter remains obscure.[4]

II

Almost as obscure is the history of the composition of the *Essay* itself. The conditions favourable to its conception were probably established with the return of Bolingbroke from exile in 1723-4, when it is evident from the correspondence that the poet was beginning to toy with ethical speculation and the statesman to assign himself the rôle of guide, philosopher, and friend.[5] The first explicit reference, however, occurs in a combined letter of Boling-

---

1. I take the title, "Of the Use of Riches", in Pope's list to cover *Moral Essays* III and IV, since it is the title Pope later gave to both of them. When first published, *Moral Essay* IV was called *Of Taste*, and later, *Of False Taste*.

2. Spence, pp. 136-7. 3. *Ibid.*, p. 315.

4. In 1740 Pope seems to have been seriously meditating a continuation of the *Essay*: see *Epilogue to the Satires*, II 255 (vol. IV, p. 327).

5. EC, VIII 393, 396, 402. Cf. also, *ibid.*, pp. 59, 63, and Spence, p. 11, for Pope's intention (as early as 1725) to write a set of maxims in opposition to La Rochefoucauld's. His treatment of the passions and virtues in *Essay* II may have been to some extent affected by this purpose.

broke and Pope to Swift (November 1729), in which Bolingbroke says that Pope is engaged on a fine scheme which will be in his hands "an original", and Pope explains that the work referred to is "a system of ethics in the Horatian way".[1] Though this doubtless refers to the ethic programme as a whole, there is every reason to believe that Pope began with the *Essay on Man*, which he always regarded as the introduction to the rest—"what a scale is to a book of maps".[2] From this time forward, and especially after May 1730, Pope seems to have been seriously intent upon the work. He wrote Swift in June (?) 1730 that he was "just now writing, or rather planning, a book, to make mankind look upon this life with comfort and pleasure, and put morality in good humour".[3] By December, hearing of Oxford's preoccupation with a "new room to lodge books in", he confides that he is "busy about a book to lodge in it" that will contain "nothing but such doctrines as are inoffensive, and consistent with the truest divinity and morality. What it will want in spirit, it will make up in truth."[4]

Except for some allusions in the following February and March which suggest that Pope has lately been engaged with Epistle II,[5] we learn nothing further till 2 August 1731. On that date Bolingbroke writes to Swift that three epistles are complete.

> The first epistle, which considers man, and the habitation of man, relatively to the whole system of universal being; the second, which considers him in his own habitation, in himself, and relatively to his particular system; and the third, which shows how
>
> A universal cause
> Works to one end, but works by various laws;
>
> how man, and beast, and vegetable are linked in a mutual dependency, parts necessary to each other, and necessary to the whole: how human societies were formed; from what spring true religion and true policy are derived; how God has made our greatest interest and our plainest duty indivisibly the same— these three epistles, I say, are finished. The fourth he is now

---

1. EC, vii 176, 175.   2. Spence, p. 16.
3. EC, vii 199.   4. *Ibid.*, viii 278.
5. *Ibid.*, vi 326; vii 221.

intent upon. It is a noble subject. He pleads the cause of God (I use Seneca's expression) against that famous charge which atheists in all ages have brought—the supposed unequal dispensations of Providence—a charge which I cannot heartily forgive your divines for admitting. You admit it indeed for an extreme good purpose, and you build on this admission the necessity of a future state of rewards and punishments. But what if you should find, that this future state will not account, in opposition to the atheist, for God's justice in the present state, which you give up? Would it not have been better to defend God's justice in this world, against these daring men, by irrefragable reasons, and to have rested the proof of the other point on revelation? I do not like concessions made against demonstration, repair or supply them how you will. The epistles I have mentioned will compose a first book; the plan of the second is settled. You will not understand by what I have said, that Pope will go so deep into the argument, or carry it so far as I have hinted.[1]

Whether having once embarked upon the fourth Epistle Pope carried it to a speedy conclusion in the autumn of 1731, it is impossible to say. At just about this time regular allusions to the *Moral Essays* begin to appear in the correspondence, and nothing further of consequence is said about the composition of the *Essay on Man* until the summer and autumn of 1733, when it is evident that Epistle IV is still undergoing revision,[2] though the other three epistles had been published for several months. The exceedingly rough state of Epistle IV in the only manuscript of the *Essay* which preserves it[3] suggests that Pope may have brought it to this condition while he was still "intent upon" it in 1731 and then diverted his energies to the poems of the second book until the time of publishing arrived. At this point, returning to the *Essay on Man*, he published and printed the first three epistles, and then, deterred by the amount of work still to be done on the fourth and distracted by the death of his mother (June 1733), continued to postpone publication until January 1734. Here again certainty recedes in speculation.

---

1. EC, VII 244–5.   2. *Ibid.*, IX 154–5; VI 345.
3. Morgan MS.

III

A good deal more is known about the publication and reception of the *Essay*. Pope was understandably proud of this work and wished it to have a fair hearing. The *Epistle to Burlington* (now usually known as the fourth *Moral Essay*) had failed of such a hearing because of a malicious interpretation by the dunces.[1] The only way to make sure that the new poem should receive a fairer trial—all the more necessary for a work dealing with matters on which doctors disagree—was to dissociate his name from the publication. Accordingly, between January 1733 and January 1734, Pope issued through his regular booksellers three important poems bearing his name,[2] and in the meantime, unacknowledged, through a different bookseller, the four epistles of the *Essay on Man*.[3] The result was all that could have been desired. According to letters from Pope to Caryll (8 and 20 March 1733), there was a time shortly after publication when the poem was believed to be the work of a divine, "Dr. Croxall, Dr. Secker, and some others" solemnly denying it.[4] During the same period, moreover, some of Pope's enemies committed themselves to praises which they could not decently retract. On 12 March, for instance, Leonard Welsted, one of Pope's oldest and bitterest enemies, wrote the unknown author that he had found the *Essay on Man* "what I had long despaired, a performance deserving the name of a poet . . . It is, indeed, above all commendation . . . If my testimony be of weight any where, you are sure to have it in the amplest manner."[5] This little comedy was intensified in April when a second victim of the *Dunciad*, Bezaleel Morrice, hailed the new poem unreservedly in verses prefixed to his own imitation of it called *An Essay on the*

---

1. See the introduction to the *Moral Essays* (vol. III, pt ii).

2. The third and first of the *Moral Essays*, and the Horatian imitation, *Sat.*, II i. *The Impertinent* (imitating Donne's fourth satire), without Pope's name, was also published during this period.

3. For exact dates, see the Note on the Text below, pp. 3–4.

4. EC, VI 339, 340. Pope is said by Warburton (Pope's *Works*, 1751, IV 34) to have told him that the *Essay* was at first assigned to Young, Desaguliers, Bolingbroke, and Paget.

5. "Testimonies of Authors", affixed to the *Dunciad* (in this edition, V 43).

Universe. [1] The uses of anonymity had proved sweet, [2] and, as Pope wrote to Jonathan Richardson on 2 March, a glut of praise was succeeding the glut of reproach raised by the *Epistle to Burlington.* "I am as much overpaid this way now as I was injured that way before." [3]

During the next five years the chorus of approbation continued strong. Besides an almost unbroken flow of pirated and authorized editions, of allusion and imitation in the work of other poets, there was a swift succession of enthusiastic notices. As poetry, the *Essay* was agreed to be throughout "equally beautiful and noble", "the sublimest piece . . . in its kind", and in fact a new species, joining the softnesses of verse with the strength and sense of prose. [4] As thought, it was admitted to be "calculated on the noblest basis of philosophy and divinity", to have the power of at once enlarging the understanding, convincing the judgment, and touching the heart, and to be proof that Pope had added to his titles of British Homer and Scourge of Dunces that of great "Columbus of the human mind". [5] In these early comments, there was scarcely a hint

1. Advertised for "this day", *Daily Journal*, 18 April.

2. So far as I have been able to discover, the poem was first publicly attributed to Pope in an epigram in the *Universal Spectator*, 23 June 1733, reprinted in the *Gentleman's Magazine*, III 319. Voltaire knew the authorship of the poem by 24 July (Audra, p. 77). Pope did not put his name to the *Essay* until it was included in editions of the *Works*, vol. II, in 1735.

3. EC, IX 503. Dr Alured Clarke wrote to Lady Sundon, 10 April 1733, that the first epistle of the unknown author's *Essay* was "the most extraordinary performance" he had met with: "I fancied for some time after I had read it, that the poet had enabled me to be a perfect hero in affliction, if it had come soon in my way to be put to the trial." The second epistle, which Clarke had also seen, he found "in many places . . . too hard to be understood" and "not comparable to the first, though it has many beauties" (*Memoirs of Viscountess Sundon*, 1847, II 195). I owe this passage to my friend John Butt.

4. The sources here cited are, in order, the *Weekly Miscellany*, 12 May 1733; the *Gentleman's Magazine*, IV (1734) 97; and the *London Evening-Post*, 17 March 1733. For a further account of "The Early Vogue of the *Essay on Man*" in England, see the unpublished Harvard dissertation of that title by R. W. Rogers, ch. I.

5. The sources are the same as those in the preceding note, with the substitution (for the third) of the *Weekly Amusement: Or, Universal Magazine*. Number I (Dublin, 1735), pp. 17–18. For similar opinions, as late as 1737, see *Common Sense; or, The Englishman's Journal* [10 Dec. 1737] *Being a Collection of Letters . . . Publish'd Weekly under that Title* (1738), I 311–12.

of the moral or theological criticism that was to dog the *Essay* later.[1]
Some of Pope's friends, we know, would have been happy to see
the poem extended to include explicit acknowledgment of revealed
religion,[2] and it is possible to uncover in the ephemera of the time
an occasional minor questioning of tendencies in the work—even,
one writer tells us, in a few "narrow minds", a disposition to discover "strong traces of Infidelity".[3] But the author of the only
philosophical discussion the poem received during these years (a
long riposte by a correspondent of the learned and serious *Present
State of the Republic of Letters*) found no quarrel with the argument of
the *Essay* beyond the objection that, omitting to give an adequate
notion of the strength of the infidel positions, the poet had affected
to conquer with too much ease.[4] Moreover, though the years
immediately following the *Essay's* appearance were one of the
fertile periods of hostile Popiana, a time when attacks on the poet's
person, manners, morals, and works sprang up like dragon's
teeth, the *Essay on Man* was left significantly alone.[5] So far as the

---

1. It is significant that the *Weekly Miscellany*, which contains very high
editorial praise of the *Essay* both as poetry and theology (cf. above), was an
extremely orthodox journal, designed, in its editor's words (16 June 1733), "to
guard the minds of the People against the Attempts of Infidels . . .: and to
defend the Church of England . . ."

2. See Warton, III 10–11.

3. The quotation is from a letter published in the *Daily Journal*, 31 July 1733.
For the minor questionings referred to, see the verses "On Some Authors
levelling the Rational Nature with the Brutal" (*Weekly Miscellany*, 11 Aug.
1733); a letter in defence of anthropocentrism against *Essay* I 131*ff* (*ibid.*,
28 Sept. 1734); a letter (signed "T.B." and probably by Pope's enemy Thomas
Burnet) interpreting *Essay*, I 86–90 and 279 as Lucretian repudiations of God
and Providence (*Prompter*, 2 Dec. 1735); and the preface to a poem by an
unidentified "Mr Bridges", *On Divine Wisdom and Providence* (1736), which says
that Pope's *Essay* is Christian in intent but capable of deistic misinterpretations.

4. *Op. cit.*, XIV (1734) 254*ff*. The writer is less interested in Pope's *Essay* than
in describing historical solutions of the problem of evil. His letter purports to be
the first of three, but the others were not published.

5. This is the more notable in that criticisms of Pope for having dedicated the
poem to a bad man (i.e. Bolingbroke) are not accompanied by criticisms of the
poem itself. See, for example, "To Mr. P–pe, upon his addressing his Poem to
that Pattern of exemplary Piety, Chastity, and Virtue, the Lord V—t B—e", in
the *Corn-Cutter's Journal*, 31 Dec. 1734.

B

English public was concerned, the evidence is overwhelming that it was not thought necessary (these are the words of one of the earliest admirers of the poem) "to give up to the Cause of Infidelity every Piece that is excellently written" or to turn its author loose with "the opprobrious name of *Infidel* or Deist tack'd to his tail".[1]

The origins of a more jaundiced attitude must be looked for on the Continent. There, from 1733, and especially from 1736, when Silhouette's French prose translation was published and ran through four editions in a year, the *Essay on Man* enjoyed an extraordinary vogue.[2] Silhouette's preface in 1736 indicates that some doubts had been expressed concerning the orthodoxy of the poem: "On a prétendu qu'il y avoit du Spinosisme dans cet essai sur l'homme." But he reminds his readers that only certain expressions have been censured in this way and these only by separating them from the whole work. "Epiloguer de la sorte, c'est agir contre les règles d'une saine critique; & même d'ailleurs on eut dû considérer qu'on ne doit pas interpréter rigoureusement et théologiquement des saillies & des essorts poétiques." The Jesuit Tournemine, Silhouette adds—"un des premiers hommes de lettres qu'il y ait en France, & reconnu pour juge compétent, soit comme théologien ou comme philosophe"—had assured him after reading the poem that it could injure none but minds already corrupted; an upright spirit would draw from it sound nourishment, enlarged views, and useful maxims. "Je suis charmé de Pope," Tournemine had said; "c'est un philosophe profond & un poète vraîment sublime."[3]

This view of the *Essay*, though confirmed in the same year by the *Mémoires de Trévoux*, an official organ of the Jesuits, was suddenly retracted in 1737 and the poem condemned in the name of both morality and religion.[4] For this reversal the translation by Du Resnel, published in the interim, was apparently responsible. Du

---

1. *Daily Journal*, 31 July 1733.

2. Audra, pp. 89–92. Cf. also the news item in the *London Evening-Post*, 15–17 Jan. 1736: "Mr. Pope's Essay on Man, having been translated into French, is in great Esteem at Paris, and in the Hands of all the polite People there."

3. Pp. xxxi–xxxiii. I use the edition numbered 21 in Audra's bibliography (*Les Traductions françaises de Pope*, Paris, 1931).

4. Audra, p. 92.

Resnel's intention, apart from converting Pope's verses into French ones, was to supply the poem with more of the system and method cherished by the Latin mind.[1] Consequently, a multitude of passages in the poem had to be deleted, others added, still others transposed, expanded, or contracted, and the whole so altered as to become substantially unrecognizable as Pope's.[2] Even the title was changed to imply something especially ambitious: having decided on a reimpression of his translation of the *Essay on Criticism* Du Resnel issued the two together in one volume as *Les Principes de la Morale et du Goût.*

Meantime, the French translations of the poem had penetrated to Lausanne, where a Swiss professor named J. P. de Crousaz seized the occasion "de pourfendre Leibniz à travers Pope".[3] In 1737 Crousaz published his *Examen de l'Essai de M. Pope sur l'Homme,* based on Silhouette's version, and the next year, having been informed that Silhouette was unfaithful to Pope's thought, a *Commentaire sur la traduction en vers . . . de l'Essai . . . sur l'Homme,* based on Du Resnel. A less happy confrontation of minds and methods could hardly have been imagined. On the one hand, a "mathématicien, philosophe et pédagogue, . . . terriblement affairé et pédant",[4] understanding no English and less interested in poetry than in infidelity; on the other hand, the elusive couplets of the *Essay on Man,* some perhaps deliberately ambiguous, many containing terms and concepts which are equivocal in the very nature of language, many others requiring for interpretation a context of intellectual and literary history that Crousaz did not choose to supply, and the whole problem further complicated for a foreign writer by translations each differing from the original. The result was that Crousaz devoted a substantial part of his labours to the criticism of expressions that had no existence in the English poem and of propositions which his victim would have

---

1. See the *Discours préliminaire* to his translation.

2. Despite considerable omissions, Du Resnel stretched Pope's 1300 lines to 2,000. On his distortions of Pope's sense, see Johnson's notes to his translation of the *Commentaire* of Crousaz, 1739 (reissued, 1742).

3. Audra, p. 92.

4. *Ibid.*

found as laughable as he.[1] What remains when all irrelevancies are stripped away is a tedious, if successful, demonstration that the poem shows logical antinomies of the sort that poets habitually use for purposes of their own, and that the principle of plenitude on which its theodicy is partly based is capable of fatalistic consequences—if carried farther than Pope carries it.

Despite its obvious faults, the attack was damaging to Pope. Crousaz's prestige as a theologian and logician, and his disingenuous method, which carefully associated the doctrines of the *Essay* with Leibnizian philosophy and Spinozism while professing to separate it from them,[2] were nicely calculated to alarm the orthodox and rouse the poet's enemies. On 22 and 25 November 1738, Curll, whose minions had previously left the poem unassailed,[3] advertised a translation of the *Commentaire*, with the observation that it was "a critical Satire upon the *Essay on Man*", to which Mr Pope would be in honour bound to make reply, and promised to "pursue M. Crousaz in his Attacks upon Mr. Pope regularly".[4] Simultaneously, on the 23rd, a translation of Crousaz's other work,

1. Johnson calls attention to many of these in the notes referred to above. An especially fine example occurs at *Essay*, III 225–6. Here Pope says that primitive men came to knowledge of God by tracing backward from their earthly fathers; Du Resnel translates this to mean that they invented portrait painting to perpetuate their fathers' likenesses; Crousaz (adding the idea of worship) censures Pope for saying that men paid their fathers' likenesses divine honours.

2. Crousaz was also disingenuous in another way. As Johnson observes in the notes cited, Crousaz repeatedly criticizes Pope for doctrines that he knew (through Silhouette's more accurate translation) were not contained in Pope's work.

3. All that one of them could find to say of the *Essay on Man* in 1735, for instance, was that it contained obscurities, being "otherwise most excellent" *The Poet finish'd in Prose* (1735), p. 11.

4. *Daily Advertiser.* The translation was by Charles Forman, whose name appears in the *Daily Advertiser* announcement on the 27th. The translation included only Crousaz's commentary on Epistle I (even this in a condensed version) and was itself friendly to Pope. Curll, however, prefaced it with a triumphantly sardonic challenge. The information in the last two sentences I owe to Audra, pp. 93–4, and G. A. Bonnard, "Note on the English Translations of Crousaz' Two Books on Pope's *Essay on Man*", in *Recueil de Travaux* [by the Faculté des Lettres] *à l'occasion du quatrième centenaire de la fondation de l'Universite* [de Lausanne], Lausanne, 1937, pp. 175–84.

the *Examen*, was published by A. Dodd, containing, the advertisement said, "a Succinct View of the System of the Fatalists, and a
Confutation of their Opinions; ... and an Enquiry what View Mr.
Pope might have in touching upon the Leibnitzian Philosophy".[1]
Advertisements of this kind, continuing throughout the autumn
and winter, were followed on 13 March 1739 by the announcement
of Ayre's *Truth. A counterpart to Mr. Pope's Essay on Man. Epistle the
First*; and, on 13 June, by the announcement of "*Truth . . . Epistle
the Second*, opposing his [Pope's] Opinions of Man as an Individual".[2] It is little wonder that Pope took alarm and gratefully
accepted the refutation of Crousaz which Warburton had been
publishing for several months, quite unsolicited, in the *History of
the Works of the Learned*.[3]

Warburton's vindication of the *Essay* is usually dismissed without
sufficient reason. It strains passages in the poem toward a literally
pietistic interpretation that they will not bear, and claims for it a
ratiocinative rigour that is impossible in poetry and probably
undesirable. Yet the work had two considerable merits. It gave an
analysis of the argument far more consonant than Crousaz's with
any meaning we may suppose the poet to have had, and it recog-

---

1. *Daily Advertiser*. This was Elizabeth Carter's translation, announced on
8 Sept. (*ibid.*) as in the press: Bonnard (*op. cit.*, p. 176) states erroneously that
her translation did not appear till 1739. The wording of the 23 November
advertisement was apparently, as Bonnard shows, suggested by Johnson.
    The same advertisement enables one to date more accurately than hitherto
the publication of Johnson's translation of the *Commentaire*. This book usually
appears with a 1742 title-page and a Cave imprint, but there is at least one copy
(in the Yale library) with a 1739 title and a Dodd imprint (cf. A. T. Hazen,
"Crousaz on Pope", *Times Lit. Suppl.*, 2 Nov. 1935, p. 704). According to the
Daily Advertiser, this translation was also (on 23 November 1738) available at
Dodd's shop. The announcement does not mention Johnson's name, but its
description of the book is unmistakably a description of Johnson's work.

2. *Daily Advertiser*. On 3 May appeared also the third edition of Bridges's *On
Divine Wisdom and Providence*, cited above, p. xvii, *n.* 3.

3. Dec., Jan., Feb., March, April: iv (1738) 425*ff*, v (1739) 56*ff*, 89*ff*, 159*ff*,
330*ff*. The five letters were collected, with the addition of a sixth, and published
as *A Vindication of Mr. Pope's Essay on Man*, 15 Nov. 1739. A seventh letter
appeared separately, 13 June 1740, and a final revision incorporating all the
letters, 10 Aug. 1742. These dates are from the *Daily Advertiser* and the *London
Evening-Post*.

nized that the principle of plenitude, however it might have been treated in the systems of Leibniz and Spinoza, had enjoyed a long untainted history among orthodox theologians. "As to the Truth of the Notion," Warburton argued, "that is another Question; and how far it clears up the very difficult controversy about the Origin of Evil, that is still *another*. . . . However, what may justify Mr. *Pope* in embracing this *Platonic* notion, is, that it has been received by the most celebrated and orthodox *Fathers* and *Divines* of the ancient and modern Church." [1]

Sheltered thereafter by Warburton, the principles of the *Essay* met but one more attack before Pope's death. This too came from across the Channel, where, in a pious poem of 1742, Louis Racine assailed Pope as an "abstrait Raisonneur, qui . . . Dans son flegme Anglican répondra *Tout est bien*", and the *Essay* as a nursery of heretical opinions, "qui sont devenus si communs parmi nous depuis la lecture de son *Essai sur l'homme*, dont les principes n'étant pas assez développés pour nous, sont cause que plusieurs personnes croient y trouver un système qui n'est peut-être pas celui de l'Auteur". [2] The kindly suggestion of the last sentence opened the way to an exchange of letters between Pope's friend Ramsay and Racine, and eventually between Racine and Pope. Pope, for his part, declared flatly that his poem was misrepresented by the translation of Du Resnel in which Racine had read it (sending a copy of Warburton's *Vindication* in proof of this), and that his opinions far from being "those of Spinoza, or even of Leibnitz" were "on the contrary conformable to those of Mons. Pascal & Mons. Fenelon: the latter of whom I would most readily imitate, in submitting all my Opinions to the Decision of the Church". [3]

---

1. *Vindication . . . In Six Letters* (2nd ed., 1740), pp. 17–18.

2. *La Religion* (7th ed., 1756), pp. 43, 233. The first quotation is from *La Religion* (Chant II 93–4); the second, from an *Avertissement* to another poem in the same volume.

3. For a facsimile of Pope's letter, see Audra, frontispiece. Racine published the letter in English in the seventh edition of *La Religion* (pp. 260–61), after Voltaire had expressed doubt of its existence. Racine also commented (p. 266) that though Pope's intentions were Christian, the poem, even in its original English, still seemed to him deistically inclined.

II: THE *ESSAY* AND "PHILOSOPHY"

I

The Crousaz-Warburton and Pope-Racine exchanges illustrate three kinds of question with which discussion of the *Essay*, down to our own day, has been preponderantly concerned. These are the question about Pope's intentions—was his poem deliberately heterodox? the question about the derivation of his doctrines— did they come from Leibniz or from others? and the question about the worth and meaning of the *Essay* as philosophy—is it sound or unsound, logical or inconsistent, shallow or something more? The persistence of these questions in the historical record necessitates pausing on them briefly before going on to another question of more importance that has been less often asked: for what poetic purpose did Pope use—in what kind of poetic world and in the service of what poetic insights—the materials that philosophy supplied?

Evidence on the subject of Pope's intentions is as conflicting as perhaps the intentions were themselves. All that we know of Pope before or after the writing of the *Essay* suggests that he was a man of religious temper, in the main a practising Christian if not an especially devout one, perhaps more warmly interested by the ethics of Christianity than by the dogmas whose divisive consequences he could see in the society around him as well as in his own incapacitated political lot. We know too that he had written for the poem an address to the Saviour modelled on Lucretius's address to Epicurus, which was eventually omitted on the advice of his friend George Berkeley.[1] This address must have said, one supposes, something roughly analogous to what Lucretius says of the philosopher, that he alone had looked into the heart of the universal mystery and brought back light to men. How far it may have committed Pope to specific doctrines like the Incarnation cannot be guessed, but it can hardly have been Socinian or Pope would not have shown it to Berkeley; nor would Pope, astute judge of audiences that he was, have vented an opinion certain to bring the English public about his ears. To this evidence must be added

1. Spence, p. 142.

the fact that Pope set down on the earliest surviving manuscript of the *Essay*, "Thy will be done, in Earth as it is in Heaven."[1] This superscription can have had no ulterior motive (the manuscript is much too rough to have circulated among Pope's acquaintance), and while it indicates nothing precise about Pope's Christianity, it is not the work of a man who is taking part in a conspiracy, as Elwin presumed, to write down the Christian religion.[2]

On the other hand, there is evidence that during the period when the *Essay* was being composed Pope had leanings toward the fashionable "natural" religion of the day. Bolingbroke's influence would have pressed him in this direction, and some of Pope's friends and acquaintances have left statements suggesting that at this time he was a professing deist.[3] What such testimony amounts to in an age when "deism" could cover anything from outright rejection of Christianity to moderate scepticism about the literal veracity of the Old Testament (the term was applied to many clergymen and to at least one archbishop)[4] is difficult to say. Pope was not the man to unburden the inmost convictions of his heart, even if Augustan conversational decorum had encouraged it (probably it would have encouraged it still less in a Roman Catholic); he liked too well, as his poems tell us, to house with both Whig and Tory, Locke and Montaigne, Aristippus and St Paul.

The only piece of evidence that bears directly on Pope's intentions *in the Essay* is the comment of the younger Richardson that the poet never dreamed of interpreting his poem as Warburton was

---

1. Morgan MS., Epistle 1, folio 6. The sentence is apparently a gloss on the final line of Epistle 1, to which it is attached as a footnote. It is, of course, impossible to date, but there seems no reason to suppose that it was written later than the Epistle.

2. This is Pattison's very exact description of Elwin's editorial attitude. See the former's *Essays* (1889), II 384.

3. Cf. Lyttelton's testimony, in Warton, III 10; and Chesterfield's in his *Works* (ed. Mahon, 1845), II 445.

4. The archbishop was Tillotson, whom, according to the deist Anthony Collins, "all English Free-Thinkers own as their Head" (*Discourse of Free-Thinking*, 1713, p. 171). On the general English blurring of orthodoxy and deism in this period, see Leslie Stephen's *English Thought in the Eighteenth Century*, I 74ff, and E. C. Mossner's detailed study, *Bishop Butler and the Age of Reason* (1936), chs. I, II, V.

to do until "the general alarm of its fatalism, and deistical tendency" broke out—"of which, however, we talked with him (my
father and I) frequently at *Twickenham*, without his appearing to
understand it otherwise, or ever thinking to alter those passages,
which we suggested as what might seem the most exceptionable".[1]
This statement can be taken in several ways. If it means, as Elwin
believed, that Pope intended and approved a generally fatalistic,
deistic, and anti-Christian meaning in the *Essay*, it is nonsense,
since it conflicts with everything we know about the author and
the poem. If it means, as Warton thought, that Pope, though not
interested in a general attack, intended that certain passages be
unmistakably heterodox, it conflicts with the strong desire evinced
by Pope in letters to his friend Caryll to reconcile the poem with
Christian teaching.[2] Richardson's statement may, in fact, mean no
more than that like other poets Pope proved enigmatic when
queried about his meanings, solemnly refusing to combat interpre-
tations of the parts which he did not see how any careful reader of
the *Essay* in its entirety could make—and with respect at least to
fatalism, he would have been absolutely right.

On the whole, the most eligible conclusion appears to be that
in 1733 Pope may have wished to have it both ways: that he had
sympathies with the liberal theology which was stirring the great
religious controversy of his time, and sympathies with an older
view; that he wanted to be enlightened and tell the truth as he
conceived it, without wanting to be un-Christian or start a fight.
The poem, we know, satisfied neither Bolingbroke nor Crousaz.[3]

---

1. *Richardsoniana* (1776), p. 265.

2. See the letters of 23 Oct. 1733 and 1 Jan. 1734 (EC, VI 345–7).

3. Though Bolingbroke never flatly expresses dissatisfaction, he hints frequently that Pope will not carry the argument to its proper conclusions. See the
last sentence of his letter to Swift (above, p. xiv); the statement in his introductory letter to his philosophical writings (*Works*, 1809, V 73) that Pope's caution
will screen his handling of philosophy "against any direct charge of hetero-
doxy"; and his often-quoted remark, reported by Warburton (*Works*, 1811, XII
335) that Pope did not "understand" the implications of his own principles. As
John Laird has lately pointed out (*Philosophical Incursions into English Literature*,
1946, p. 37), this remark need not have been malicious. It is more likely to have
been testimony of a fundamental divergence between the real convictions and
interests of the two men, which Bolingbroke perhaps grasped more clearly than
Pope. Thus Bolingbroke acknowledged in the "Advertisement" preceding his

It did not unequivocally embrace explicit Christian doctrines, but
it did not unequivocally oppose them; and it kept a number of
them present by implication just beneath the text. It resembles in
that respect those collections of eighteenth-century sermons in
which a first series in defence of religion on natural grounds is
combined with a second series in defence of revelation. Pope has
telescoped the two and submerged the second, but the duality of
his poem expresses the duality of his age, and in all likelihood,
during the time when Bolingbroke's ascendancy was greatest, of
his mind. Five or six years later, when, as we have seen, circumstances forced him to decide which element in the *Essay* he was
prepared to underwrite, he decided to prefer the element stressed
by Warburton. This decision is hardly open to the ridicule it has
received. What had to count with Pope at that time was not
whether his thought had ever enclosed a dark and a bright angel,
but which one he was now going, volitionally, to embrace.

II

The problem of Pope's intentions blurred easily for the eighteenth century into the problem of his sources, since it was usually
assumed that the meaning of the *Essay* must be approximately
equivalent to that of the writers who were supposed to have
influenced it. On the Continent, as has been noticed, Leibniz was
the favourite source, with the result that the poem there became
the battlefield for a struggle between pro- and anti-Leibnizians
which had very little to do with its actual contents.[1] In England,
after 1754, the favoured source was Bolingbroke, among whose
Letters, or Essays address'd to Alexander Pope (published posthumously
in that year) was a series of *Fragments or Minutes of Essays*, which
revealed a number of parallels of phrasing and idea with the *Essay*

Fragments or Minutes (see below, p. xxix, *n.* 3) that the friends (i.e. Pope) for
whom he is writing these pieces will find "their own opinions and prejudices . . .
frequently contradictéd" (*Works*, 1809, VII 278); and in the introductory letter
referred to above, he puts into Pope's mouth the demurrer "that if any doubts
arise in our minds concerning religion, we must have recourse to [the priest]".
Op. cit., V 103.

1. The rôle of the *Essay* in this struggle is illuminated by R. W. Rogers in the
Harvard dissertation (ch. II) referred to above, p. xvi, *n.* 4.

on Man.[1] To these two names, Warton and later critics added Shaftesbury, and Archbishop William King, whose *De Origine Mali*, published in 1701 and translated with copious annotations in 1731,[2] was probably the most influential of eighteenth-century theodicies in prose.[3]

Of these writers, Leibniz is the one most readily dismissed. The problem of his influence on Pope has been canvassed elsewhere with negative results.[4] Pope said himself that he had never read the *Théodicée*.[5] The *Essay* contains nothing not derivable from other sources. And though it is possible that some of Leibniz's thought reached Pope by way of Bolingbroke or Shaftesbury, what filtered into the poem, if anything, was precisely what was not characteristically Leibnizian.

Shaftesbury and King have better claims. Pope had read Shaftesbury, at any rate *The Moralists*, to which he alludes with a smile in the fourth book of the *Dunciad*. That section of the *Characteristics*, when placed beside the *Essay* without reference either to the general climate of the age or other literature early and late, might lead to the judgment made by Herder (and many since)[6]

---

1. The *Letters, or Essays*, as a whole, includes four long essays besides the shorter *Fragments or Minutes*; but only the latter have been seriously brought forward as Pope's sources.

2. *An Essay on the Origin of Evil*, ed. and tr. Edmund Law. The book, though dated 1731, was published in November 1730 (*Monthly Chronicle*, III 227), and read by John Wesley before 11 December (see his *Journal*, ed. Curnock, 1909–16, VIII 272–5).

3. The influence of Shaftesbury is noticed (and exaggerated) as early as 1734, by the correspondent of the *Present State of the Republic of Letters* (above, p. xvii). King's editor, Law, called attention to the influence of King in the 1781 edition of King's work—as Moses Mendelssohn had before in the *Anhang* to *Pope ein Metaphysiker!* (1755).

4. By C. A. Moore, "Did Leibniz Influence Pope's *Essay*?" in *Journ. Engl. and Germ. Philol.*, XVI (1917) 84–102.

5. Pope to Warburton, 2 Feb. 1739. First published by A. W. Evans in *Warburton and the Warburtonians* (1932), p. 79.

6. Herder's *Adrastea*, Erst. Band, Zw. Stück (1801), in *Werke*, ed. Suphan (Berlin, 1877–1913), XXIII 154. (I am indebted to my colleague Heinz Bluhm for help in verifying this reference.) Voltaire had spoken to the same effect in the 1756 revision of the *Lettres Philosophiques* (Lettre 22), and the opinion has been passed down from one student of Shaftesbury to the next.

that without Shaftesbury Pope could hardly have written the best verses in his poem. But the judgment was premature. Some of the larger concepts of the poem, like the idea of universal harmony, the duty of the individual to accord with the whole, the serenity of virtue as pictured in Epistle IV, may be owing to Shaftesbury. But they may equally well be owing to the Stoic and Platonic writers— Cicero, Seneca, Aurelius, Epictetus, Simplicius,[1] etc.—whom every educated neo-classicist knew. Of the aesthetic intuitionism which we think of to-day as Shaftesbury's particular contribution to ethics, there is not a trace in the *Essay on Man*; and of the view of the human situation that Pope presents in Epistle II, there is hardly more than a trace in the *Characteristics*. The sensible conclusion about Shaftesbury is that Pope may have adopted a good deal from him, need not have adopted anything, and probably did adopt, here and there, an illustration.[2]

The case for King must be qualified with the same reservations. As a formal theodicy trying to account rationally for the presence of evils in a world made by a good Creator, the *De Origine Mali* inevitably contains a good deal that the *Essay on Man* also contains. It makes emphatic use of the principle of plenitude, with its usual corollaries that nothing created can be perfect (cf. Pope's "and what created perfect?"), but that everything is as perfect as its rank and the ends assigned it demand (cf. Pope's "man's as perfect as he ought"). It draws out the inference that in a full world man's dislocating himself from his appropriate rank might lead to similar dislocations above and below (Pope's "on superior powers Were we

---

1. Simplicius, the least familiar of these writers, had been made easily available in George Stanhope's translation, *Epictetus His Morals With Simplicius His Comment*, 1694 (4th ed., 1721).

2. C. A. Moore gives an excellent account in "Shaftesbury and the Ethical Poets in England" (*Publ. Mod. Lang. Assoc.*, XXXI (1916) 264–325) of the elements in Shaftesbury which most appealed to Augustan poets (including Pope); but he over-stresses the direct influence of Shaftesbury's writings, which, as R. S. Crane has long insisted (*Philol. Quart.*, XI (1932) 204–6; *Journ. Engl. Lit. Hist.*, I (1934) 205–30), are less correctly to be regarded as "sources" of the literature of the age than as parallel phenomena, stemming from a common tradition. For other work corrective of Moore's position, but tending to exaggerate a different one, see the studies of Newtonianism by Herbert Drennon, listed in A. D. McKillop's *The Background of Thomson's Seasons* (1942), p. 6, *n.* 22. McKillop's own treatment of the problem is very sound.

to press, inferior might on ours"); it stresses the conviction that God so orders the evil men do as to turn it to ultimate good (Pope, Epistle II 237–40); it supplies a justification of man's living by the deaths of other animals that Pope refers to a considerably larger context in Epistle III; and it contains a variety of major and minor parallels with Pope's argument that makes the poet's use of it practically certain.[1] Here again, however, the significant ideas are traditional; for most of what King says, Pope could (and may) have gone to Simplicius and other Platonists. The real differentia of the piece, its formal structure and methodical treatment of the types of evil point by point, is just what Pope does not use. Nor is there anything from King in most of the matter of about three quarters of the poem.

The problem of Bolingbroke's influence is complicated by two factors about which our knowledge is insufficient: what Bolingbroke communicated to Pope in their philosophical conversations; what Bolingbroke communicated to Pope in a written "dissertation" or "letter" that may have existed but is now lost.[2] The published *Fragments or Minutes of Essays*—despite the long-established custom of citing them—cannot be very seriously considered as sources of Pope's work. The chronology is all against it. Bolingbroke's statements in his introductory letter to his philosophical writings make it very plain that he is just at that moment beginning to *write* on the subjects they have previously discussed, and this introductory letter cannot be dated earlier than 14 December 1731—about four months after the date when three epistles were completed and Pope was intent upon the fourth.[3] Parallels of

1. The best account of King's work is to be found in A. O. Lovejoy's *The Great Chain of Being* (1936), ch. VII. Law's notes to King's work are fertile in quotations from all sorts of physico-theological writings and may have directed Pope's attention to these.

2. For the available evidence on this last, see the first of George Sherburn's "Two Notes on the *Essay on Man*", *Philol. Quart.*, XII (1922) 402, and his "Pope at Work", *Essays on the Eighteenth Century Presented to David Nichol Smith* (1945), p. 52.

3. The letter, as Roscoe pointed out (Pope's *Works*, 1824, I 397*ff*), alludes to the misinterpretations of *Moral Essay* IV, which followed its publication, 14 Dec. 1731; yet by the preceding August, Pope had finished three epistles and was working on the fourth (above, p. xiii). The internal evidence of Bolingbroke's *Fragments*, while not decisive, also favours the conclusion that they were written later than the *Essay on Man*. This evidence is summarized briefly in Appendix A.

phrasing in the published pieces must therefore be considered Pope's influence upon his friend, a supposition the more likely in that Pope's way of stating these ideas has seemed memorable to others besides Bolingbroke.[1]

This leaves us with the philosophical conversations and the mysterious dissertation. If one may assume (granting that anything one says on this point is speculation) that these did not differ radically in content or point of view from the published writings, the probabilities of their influence on the *Essay* may be described approximately as follows:

1. They can have contributed very little of the matter dealt with in Pope's Epistle II.

2. They may have contributed something to Epistle IV, for which Pope is said to have had "very large (prose) collections on yᵉ Happiness of Contentment".[2] There is no certainty, however, that he had them from Bolingbroke; the theme is a traditional one which, as Pope develops it, reminds one less of Bolingbroke's characteristic ways of thinking than of Pope's. The emphasis that Pope is likeliest to have taken from Bolingbroke (though it too is omnipresent in Platonism and Stoicism) is that terrestrial happiness is adequate to justify the ways of God. This would have pleased Bolingbroke, who did not like arguments for a next world to be founded on the unequal dispensations of Providence in this one.

3. In the real core of their argument—the approach to the problems of man's life, the kinds of evidence drawn on, the texture of attitudes—Pope's *Essay* and Bolingbroke's philosophy as we know it are sharply at odds, more at odds than the difference between poetry and prose required. Pope assimilates into his

---

1. That the phrasal influence goes from Pope to Bolingbroke rather than vice-versa has been repeatedly pointed out (though so far without much effect): e.g. by Warburton in the fourth letter of his *View of Lord Bolingbroke's Philosophy* (1755), *Works* (1811), XII 335; by Ruffhead in his *Life of Pope* (1769), p. 217; by George Ensor in his *The Independent Man* (2 vols., 1806); and by Roscoe in his edition of Pope (1824), I 407. I have not seen a copy of Ensor's book, but there is a full description of his position on Pope's *Essay* in the *Monthly Review*, LVII (1808) 413–15.

2. From a note by Spence, first printed in George Sherburn's "Pope at Work", *op. cit.*, p. 50 (above, p. xxix, *n.* 2).

account of the universe and man's life a great deal that Bolingbroke was careful to eradicate from his: the classical, medieval, and Renaissance ontosophy that supposes the order of the universe to be what Shakespeare's Ulysses describes in *Troilus and Cressida*; the strong humanistic mistrust of natural philosophy as competitor of ethics; the appeal to intuition for the distinction of right and wrong; the reality of the moral attributes of God; ruling angels, seraphs, faith, hope, charity, etc. Similarly, Pope rejects in his account the two points on which Bolingbroke was most insistent: that human knowledge, stemming entirely from sensation, pronounces nothing about angels, chains of love, intuitive morality, a next world, or an objective supra-human moral order; and that good and evil, having no foundation outside the human scheme, are ideas inapplicable to God, everything that God has done being right for the simple reason that He has done it.[1]

4. With these important differences (differences, as will be suggested later, largely determining the meaning of the *Essay* as a whole), Bolingbroke's thought may be said to have transmitted to the poet the outlines of his argument and an unknown number of its subsidiary ideas. It cannot be said to have done more, because everything Pope incorporated in the poem was available to him from other sources: his reading; the talk of the town; above all, the traditional patterns of theodicy and ethics on which Bolingbroke, Shaftesbury, King, and Leibniz alike drew. There has been a certain naïveté in the view, so long held, that Pope's mind was a *tabula rasa*, some contemporary's the hard stylus. Pope had a stylus of his own.

---

1. For discussion of some of the fundamental differences between Pope's thought and Bolingbroke's, see John Laird's *Philosophical Incursions into English Literature* (1946), 40–42, 50–51. Laird's argument, though not friendly to Pope's poem, rightly opposes "the silly idea that he [Pope] simply put into tuneful rhyme" materials derived from Bolingbroke; noting that Pope's homage at the close of the *Essay* committed him to having accepted from Bolingbroke only the five cardinal points it specified—see *Essay*, IV 394–8. The careful reader will observe, however, that the peroration nowhere commits Pope to having accepted *from Bolingbroke* even these points—which are, in any case, commonplaces.

III

In the parts of his poem that deal with theodicy, mainly Epistle I and the early divisions of Epistle IV, Pope uses the traditional explanations of evil, wherever he may have derived them, in the traditional ways. For physical evils he relies on the accepted postulate that what man knows as ill is good in its relation to a larger plan enclosing him that he cannot comprehend: partial ill equals universal good. He does not say, though he has sometimes been supposed to, that physical events which are in accord with the good of the universe are for that reason good for men: universal good equals partial good. The evils that men experience are real enough—only, they do not arise from any moral fault in God. They arise instead from inherent limitations of His omnipotence (such as most theology recognizes, e.g. "God cannot will a contradiction") which in discussions of physical evil take the form of divinely established laws of causality, operations of the system of nature. These, as implemented acts of His own will for the larger good, God cannot be supposed to wish to alter for the good of the part, except on the rarest occasions. From this cause, physical evils. From this cause also, their impartial distribution.[1] The rain, and the tempest, fall alike on the just and unjust. "Not even a God," says Plotinus, "would have the right to deal a blow for the unwarlike: the law decrees that to come safe out of battle is for fighting men, not for those that pray. The harvest comes not home for praying but for tilling; healthy days are not for those that neglect their health: we have no right to complain of the ignoble getting the richer harvest if they are the only workers in the fields, or the best."[2] This is precisely Pope's position.

The kind of evil which formal theodicies call metaphysical (i.e. that which is seen in the imperfections of one kind of creature when compared with another) Pope explains on the principle of plenitude. The gist of his argument was mentioned in discussing King:

1. I am here including Pope's return to the question of physical evils, this time under the aspect of their distribution among good and evil men, in *Essay* IV 77–166.
2. Cf. Plotinus, *Enneads*, III 2, 8 (tr. Mackenna, 1921); and Pope's *Essay*, IV 99–102, 149–56.

that nothing created can be perfect, but that everything created is as perfect as it need be. The argument rests on the assumption, to-day thoroughly familiar, that God could not rest in his own perfections till He had communicated as many degrees of perfection (kinds of being, each with its special powers) to the universe as possible—the process of communication being thought of as a process of descent, from the highest degrees to the lowest. As a basis for theodicy, the assumption had the advantage of explaining man's mental and physical limitations (he had the degree of perfection suited to his state and place), of throwing further light on physical evils (many of these resulting from one "good" thing's becoming "corruptive of another", as the wolf of the lamb),[1] and best of all, of explaining moral evil. In the poem, Pope takes largely for granted the acceptance of the principle with respect to physical and metaphysical evil. His task is to apply it to moral evil—and it is just here that what he says has been oftenest misunderstood.

The traditional philosophical way of accounting for moral evil, in pagan and Christian writers both, has been to use the principle of plenitude: to recognize the possibility of sinning (though not of course the necessity) as one of the assigned limitations of man's rank in the design of the whole. Thus Aquinas: "Perfect goodness would not be found in things, unless there were degrees of goodness," both the goodness "unable to fail from goodness" and also "that which can fail". Moral evil follows "because that which can fail, at times does fail". "Therefore it does not belong to the divine providence to ward off evil entirely from things."[2] This is exactly the bearing of Pope's comment about Borgia and Catiline. God is not to be blamed for having, in the interest of the whole, constituted man a system of psychological forces (i.e. reason and passion) such that he is capable of falling, any more than He is to be blamed for having established, in the same interest, a system of natural forces that sometimes produces earthquakes and plagues. Pope's attitude is further grounded in good authorities by the argument, also mentioned in discussing King, that God manipu-

---

1. Aquinas's example. *Sum. c. gent.*, II xli.

2. *Sum. c. gent.*, III lxxi. Cf. *Sum. theol.*, Pt I, 1st number, q. 48, a.2. Also, Plotinus, *Enneads*, III 2 and III 3, esp. III 2, 9, and III 3, 3.

C

lates the evil men do on behalf of the common good. Augustine
puts this as succinctly as Pope does: As bad men use to ill purpose
the goods of the world, God, who is good, uses bad men to good
purpose. The painter knows where to place black in the scheme of
his picture, and God knows where to place wicked men in the
scheme of his world.[1]

All these abstract pieces of his argument Pope catches up like
his predecessors in the metaphor of harmony-from-discord that
has influenced Western thinking for more than twenty centuries.[2]
It may be that the ultimate appeal of this metaphor has lain in
giving imaginative configuration to the average human being's
sense that he is, and yet is not, at home in a world he never made.
At any rate, it has had the special virtue for theodicy of recognizing
the fact of evil while restricting its significance. It enabled one to
take account of the observed heterogeneity and conflict of things,
but reconcile them; as, for example, in the thought of Heraclitus,
its probable inventor, who asserted that the universal discord—
"everything happens by strife"[3]—was the ground of the universal
union—"as with the bow and the lyre, so with the world: it is the
tension of opposing forces that makes the structure one."[4] Thus
the image brought together in one perspective man's present
suffering and his faith, the partial and the whole views; and in
such a way that even its commonest linguistic formulations (*concors
discordia rerum*) dramatized the triumph of cosmos over chaos,[5] and
its commonest analogies (the world as picture, play, poem, building, etc.) all suggested, like the parent image, that in some higher
dialectic than men could grasp the thesis and antithesis of experi-

1. *Sermo* CCCI, c.v. (in Migne's *Patrol. lat.*, XXXVIII 1382): "Sicut enim mali
homines male utuntur creaturis bonis; sic Creator bonus bene utitur hominibus
malis. . . Pictor novit ubi ponat nigrum colorem, ut sit decora pictura; et Deus
nescit ubi ponat peccatorem ut sit creatura ordinata?" I have translated freely.

2. For an exhaustive (and fascinating) discussion of the history and influence
of this metaphor, see Leo Spitzer's "Classical and Christian Ideas of World
Harmony", in *Traditio*, II (1944) 409–64, III (1945) 307–64.

3. Diels, *Fragmente der Vorsokratiker* (ed. Krantz, 1934), I 152, 169 (frags. 8
and 80).

4. *Ibid.*, p. 162 (frag. 51). I adopt the translations (both here and above)
given by J. C. Adams in *The Vitality of Platonism* (1911), pp. 97, 163, 164.

5. On this point, see Leo Spitzer's article, p. 415 (cited above, *n.* 2).

enced evil would be resolved: "All discord, harmony not under-stood". In Stoic, neo-Platonic, and Christian theodicies, as also in Pope's *Essay*, this metaphor spreads its fine reticulations through the abstract planes of argument and gives a concrete definition to the position from which theodicy has never shrunk: that in a world where all is right there is nevertheless much for man to do. "Re-member," warns Epictetus in a typical passage, "that the World is a Theatre, and that your Part in this Play of Life is determined by the Poet." That is God's business. But remember, too, "that the playing of the Part assigned you, commendably, depends upon yourself. This is your Business."[1]

The transition from God's to man's business marks the concern with ethics that all traditional theodicies imply; it is the transition that Pope makes when he turns from Epistle I to Epistle II. In the *Essay on Man*, the necessary framework to all ethical considerations is man's attitude with respect to the universe, his firm acceptance of the proposition that all things, taken together, are right. This is, of course, the point to which the poet addresses himself in the first Epistle. Within this framework, man's other relationships, to himself and to society, can be discussed, and finally the result of appropriate attitudes in all these fields, which is inward happiness: indestructible because no one can take the attitudes away, equal because all men have power to achieve them, independent of externals because the individual can will good even if fortune incapacitates him from carrying out his will, and inexhaustible for the same reason. Many of these conceptions originated with or were chiefly transmitted by the Stoics, and in this sense the general structure and theme of Pope's ethics are strongly Stoic.[2]

---

1. Epictetus, *Encheiridion*, c. 17. Stanhope's translation (4th ed., 1721), p. 123.

2. W. L. Davidson, *The Stoic Creed* (1907), p. 176, observes that the *Essay on Man* "is simply Stoicism in verse". This is true; but so is the observation of A. O. Lovejoy (*The Great Chain of Being*, 1936, p. 60) that the poem is, in part, "one of the footnotes to Plato" (cf. also Paul Shorey's *Platonism Ancient and Modern*, 1938, pp. 44, 175, 208ff), and the observation of E. H. Gillett, *God in Human Thought* (1874) II 697, that the poem reflects with amazing exactitude the ideas and language of the theologians and moralists of its time. The fact is, of course, that like most poems of weight, the *Essay* is in one sense strikingly con-temporary and in another sense strikingly universal.

Like most writers outside the Stoic school, however, Pope allows relevance and value to man's passions—accepting the traditional division of human nature into reason and appetitive instinct, and regarding the passions as useful rather than reprehensible expressions of this instinct. Here Pope follows the Aristotelian and scholastic tradition, with the purpose of making the ethical situation include the whole of human nature, not the reason alone. For Pope, though man has affinities with the Godlike-rational, he must recognize (as the Stoics did not, and hence their "pride") that he has equally powerful affinities with the animal-sensitive and that his problem is to unite both characters in the peculiar synthesis that constitutes the art of being human.

It is in this connection that the ruling passion becomes important for Pope's system. There is nothing original about the conception, which was of course implied in humoural psychology and medicine, in the dominant humour of dramatic theory, in the Theophrastian character, and elsewhere, though Pope's treatment is considerably the most complete. If Pope has a particular indebtedness on this matter, it is possibly to Bacon and Montaigne, both of whom seem to have seen in the ruling passion a kind of "forme maistresse", around which the other elements of personality must be organized and without which no lasting consistency of character can be attained.[1] This is at any rate one of its significances for the *Essay*. If we may assume, as some modern psychologies suggest, that human beings pass from chaotic to better organized states by ways which we still know little about, the ruling passion might be called Pope's guess at one of the ways. Lacking this passion, man would be in Pope's view a vessel tossed in contrary directions by the aimless succession of his desires; having it, he goes with some stability to his main objectives. This conception is central to the second Epistle, where it is obvious from the imagery that Pope is thinking of character as a creative achievement, an artistic result, something built out of chaos as God built the world. The ruling passion, which God sends, affords a focal point for this activity. The direction of the character is thus a *datum*, but what man makes of it, and whether it leads to virtue or to vice, depends upon his skill.

---

1. The phrase is Montaigne's: *Essais*, III ii (ed. Villey, Paris, 1922–3), III 35. Cf. also Bacon's essay "Of Empire".

The other significance of this passion for Pope's theory springs
from its relation to the divine plan. Sent by a higher power, it
functions within the providential scheme not only to stabilize
character toward the given objective, but to differentiate men
toward differing objectives—so that the world's work may be
accomplished—and toward differing satisfactions—so that each
may have his peculiar contentment. When the ruling passion is
allowed to grow unregulated to the extreme at which it becomes
a vice, as it is, for instance, by the Borgias and Catilines, God
harmonizes these vices (as we have seen in discussing theodicy)
in the spirit of Augustine's sentence: "no man's sin does either hurt
Thee, or disturb the order of Thy government, first or last."[1]
God's direction and supervision of ruling passions is therefore a
phase of Pope's theodicy as well as of his ethics, the object of both
being, at this point, to show that man's dual nature, however
ticklish in the management it requires and though like any good
it may be abused, is to be accepted with gratitude and resignation
from a wise and benevolent Creator. In the movement of the
faculties within man, and in the movement of men in the exterior
world, it is the tension of opposing forces that makes the structure
one.

In writing of the ruling and other passions in this double
context, Pope makes use of expressions which, though confusing,
are thoroughly characteristic of his time and of his theme. Psychological treatises of the sixteenth and seventeenth centuries are
likely to deviate, on successive pages, from a description of passions
as "tempestes qui desbauchent honteusement l'ame de sa tran-
quillité" to a description of them as "sollicitations acheminants
l'ame aux actions vertueuses"[2]; and they are likely to deviate,
correspondingly, from a rigoristic definition of virtue: virtue is
action not motivated by the affective or "lower" elements in
human nature, to a quasi-utilitarian one: virtue is action having
good effects, to which the passions are frequently the best incen-

---

1. *Confessions*, XII xi (tr. Loeb).
2. The phrases are Montaigne's (*Essais*, II xii, ed. Villey, Paris, 1922–3, II
322), in whose thought this double attitude goes deep. For a typical English
example, cf. p. 33 of Henry More's *Enchiridion Ethicum* (Engl. tr. 1690, ed. Facs.
Text Soc., N.Y. 1930) with pp. 82–3; and cf. also pp. 37, 38.

tive.[1] Such thinking betrays a lack of inner self-consistency, but has perhaps compensatory strengths. Popular thought on many subjects (together with the thought of philosophers, as criticisms of their systems show) is often less significant for coherence than for keeping alive, together, conflicting but valuable points of view. Some of these conflicting points of view for seventeenth- and eighteenth-century ethics were that motive is the right standard of human virtue—but so is result; that man's affective nature is inferior to the best that is in him—but a contributory cause of what is best; that man is pitiable or contemptible when looked at in himself—yet somehow strong and good when looked at with reference to his potentialities. If, as Hulme says,[2] the starting point of religious attitudes is always the kind of subject found in Pascal, the vanity of desire, their ending point is always in the value of some aspect of the agent in whom the vain desires take place: *misère*, but not without *grandeur*.

It is in this light that Pope's language about the passions must be read. His double attitude, announced in the famous opening lines of this second Epistle, is carried through it with deliberation. Thus he speaks of the formation of human character as though it were simultaneously man's achievement and a free gift of God, like Grace; of reason as a God within the mind and also a deluded queen; of the ruling passion as a disease and yet divine; of good and evil as absolutes known intuitively and yet in practice blurred beyond distinction. In the same way, shifting between the rigoristic and unrigoristic terminologies, he calls the results of affective actions good, their self-regarding motives, bad; so that while he is celebrating on one hand the utility of the passions, he is on the other constantly referring them to a context of frailties, vanities, imperfections, wants. The pursuits to which our passions spur us, it appears, genuinely beautify our days, but we must not fail to acknowledge them, in the long run, painted clouds; nature's law is kindly (nature being here the inclusive empirical nature of man), but the life that nature (in this sense) leads to is a poor play,

---

1. More illustrates this throughout the treatise cited above. For a general discussion of rigoristic thought, cf. F. B. Kaye's introduction to his edition of Mandeville's *Fable of the Bees* (1924).

2. T. E. Hulme, *Speculations* (N.Y. 1924), p. 22.

signifying not very much, and lighting mainly the incorrigible child in man to rest.

The prevailing tone of this second Epistle, though man is included in his capacity as world's glory as well as jest, emphasizes the latter aspect of him because of the Epistle's place in the total scheme. Pope's subject at this point is primarily man in himself, with only secondary recognition of his relation to the larger order that has been seen in the first Epistle to embrace him. Epistle II thus represents the second step in what Pope conceives as the formation of proper religious and moral attitudes: it asks the Psalmist's question, "What is man that thou art mindful of him?" The third and fourth Epistles give this question a gradual answer by replacing man in the social and cosmic orders. In the third, as the reader will have noticed, the leading ideas are drawn from Stoic and other ancient idealist doctrines, shored, as such materials usually were in the late seventeenth and early eighteenth centuries, against the ethical ruin that Hobbism was felt to imply. Hence, in part, the strong insistence on the naturalness of society to man, on the "state of nature" as a condition of concord rather than war, on the necessary foundation of any stable society in the principle of love rather than fear, and on the reconcilability of self-love and social, of king and peasant, in man's political and social institutions, according as these seek their sanction and their model in the cosmic order willed by God: again, the tension of opposing forces must make the structures one. What the fourth Epistle adds to this is a sustained and brilliant Stoic account of the pre-eminence of virtue over externals, partly by way of theodicy, vindicating Providence for the unequal distribution of these goods, partly by way of ethics, showing where true ethical objectives lie.

In these latter two Epistles, the double view of man that Pope announces in Epistle II is not of course ignored. It is present in the recognition that the "fierce embrace", and not alone the loyalties and charities that flow from it, creates and helps sustain the family unit; in the diptych portrait of the man of the state of innocence and the man of times to come; in the reigns of love and fear; as well as in the systematically alternating allusions to good men and bad men throughout Epistle IV, coming to a climax in the juxtaposition of the modest man of virtue with those in whom "guilt and greatness equal ran". Yet the progress of these Epistles, as earlier suggested, is toward a gradual catching up of human nature's actualities in its potentialities (man no longer "in himself"), and the situation with which the final lines deal is one in which man can be said to have captured his "true" nature, happiness, and virtue by discovering his relations to a divine and human *ordre naturel*. We should be mistaken to suppose, as sometimes has been done, that the tough-minded and soft-minded views of the human predicament are a weakness in Pope's argument or irrelevant to its meaning. His poem would be weaker if it excluded either one. Pope simply says here, rather brilliantly, what most of the older ethical systems have taught: that there is a sense in which man as he is and the worldly objects he pursues have a reality and validity in their own right—

> To these we owe true friendship, love sincere,
> Each home-felt joy that life inherits here;[1]

and another sense in which, standing off from them, man realizes that his real home is elsewhere, his real values different, and that the very things given him to constitute his happiness and self-fulfilment on one plane are insufficient to it on a higher. Seen from this higher plane, the home-felt joys convert to bubbles laughing in Folly's cup, and the painfully won successes at the naturalistic level become only another stage to be transcended. Man must lose his soul to find it; in Epistles III and IV, Pope shows him doing so.

When Pope stated in his "Design"[2] that he had steered between the extremes of doctrines seemingly opposite, he may have meant the Stoic and Epicurean, with their respective positions on the dignity and (in the popular view of Epicureanism) ingloriousness of man, and on apathy and activity as the supreme ethical goods. Or he may have meant the egoistic theory of Hobbes and Mandeville on the one hand, and the benevolistic theory of Shaftesbury and Hutcheson on the other, from both of which he can be said to have incorporated attitudes without accepting either wholly. Whatever Pope may have meant, his real "steering between" is of the kind that has just been noticed.

---

1. *Essay*, II 255–6.   2. Below, pp. 7–8.

IV

If we were to stop now to take stock of the *Essay* for its philosophical substance alone, it would be equally easy to underrate or
exaggerate its worth. Its one claim to originality of a sort lies in
the developed theory of the ruling passion, particularly in that
passion's psychological aspect as the focus of personality; but all
the materials for this, though no one else seems to have presented
the case so fully as Pope, were implicit in older psychologies, and
the theory is not in any case an adequate one. Nothing else in the
Essay at the philosophical level can be called original at all. The
wide European influence of its argument for a considerable period
on men of thought (e.g. Kant) must be set down to other virtues.[1]

With respect to logical coherence, the disposition since the
eighteenth century has been to rate Pope's scheme too low. The
Essay does not of course contain a *système* in the Continental sense,
despite the eagerness of many distinguished Continentals to find
one in it during the first two decades of its existence.[2] Nor does the

1. Kant quotes the *Essay* frequently in his writings, especially in the *Allge-
meine Naturgeschichte und Theorie des Himmels* (1755), which in A. O. Lovejoy's
opinion is to a large extent "a prose amplification and extension of the First
Epistle" (*The Great Chain of Being*, 1936, p. 357, *n.* 24). The general European
popularity of the *Essay* during the first hundred years or more of its existence
can hardly be exaggerated. It was translated into Czech, Danish, Dutch (6),
French (16), German (24±), Hungarian (2), Icelandic, Italian (18±),
Latin (5), Polish (5), Portuguese (2), Rumanian, Russian (4), Spanish (3),
Swedish (4), Turkish, Welsh (2). The figures in parentheses indicate the
number of known separate translations, including a few partial ones. These
figures (based mainly on standard secondary sources, and on correspondence
with European libraries, for the reason that the translations themselves are
rarely available in England or America) are of course tentative, and when
followed by a ± sign, especially so. They are the result of researches undertaken
at Yale by Miss Rebecca Price, who has kindly permitted me to use them.

2. For example, the Prussian Royal Academy proposed an examination of
Pope's "system" as subject for a prize philosophical essay in 1755. (A brief
account of the affair is given in A. Harnach's *Geschichte der kgl. preuss. Akad. der
Wissensch. zu Berlin* (Berlin, 1900), I 403ff.) The misguided gravity of the
academy's approach to the *Essay on Man* provoked the well-known pamphlet—
Pope ein Metaphysiker! (1755)—in which Lessing and Mendelssohn showed how
fundamentally different Pope's thought was from that of Leibniz and descanted
on the absurdity of looking for metaphysical systems in the works of poets. Kant

poem contain a system in the less formal sense of a fully expounded philosophy of life: Pope ignores too many subjects that any such philosophy, including his own, would have required. The *Essay* is also short in the logical virtues of delimitation and consistency in the use of terms, in systematic considerations of ethical cruxes like motivation, obligation, etc., and in careful definitions, at the level of logical coherence, of such relations as that between the pleasure-seeking of Epistle II and the inward happiness of Epistle IV. (Their significance for the larger outlook on man is clear, as we have seen.) But the absence of such virtues from the *Essay* need not surprise us, since they are also absent from a majority of ethical treatises, particularly those of Pope's day, when ethics was just beginning to become an independent study. The significant difference between Pope's work and the work of men like Hobbes or Hume is not, primarily, that the *Essay* is incomplete or incoherent at some points (Hobbes's system, as is well known, contains a wide variety of contradictions and in part refutes itself), but that it does not offer, philosophically speaking, any novel insights or fruitful reorientations of the old. Its materials are painstakingly traditional and its insights and reorientations (some of which will be looked at later) are not made inside the area of philosophical utility. Even in this area, however, Pope is more competent than has often been supposed. Much of the *Essay* is well argued, and if read within the limits of its subject matter and design—as an *essay* in four parts on some of the permanent concerns of men—its thought will be seen to have a high degree of unity and Warton's judgment of it to have been remarkably exact: "as close a piece of argument, admitting its principles, as perhaps can be found in verse".[1] The qualification of the final phrase should not be overlooked.

One's judgments of the *value* of Pope's philosophy, its soundness, will depend of course on several considerations—the kind of con-

---

made some jottings toward a contribution to the contest (preserved in Rudolf Reicke's *Lose Blätter aus Kants Nachlass*, Königsberg, 1889, I 293*ff*). No finished piece has survived, but the jottings show that Kant found Pope's ideas superior to Leibniz's: see his notation (*op. cit.*, I 296): "Vergleichung des Lehrbegriffs des Pope mit dem optimismus und vorzug des ersteren."

1. *Essay on Pope* (1806), II 55.

siderations, for instance, that determine one's attitude toward Platonic "Forms" or the soul's ascent to highest Beauty: are these conceptions nonsense, or do they point to some kind of truth? Were the principle of plenitude and the chain of being, to take instances closer to Pope, preposterous—chimeras that philosophy is today well rid of; or did they reflect confusedly, and perhaps with much distortion, insights that we miss because we have changed the angle of the glass? Is the explanation of the universe they led to partly true or wholly false, significant even if mistaken, or absurdly callow? A philosophically trained Scot of about a hundred years ago declared Pope's poem "a valuable summary of all that human reason has been able hitherto to advance in justification of the moral government of God"; in our day another philosophically trained Scot refers to its four Epistles as "the unconvincing four".[1] Which is right?

Without pretending to answer these questions (every reader of the poem must face them for himself), one may point to certain qualifications that need to be made in the popular judgment of Pope's work as shallow. This term, as it has been used in criticism of the *Essay*, seems to embrace four distinguishable senses that may be taken up in turn.

1. The ideas of the poem are unoriginal, in fact commonplaces of Western thought. This is the substance of Johnson's comment ("Surely a man of no very comprehensive search may venture to say that he has heard all this before"), and it is as usual eminently sound.[2] Shallowness in this sense is not a very damaging criticism, however, since ideas become commonplaces to the extent that they have seemed to answer to some aspect of truth.

2. Pope's philosophy cannot solve the problem of evil. This indictment is also just, but not particularly interesting. It is uninteresting not so much because no other philosophy has solved the problem either (Pope's explanation standing, as Leslie Stephen

---

1. Dugald Stewart, *Philosophy of the Active and Moral Powers* (Edinburgh, 1828), II 127. John Laird, *Philosophical Incursions into English Literature* (1946), p. 38.

2. "Pope", *Lives of the Poets*, ed. Hill (1905), III 244. On the level of thought, this is Johnson's main point, though he attacks (as always) the concept of the chain of being.

said,[1] at the threshold of a door into which no one has entered far),
as because the purport of the classical theodicies Pope follows is
precisely that the problem is insoluble by man. These theodicies
assert that the universe is ultimately rational instead of arbitrary,
they do not assert that men can fully understand it: "The book of
this law we are neither able nor worthy to look into. That little
thereof which we darkly apprehend we admire, the rest with religious ignorance we humbly and meekly adore."[2] In this respect
they resemble the Christian solution, acknowledging a mystery
but seeking what light they can.

3. A further sense of shallow may be defined by quoting a judgment of Pope's poem uttered on its two-hundreth anniversary:
"The wisdom which teaches us not to weep cannot dry our tears,
still less can it draw them forth."[3] Putting aside (as a curiosity) the
theory of poetry this remark implies, one can accept its truth. But
to apply it to Pope's *Essay*, or any theodicy, is to misconceive the
genre. There are times when we suffer evil, there are times when
we speculate about it. One cannot imagine a mourner comforted
by theodicy because one cannot imagine a letter of consolation
beginning "The *reason* that . . .". The nature of suffering is to turn
the mind upon itself and toward the condition of the Phoenix—
as if "then can bee None of that kinde of which he is, but hee".
The nature of theodicy is to dilate the mind outward toward some
significance in which the individual grief is lost: the burial service
of the Book of Common Prayer, though not strictly a theodicy, is
typical in this respect. On the other hand, to the man recovering
from suffering, theodicy may again have something to say.

4. In the sense in which it is most commonly applied to Pope's
philosophy, shallow is simply a pejorative term for philosophical
optimism. This kind of optimism, every one to-day knows, does not
mean what nineteenth-century theorists meant when they said
that the outlook for mankind was optimistic; it means that the
physical evils and limitations afflicting men, and the freedom which
without requiring men to sin makes them capable of sinning, so
inhere in the structure of the universe that the outlook for mankind

---

1. Unsigned review, "Mr. Elwin's Edition of Pope", in *Fraser's Magazine* (new
sér.), III (1871) 301.

2. Hooker, I ii 5. 3. *Times Lit. Suppl.*, 10 Aug. 1933, p. 530.

will never be very optimistic. The two recurring objections to this philosophy have been that it is cheerless, and that it is fatalistic. Both will bear examination.

As a protest against the cheerlessness of optimism, Voltaire's poem on the Lisbon earthquake is typical and has often been praised for exposing the real bleakness of the creed.

> Philosophes trompés qui criez: "Tout est bien";
> Accourez, contemplez ces ruines affreuses. . . .
> Direz-vous: "C'est l'effet des éternelles lois
> Que d'un Dieu libre et bon nécessitent le choix"?[1]

"Yes" is not the answer anticipated by Voltaire's question, but it is of course the right answer, if one believes in the benevolence of God. What Voltaire ignores is that the *éternelles lois* are simply a way of conceptualizing the limitations that theology and theodicy have always placed on God's omnipotence in order the better to defend His goodness. In the poem on Lisbon, Voltaire gives up, implicitly but fundamentally, His goodness.[2] Nor does the history of thought suggest that, for theism, there is any other alternative, once the "eternal laws" are dismissed.[3] Either God is willing to avoid evils but not fully able, or He is able and not fully willing.[4]

---

1. *Poème sur le Désastre de Lisbonne*, 4–5, 15–16.

2. Rousseau put the issue very plainly in his letter to Voltaire after reading the poem (18 Aug. 1756): "Si l'embarras de l'origine du mal vous forçait d'altérer quelqu'une des perfections de Dieu, pourquoi vouloir justifier sa puissance aux dépens de sa bonté?" The same might be said of *Candide*. The theme of *cultiver-son-jardin*, as Paul Hazard has remarked, is essentially a shrivelling oneself up, "pour donner moins de prise au mal triomphant". "Le Problème du mal dans la conscience européenne du xviiie siècle", *Romanic Review*, xxxii (1941) 163.

3. This statement does not of course apply to modern "evolutionary" theisms (God as Becoming not Being), where the difficulties are of a different sort.

4. I condense here the classical formulation (God is both able and willing, neither able nor willing, willing but not able, able but not willing) to the alternatives really at stake in the attitudes of Pope's poem and Voltaire's. Though one cannot but admire the outraged humanitarianism of Voltaire's poem, one has only to place the challenge (it has been called a defiance) of its closing lines beside the close of Pope's first epistle (to say nothing of still finer passages in more spiritual writers than Pope) to see that Voltaire is religiously immature.

The former outlook may indeed be cheerless—if cheer is to be made the test. The latter is bleak at the very core.

The second objection—that optimism paralyses ethics[1]—has more philosophically to commend it. To the question why, if the world is already as right as it can be, we should try to alter any ill, there is probably no answer that will satisfy a logician. The great theologies have all skirted it by some species of ambivalence. Nature, for example, in Stoic theodicy, means the divine unity and sum of things which man is to accept as right; but the "nature" to be accepted as right in Stoic ethics is only man's higher self. In neo-Platonic theodicy, man has an assigned "perfection", against which he must not rebel; but as this is also a *degree* of perfection, he aspires in neo-Platonic ethics to close the gap between himself and the degrees above. Christian thinking shows a similar antinomy— to mention only one—in the paradox of the Fortunate Fall.[2] Though the presence of such ambivalences in a variety of religious philosophies supplies no answer to the logical problem, it suggests that psychologically the combination of acceptance as a state of mind with moral effort as a rule of conduct is both possible and sound: Stoicism, neo-Platonism, Christianity—the chief optimisms of the West—have been its chief teachers of moral discipline. With a little introspection one can perhaps see why. The man who works best or the soldier who fights best is likely to be the one who believes that he will be spared *unnecessary* hardships, not the one who thinks that the High Command is wasteful, or indifferent to him, or that there is no High Command.

Even, however, if one prefers logical to psychological truth, it is well to bear in mind (before dismissing Pope and the tradition he represents) the comment of a distinguished philosopher of our own day on its character: "We are told by logicians that a proposition must be either true or false, and that there is no middle term. But in practice, we may know that a proposition expresses an important truth, but that it is subject to limitations and qualifications which at present remain undiscovered."[3]

---

1. The objection, for example, of J. M. Robertson, *Pioneer Humanists* (1907), p. 210.

2. On its long history, see A. O. Lovejoy, "Milton and the Paradox of the Fortunate Fall", *Journ. Engl. Lit. Hist.*, iv (1937) 161–79.

3. A. N. Whitehead, *Science and the Modern World* (Cambridge, 1926), p. 255.

III: THE *ESSAY* AS A POEM

I

It will perhaps have occurred to the reader that the ideas so far discussed, either of theodicy or ethics, do not quite account for Pope's poem. In the field of theodicy, we have seen Pope taking over established arguments, yet the space they occupy in his poem is surprisingly limited and the arrangement they have been given quite unlike, say, the systematic organization that Pope knew in the treatise of Archbishop King or perhaps others. Similarly, the approach to the *Essay* as a system of ethics, while it illuminates, as has been observed, a good deal in the larger outlines of the thought, does not adequately explain some of the most forcible impressions that a reader of the poem receives—for example, the passionate concern with "pride"; or indeed the absence of some of the subject-matters that we have already noticed a fully purposeful system of ethics should include. These differences are in part of course the differences of poetry from prose—the philosopher's job, said Bolingbroke, being to dilate, press, prove, convince; the poet's to hint, to touch with short and spirited strokes, to warm the affections.[1] But this explanation is not sufficient. Almost all the philosophical materials in the *Essay* can be paralleled in Thomson's *Seasons*,[2] yet two poems could hardly be less alike. The question we are brought to, therefore, is that earlier suggested concerning the kind of poetic meaning Pope has used philosophy to construct— a question that can best be answered by examining the *Essay* in the light of Renaissance thought and literature. Here the ideas that we have dealt with so far on the philosophical plane can be studied in formulations elaborated and particularized by the literary imagination of centuries, and arranged in a pattern or formed *Weltanschauung* that seeks to take hold of the relations of God and man not through theorem but through symbol. What we are now approaching, therefore, is a body of materials that stands closer to the poetic centre of the *Essay on Man* than either pure theodicy or pure ethics; and which, having a good deal less to do with the

1. Introductory letter to Pope. *Works* (1809) v 79.
2. This will be particularly clear to readers of A. D. McKillop's *The Background of Thomson's Seasons*, 1942.

ideas, postulates, conclusions (and right or wrong) of the poem's logical meaning and organization, has a good deal more to do with its implicit organization, its attitudes, images, emotions, and its developing theme.

In Renaissance thinking, as a number of recent studies have emphasized,[1] one of the most striking features is the powerful conception of the universe as order, with its twofold aspect of hierarchy (the principle of plenitude circumstantially filled out) and union. For Hooker, echoing Aquinas, and aiming to put ecclesiastical polity on a metaphysical foundation, the unifying principle is law: a law differently denominated according to the kinds of creature subject to it—natural law for natural objects, celestial law for angels, laws of reason, of revelation, of magistrates, for men—but always fundamentally a single ordinance operative to a single end, the integrity of the whole. "Of Law there can be no less acknowledged, than that her seat is the bosom of God, her voice the harmony of the world."[2] Writers in the Platonic tradition, on the other hand, are more likely to conceive the unifying principle as love. To the several varieties of this force they attribute the reconciliation of the warring elements, the maintenance in their places of stars and earth and ocean, the cohesion of human societies, man and woman, friend and friend; yet love, like law, is finally one, the circulating current of "the everlasting Chaine"

> Which together all things tyed,
> And unmoved doth them retayne,
> And by which they shall abide:
> That concent we cleerly find
> Which doth things together draw. . . .[3]

A third principle is the *concors discordia* we have also already met

---

1. Hardin Craig, *The Enchanted Glass*, 1936; E. M. W. Tillyard, *The Elizabethan World Picture*, 1944; *Shakespeare's History Plays*, 1944; Theodore Spencer, *Shakespeare and the Nature of Man*, 1945; Douglas Bush, *The Renaissance and English Humanism*, 1939; *Paradise Lost in Our Time*, 1945; C. S. Lewis, *Preface to Paradise Lost*, 1942.

2. Hooker, I xvi 8.

3. Drayton's seventh eclogue (*Pastorals*, 1619), 169 *ff*; these verses are not in the 1593 edition.

with—applied in the Renaissance, as earlier, to stress the unifica-
tion in "comely agreement" of warring opposites: contrary motions
of the Ptolemaic spheres, the poise of the planets against each
other's influence, the clashing elements, the mixture of hostile
humours in the body, the strife of reason and passion in the soul,
the skill of painter and musician, who shape conflicting sounds and
colours into harmony, and a variety of other "concording enmi-
ties," including civil state:

> Then did *Heraclitus* conceiue it right,
> Who did affirme the *parents* of all things
> To be good *concord* in a *discord* pight. . . .

> A body *politike*, or publike *state*,
> Hath like dissents, which yet assenting stands:
> The *King*, the *subiect*, and the magistrate,
> *Noble* and *base*, *rich*, *poore*, *peace*, and warlike *bands*,
>   *Law*, *religion*, *idle*, working *handes*,
>   *Old*, *yong*, *weake*, *strong*, good men and euill bee
>   Dislike in parts, yet in *consort* agree.[1]

What all three of these principles stress is thus an order that by
stratification makes union possible. Without "degree", there would
be perpetual struggle, each thing meeting each other thing, as
Shakespeare's Ulysses says, "in mere oppugnancy". With degree,
all kinds of creatures can co-operate, and, in the senses that seem
to have mattered most to Renaissance minds, approach equality.
Equality in that all are necessary (each having its assigned work and
place); all are superior and inferior to other kinds above and
below; all are mutually dependent ("The noblest creatures neede
the vil'st on ground, The vil'st are servèd by the honor'd, most"[2]);
and all share—here we reach the principle of unity that underlies
all the others—in the immanence of God. As in a graded row of
vessels, though the capacities of creatures may be unequal, all
are equally "filled" by Him.

---

1. The quotations are from John Norden's *Vicissitudo Rerum* (1600), stas. 84,
95. *Shaks. Assoc. Facs.*, No. 4 (1931).
2. John Davies of Hereford, *Mirum in Modum*, *Works*, ed. Grosart (1878),
I 22.

Inside this macrocosmic order, as the Renaissance conceived it, stood microcosmic man, involved in a kind of triple pattern of glory, ruin, and restoration. As the details of the pattern may be studied elsewhere, it will answer our purpose to summarize only the chief points here. Man was glorious owing to his critical position in the Creation. All the powers of the inferior levels being concentred in him, and his own peculiar property of reason linking him with those above, he could be looked on as the indispensable link tying together the spiritual and corporeal creations—"the last Touch, the Master-piece, the Honour, and Ornament, nay, the Prodigy . . . of Nature".[1] This is of course the view of man reflected in the first part of Hamlet's famous comment ("What a piece of work is a man!"), in Milton's portraiture of Adam and Eve before the Fall, and in those bold predications that look out of the pages of the humanistic prose-writers with faces from another world. "As every creature," says Erasmus, "most readily learns that for which it is created, therefore will Man, with but slight effort, be brought to follow that to which Nature has given him so strong an instinct, viz. excellence. . . . What is the proper nature of Man? Surely it is to live the life of Reason, for reason is the peculiar prerogative of man."[2]

But this masterpiece of nature was also its ruined masterpiece, as no Renaissance mind ever forgot. Compounded as he had been of the faculties of the lower creatures, it was in man's power to live according to their natures rather than his own, and on a memorable occasion he had elected to do so. The favourite juxtaposition for Renaissance minds was not therefore that of glorious man and glorious macrocosm but glorious macrocosm and inglorious man— as in Milton's poem "On Time" or Vaughan's on "Man", where on the one hand is nature's chime, nature's obedience and stability, and on the other, disproportioned sin, man's disobedience and instability. For sin is regularly conceived of, in the literature we are discussing, not as the purely personal transaction that it has come to be thought by many since, but as a violation through self-will of the universal order, unity, and law: it is the creature's turning

---

1. Charron, I i.

2. Erasmus, *De pueris instituendis*. I use the translation given in W. H. Woodward's *Erasmus Concerning . . . Education* (1904), pp. 190, 192.

away from its creatureliness, from its "due" subordination, from its proper action according to the law of its proper nature. The sin of the angels, says Hooker, could not have been "but by reflex of their understanding upon themselves; when being held with admiration of their own sublimity and honour, the memory of their subordination unto God and their dependency on him was drowned in this conceit; whereupon their adoration, love, and imitation of God could not choose but be also interrupted."[1] It is the same point, in different terms, that Whichcote the seventeenth-century Platonist makes, when he declares that "the ways and dealings of *God* with his Creatures are all *Accountable* in a way of Reason; but . . . *Sinners* vary from the Reason of Things; and take upon them to Over-rule. . . ."[2]

This sense of intimacy between man and the order that contains him supports the third stage in the pattern above alluded to: his regeneration. Potentially glorious, actually ruined, human nature could be redeemed. "If we wil consider man in the first estate that God created him," says a sixteenth-century handbook of popular philosophy, "it [he] is the chiefe and principal of Gods worke . . . But if we consider him in the estate of the generall corruption spred all ouer the posteritie of Adam, we shall see him nooseled in sinne, monstrous, fearfull, deformed. . . But if we will consider [him] afterwards as being made all new by the immortall seede of God's word, ye [we?] shall see him restored. . ."[3] The means of redemption envisaged in this quotation are specifically Christian, but there were others—the way up of the neo-Platonists by mystical ascent, the more sober way up by the scale of nature (God's other revelation)

> whereon
> In contemplation of created things
> By steps we may ascend to God.[4]

To be restored by the latter method, the method most typical of Renaissance humanism, man's proper studies had to be the univer-

---

1. I iv 3.

2. *Moral and Religious Aphorisms*, Century VII, No. 646 (ed. Salter, 1753).

3. Pierre Boaistuau, *Theatrum Mundi* (tr. Alday, 1566?), f.T7. I owe this passage to E. M. W. Tillyard's *Elizabethan World Picture*, p. 73.

4. *Par. Lost*, v 510–12.

sal order and himself—two studies that were in effect the same. Knowledge of the order restored man to self-knowledge lost at the Fall by reminding him of his likeness to the lower levels—how "he ought to love them and think upon his likeness to them and his brotherhood with them, and by their means humble himself and rub his soul against them" [1]—and also of his inherent superiority— "because he is placed over them in most excellent rank and dignity". [2] In the same manner, self-knowledge restored man to knowledge of the order lost at the Fall, because it showed him that he was not an animal and therefore should not act like one, but at the same time that he was not an angel and therefore could not act like one: it was Eve's desire for something more than humanity that had led to "all that woe". Charron puts the whole matter very well in the opening exhortation of his *De la Sagesse*, which takes the identity of the two knowledges for granted. [3] On the one hand, he says, self-knowledge is man's best defence against his inordinate proud desire to transgress his creaturely bounds. Each of the other creatures "takes care of itself . . . hath Bounds set to its Desires, . . . nor hath any Aim beyond such a certain Compass: And yet thou, O vain Man, . . . wilt be grasping at the Universe, . . . pretendest to Knowledge unlimited, and takest upon thee to controul and to judge every Thing. . .". But on the other hand, self-knowledge is the only true means to what Milton later called the repairing the ruin of our first parents "by regaining to know God aright". "It must needs be so," says Charron, "because there is no other thing capable of being known to us, which carries such lively Stroaks, such express Images and Characters, such clear and convincing Testimonies of God, as Man does."

---

1. Raymond Sebon, *Theologia naturalis*, c. LIX (Venice, 1581): "Ille enim debet amare, & cogitare similitudinem, quam habet cum eis & fraternitatem, & humiliare se per eas, & fricare animam suam cum eis."

2. *Ibid.*: ". . . quia est in nobilitate excellentissima, & dignitate constitutus super eas".

3. Charron, I, Introd.

II

Against this Renaissance background, a number of important elements in the *Essay on Man* stand out in their full significance. In fact, it may not be unfair to say that while Pope's poem is in all its surface aspects a work of the Augustan period, its underlying themes have much in common with the kinds of meaning that Renaissance poets constructed out of the materials that have just now been discussed. Readers of Shakespeare, for example, have long sensed in several of the plays a structural pattern that asserts some form of equilibrium or order, usually with reference to the universal order, which is then violated in one or several ways, and reestablished at the close. This is perhaps what takes place, in part, in *Hamlet, Macbeth, Othello*, more plainly in *King Lear* and *The Tempest*, and it seems to be a theme common to tragic poetry, both Shakespearian and Greek. It is also, of course, and particularly, the theme of Milton in *Paradise Lost*. As every one knows, the central conflict in Milton's epic is that between the hierarchical order, coherence, law, love, harmony, unity, and happiness of a world created and sustained according to God's purposes, and the chaos, rebellion, dissension, hatred, and misery brought into it by man's and Satan's unwillingness to be contented with these purposes and their part in them. The opening books show the self-will of the fallen angels that enslaves them while they aspire above themselves; the next books, the delighted freedom of those who keep their state and place in the discipline of "degree". In the middle books there is the violation of order in the war in heaven, and the re-assertion of order in the Creation of the World. The poem ends with further violations, this time man's, and a further reestablishment of order in Michael's exposition of redemption at the close. In the meantime, there has been persistent counterpointing of scenes of order and disorder, religious humility and irreligious pride: darkness, pandemonium, and Satanic *hubris* against light, concord, and the Son's self-abnegation; hell in Satan's heart and ugliness in his disguises against the beauty, innocence, and trust of his intended victims; Eve and Adam immediately after the Fall against Eve and Adam in innocence and later in repentance; the violences of future history against the paradise to be regained within the soul; and so on through a dozen similar confrontations.

A great many of these Renaissance materials are also in Pope's
Essay. The poem that Pope makes of them is to be sure a different
one from Milton's, but within his four epistles, seen as parts of a
developing whole, Pope manages to precipitate a meaning that,
like Milton's, is in one sense the story of a conflict between religious
humility and irreligious pride, and in another sense, the story of
universal order, the ways it can be violated, and the ways it must
be restored.

To begin with order, Pope's conception of it has the spaciousness, intensity, and indeed the explicit forms that we have elsewhere
seen. In Pope's world, the ordering principle of hierarchy prevails
throughout the astronomical universe, throughout the scale of
creatures from "the green myriads in the peopled grass" to ruling
angels in their spheres, throughout the body politic and social
classes. Because hierarchy prevails, law prevails: hierarchy *is* law
in Pope's world—"Heaven's first law"—as it was in Hooker's and
Milton's; the creature who rebels and disobeys the laws of hierarchy
sins against God—like Lucifer if he seeks to overpass his level in
the scale, like Nimrod if he seeks to bring in tyranny at his own
level. The consequence in either case is to "invert the world, and
counter-work its Cause"[1]—the reason being that hierarchy is for
Pope, as for the tradition we have examined, the means to union:
a fellowship properly sustained not by violence but by love. In the
Essay on Man it is the Platonic power of love circulating up and
down the "everlasting Chaine" that binds the elements, plants,
animals, men and angels in one mutually dependent system;
through love, the beasts mate and men come into families; civil
societies in their origins and rightful formulations are based on
love, as are religions; and man's proper understanding of the
order that embraces him is to see it as not merely stratified but
co-operative, a "union of the rising whole", where his duties begin
and end in love of God and love of man. But again, in Pope as
elsewhere, the fellowship and the hierarchy are but other ways of
visualizing the Heraclitean *concors discordia,* where every member
of the universal orchestra contributes something and all are
reconciled by a Providence that both composes and conducts.
Thus the equilibrium of opposites by which God established a

---

1. *Essay,* I 123*ff,* III 241*ff.*

cosmos out of the chaos of the elements must be matched in the individual's life by an equilibrium of passions—established, as we have seen in discussing Pope's ethics, by "the God within the mind", through the aid of the God-inspired bias or ruling passion. This same kind of creative equilibrium must be realized in the societies of civil state and ultimately in the imaginative act whereby "the whole worlds of Reason, life, and sense" are grasped and held "in one close system of benevolence"—as they are by God.[1]

As all these ways of apprehending it imply, Pope sees the universal order, like his predecessors, as a spiritualized and spiritualizing One. In His transcendence, God ordained and keeps it so; in His immanence, He flows through it; composing and conducting, He is the music too. Pope's vivid sense of this mystery, of the fact that there is both diversity and unity, both a mighty maze and yet a plan, is one of the striking features of his poem. It is present everywhere, not only in the larger structure, where it is made the basis in each epistle for a new phase of the argument, but also in the remarkable width of imagery and allusion—weeds, oaks, poor Indians, Newtons, serpents, Gods, bubbles, seas, falcons, insects, cobblers, kings, Cains, Abels, Caesars, Tituses, Chartreses, Bethels, to mention only a few—whose inclusion in the poem's universe dramatizes the infinite variety comprehended and reconciled in God's.

Pope's fullest explicit treatment of this idea properly occurs at the close of the first Epistle, where the self-assertiveness that makes theodicy necessary is dwarfed and drowned in a brilliant picturing of the Many resolved in One.

> All are but parts of one stupendous whole,
> Whose body Nature is, and God the soul;
> That, chang'd thro' all, and yet in all the same,
> Great in the earth, as in th'æthereal frame,
> Warms in the sun, refreshes in the breeze,
> Glows in the stars, and blossoms in the trees,
> Lives thro' all life, extends thro' all extent,
> Spreads undivided, operates unspent,
> Breathes in our soul, informs our mortal part,
> As full, as perfect, in a hair as heart;

---

1. See *Essay*, iii–iv.

> As full, as perfect, in vile Man that mourns,
> As the rapt Seraph that adores and burns;
> To him no high, no low, no great, no small;
> He fills, he bounds, connects, and equals all. [1]

These lines are sometimes spoken of as pantheistic, but the interpretation is incorrect; like the poem as a whole, they recognize God's transcendence and not his immanence alone. Their theme is that the objects of the universe are particular and disjunct, yet that it is still a *uni*verse: there is something that is "changed through all, and yet in all the same". One aspect of Creation is the graded differentness of things, which the lines express by moving outward from the earth to the ethereal frame, and back again from the sun and stars to the winds and trees—as also by showing the soul superior to the body, the heart nobler than the hair, and the seraph (who in the highest order of angels adores and burns) as infinitely surpassing man, who in ignorance of the blessed vision mourns. But the other aspect of Creation is that heart and hair, man and angel, are pervaded by one essence, as, on a biological analogy, man and mollusc and amoeba immensely differ, yet all share something of which the common principle is the single cell. Being transcendent in Pope's conception, God is made the subject of the seraph's rapt adoration and also the active agent who fills, bounds, connects, and makes all equal. But at the same time He is felt as immanent, a power to whom, as the contrasting half of the couplet indicates, there is no high, no low, no great, no small, for all things live and move and have their being in Him.

An analogy to Pope's meaning—an especially relevant one in that Pope clearly echoes the passage in lines immediately preceding those under discussion—is St Paul's description of the mystery of Christian unity in Christ. Asked which of the spiritual gifts are preferable, St Paul replies by putting the emphasis on the union of them all. "If the foot shall say, because I am not the hand, I am not of the body; is it therefore not of the body? and if the ear shall say, because I am not the eye, I am not of the body; is it therefore not of the body? . . . But now are many members. Yet but one body. And the eye cannot say to the hand, I have no need of thee;

---

1. *Essay*, 1 267–80.

nor again the head to the feet, I have no need of you. . . For God hath tempered the body together, having given more abundant honour to that part which lacked: that there should be no schism in the body, but that the members should have the same care for one another." Some such conviction of union, organism, wholeness, seems to be very deeply rooted in religious feeling, and the centrality of this conviction in the *Essay on Man*, its assertion and reassertion, should help remind us that Pope's poem stems from the great tradition.

Inside this splendid union of the whole, as Pope conceives it, man is a potential violator, an irritant, a threat. In *Paradise Lost*, God is made to say to the assembled angels over whom He has decreed His Son shall rule: "Him who disobeys Me disobeys Me, breaks union, and that day Cast out from God and blessed vision, falls."[1] If Pope's poem is like Milton's partly a celebration of ideal union, it is also partly (and again like Milton's) an accounting of the ways union can be broken and men fall. In the first epistle, the subject is man's rebellion against his level in the universal chain. When in his pride he aspires above himself, the fact he revolts against is that he has a human not an angelic nature, subject by its constitution to passion and hence to moral evil; though he is equally capable of stooping below himself to envy purely physical powers. Either alternative involves the breaking of order, union, full consent of things, and the consequence, in Pope's world as in Shakespeare's, is that "chaos, when degree is suffocate, Follows the choking:"

> And if each system in gradation roll,
> Alike essential to th' amazing whole;
> The least confusion but in one, not all
> That system only, but the whole must fall.
> Let Earth unbalanc'd from her orbit fly,
> Planets and Suns run lawless thro' the sky,
> Let ruling Angels from their spheres be hurl'd,
> Being on being wreck'd, and world on world,
> Heav'n's whole foundations to their centre nod,
> And Nature tremble to the throne of God.[2]

---

1. *Par. Lost*, v 611–13.   2. *Essay*, i 247–56.

Placed immediately before the Pauline illustration from the body
and the members, and the lines earlier quoted on the One and
Many, this passage effectively images (somewhat in the manner of
Milton's war in heaven) the clash of irreligious pride with religious
resignation—the latter of which (cf. Milton's Abdiel), instead of
seeking to uncreate the universe, accords its will with God's and
accepts the creed that in differing words most religious poetry
has subscribed to:

> All Nature is but Art, unknown to thee;
> All Chance, Direction, which thou canst not see;
> All Discord, Harmony not understood;
> All partial Evil, universal Good:
> And, spite of Pride, in erring Reason's spite,
> One truth is clear, "Whatever IS, is RIGHT."[1]

The remaining epistles further elaborate this theme of pride. In
the second, the kinds of conduct to be repudiated are all those
that tend to make man glorify himself as a creature of mind alone
(hence the corrective value of self-knowledge in the sense previously
discussed) and thus deviate from "Nature's road". Typical
instances are the pretensions of natural philosophy, of Platonist
metaphysics, and of neo-Platonist mysticism, which fancies it
can put off body altogether. For the essential fact about man in
this Epistle—even about Newton, whose intellectual grasp, though
great, falls far below the pure intelligence of the angels—is his
duality of body and spirit, which it is his responsibility to come to
terms with. On the other hand, in the third Epistle, the projects
repudiated are all those by which man undertakes to set himself
apart from the fellowship of created things that reaches from the
atoms to the angels. This, like the hierarchical order stressed in the
first Epistle and the duality of man's being stressed in the second,
is also a law of God. But man in his pride of reason, progress,
civilization, is always striving to suppose that he is above nature
or outside it, and has left its teachings irrevocably behind. Hence
his insolent assumption that the lower creatures exist exclusively
for him, which is a prelude to the tyrant's insolent assumption that
other men exist for him. The facts are, if man will but choose to

---

1. *Essay*, I 289–94.

see them, that he and the lower creatures have been made mutually
dependent, the instinctive nature of the latter so unerring within
its limits that he has no cause to gloat; that his societies originate
like theirs from instinct, the arts supporting these societies from
instinctive processes, the loyalties that unite societies from instinctive principles of love; and that in its highest manifestations the
civilized life on which he prides himself is an application, not a
rejection, of the mutuality of the cosmic whole:

> Where small and great, where weak and mighty, made
> To serve, not suffer, strengthen, not invade,
> More pow'rful each as needful to the rest,
> And, in proportion as it blesses, blest,
> Draw to one point, and to one centre bring
> Beast, Man, or Angel, Servant, Lord, or King. [1]

When men have accepted this mutuality, they have "walk'd with
beast, joint tenant of the shade", known that not right divine but
virtue "A Prince the Father of a People made", and with confidence in the rightness of the Creator's plan, "understood A
sov'reign being but a sov'reign good"; when they have violated
it, they have been tyrannous in the realm of nature, tyrannous in
civil life, tyrannous in religion:

> Zeal then, not charity, became the guide
> And hell was built on spite, and heav'n on pride. [2]

Here again Pope juxtaposes in a group of powerful contrasts the
attitude of irreligious pride, as it tries to abstract itself from the
scheme of God and nature, and the attitude of religious humility,
which knows that neither political science nor punctilious dogmas
can be substitutes for rectitude of life.

To this theme the fourth Epistle supplies a final dimension. The
lines with which Pope prefaces his account of the vanity of human
wishes sum up significantly the deep-rooted conviction of the
entire *Essay* that man's efforts to set himself apart from God and
nature—in this instance, to find his happiness in principles
incompatible with the whole—are blasphemous.

---

1. *Essay*, III 297–302.   2. *Ibid.*, 261–2.

> O sons of earth! attempt ye still to rise,
> By mountains pil'd on mountains, to the skies.
> Heav'n still with laughter the vain toil surveys,
> And buries madmen in the heaps they raise.[1]

Pope concentrates in these lines[2] familiar instances of pride rebelling against the Lord—the Titans, the insurgent kings of the second Psalm—in order to make us see against this context the meaning of the world's obsession with material goods, with which much of the remainder of the poem deals. Pope's point is not simply that materialism buries the soul in the heaps it raises, but that the pursuit of material values is an act of *hubris*, a further denial, like the denials of order, man's duality, and cosmic fellowship, of the law of God.

This theme of order and violation—religious humility versus irreligious pride—is completed in the *Essay*, as in the general pattern of thought that lies behind it, with a scheme of regeneration, restoration, reunion, between man and nature and God. In part, this thesis is formulated through a cluster of meanings gradually developed around the Pauline triad, faith, hope, and charity. Hope appears in the poem on both the natural and theological levels. On the natural level, it is what springs eternal in the human breast, a member of pleasure's family, a compensation for lost happiness, a primary bond in the social unit of the family. On the theological level, it is the expectancy (without the certainty) of immortal life that heaven supplies as man's portion in his present state, an expectancy that remains in the hour of death, helps to neutralize the fear of extinction, compensates the choosing of goodness above external goods. The kind of future life expected may vary from religion to religion, but what is to be avoided is a "weak hope", which is equivalent to a lack of faith in the unity and rightness of the whole, leading to the superstitious practice of religion as a form of magic.

Faith is defined at the close of the first Epistle, though not by name, as a frame of mind which does not impugn the rightness of the whole but trusts God's goodness, both in this life and the next.

---

1. *Essay*, IV 73–6.

2. I have commented on them more fully in "On Reading Pope", *College English*, VII (Feb. 1946) 271–2.

For true faith is love of God, not fear of him, as true polity and
morality are love of man, and dissensions as to the letter in which
faith is to be defined should not blind men to the spirit they are
defining, which is charity. In one sense, therefore, faith, hope, and
charity are all aspects of the proper response of man to God and
His divine Creation, a relationship clearly emphasized in the close
of the fourth Epistle. Here the "virtue" the poem celebrates—
described in Pope's gloss to the passage as constituting "a Happiness whose Object is *Universal* and whose Prospect *Eternal*"[1]—is
plainly charity. The good man arrives at this through coming to
understand that the principle of the ordered fellowship is love and
applying this principle within himself; or, to put it in different
terms, hope leads him from goal to goal, by taking him from the
individualism of Epistle II, where every man seeks a several goal,
through the sociality of Epistle III, where he finds his soul by losing
it ("mean self-love" becoming a scale to measure others' wants by
his own), to the charity which is supreme felicity of Epistle IV.
Thus the attitude of acceptance is gradually blended with and
made the condition of moral achievement.

   In a more important way, imaginatively, the thesis of restoration
is explicit in the very structure of Pope's poem. Not simply because
the breaking of union which each epistle condemns implies the
desirability of reunion, but because all four epistles conclude with
picturizations of a reunited world from different points of view and
there is an unmistakable progress in them. The whole in which man
is included, in the lines earlier noticed on the One and Many, is
stupendous and it minimizes him: he is present, but mainly as the
lower term of a disproportion of which the upper term is the highest
order of created things. Unlike the seraph, man lacks the beatific
vision, he is vile, and mourns. At the close of the second Epistle,
on the other hand, he has travelled a certain distance. One of the
functions of this epistle is to effect a transition from a mood of
theodicy ("submit", "submit") to a mood of ethics.[2] The Borgias
and the Catilines of the first epistle, whose abuse of free will
was to be expected in the "general order" (though not required)

---

   1. Pope's note at *Essay*, IV 309 *ff.*
   2. This point is made in G. Wilson Knight's *The Burning Oracle* (1939),
pp. 167–8.

become the Nero who "reigns a Titus, if he will", the Catiline whose fiery soul "In Decius charms, in Curtius is divine". Man when compared with Providence is still a poor thing, a fool where God is wise, an individualist pursuing his own ends that are only reconciled with the larger scheme by a superior power; but he is now squarely in the centre of the picture, he is capable of virtues, and if his ways of fulfilling himself seem, when looked at from a higher view, partly delusive as well as genuine, they are after all an aspect of his reality with which the higher view must come to terms: "In Folly's cup still laughs the bubble, joy." There is pity mingled with the irony in Pope's portrait of man the eternal child.

For these passional, instinctive, self-fulfilling elements in human nature are forces helping man towards his goal, as the third Epistle shows. Through compassion, pride, interest, luxury, he subserves the fellowship of lower creatures, his self-considering instincts guide him into wedlock, family, commonwealth; misapplied, they carry him to despotism and superstition, but rectified, to true religion and government by law.[1] In the picture of reunion with which the third Epistle closes, man is no longer diminished nor even deluded, but the composer of "th' according music of a well-mix'd State", a creative agent reproducing in his society the harmony of God's, delineating thus His shadow if not His image, living "supported", but nevertheless contributing: "The strength he gains is from th' embrace he gives." And in the corresponding passage of the fourth Epistle (which brings together, it should be noted, the leading themes of all: acceptance, self-love, sociality, happiness), man no longer reflects the shadow but the image. When he has thrown an ever-widening circle of love about the whole—extending the embrace he gives to include his neighbours, enemies, and the whole worlds of reason, life, and sense—self-love transcends itself in charity, *eros* in *agape*, and man reflects to heaven an experience of complex unity creatively achieved among dissimilars (the Many resolved in *Man*), which is akin to and indeed is the mirror image of the complex unity of existents sustained in the mind of God:

---

1. In its fable of the innocence, fall, and redemption of society, this epistle contains a paradigm of the theme we are discussing.

> God loves from Whole to Parts: but human soul
> Must rise from Individual to the Whole.
> Self-love but serves the virtuous mind to wake,
> As the small pebble stirs the peaceful lake;
> The centre mov'd, a circle strait succeeds,
> Another still, and still another spreads,
> Friend, parent, neighbour, first it will embrace,
> His country next, and next all human race,
> Wide and more wide, th' o'erflowings of the mind
> Take every creature in, of every kind;
> Earth smiles around, with boundless bounty blest,
> And Heav'n beholds its image in his breast.[1]

Beginning with a reminder of a paradise man has lost, the poem ends with a paradise he can regain.

III

Attention to some of the thematic patterns of Pope's poem, suggested in the preceding pages, helps to clarify its relations to the vital interests of its time. As we all know, poems of the dimensions of the *Essay on Man* are not likely to be carried through to completion on the mere suggestion of a philosophically minded friend, yet we have been too long content with precisely this hypothesis in the case of Pope. Poems demand some kind of spiritual motivation, correspond in some way to the needs of an author or an age—needs not necessarily consciously formulated, but felt. In seeking to define such factors, we are always frankly in the realm of speculation, but the speculation can be helpful in so far as it calls attention to permanent qualities of the poem. If one were to conjecture about the *Essay on Man* in this way, one would perhaps select for emphasis the following points.

For one thing, the poem obviously shares the general urgency of modern literature, much accelerated during the seventeenth century, to internalize and translate toward higher levels of abstraction matters that in an earlier age supplied the unglossed objective content of tale, romance, myth, and mystery. Spenser

---

1. *Essay*, IV 361-72.

uses elements of romance, but semi-conceptualized in allegory; his giant is a real giant, but he is named Despair, not Hercules. Milton, for whom already the trappings of romance had ceased to be "available", turned to the one kind of heroic story he could subscribe to, and even there conceptualized it at all important points. In *Paradise Lost* the prohibition of the apple is no longer an adventitious command beset with mysteries as it is in Genesis, but a rationalized symbol of obedience or disobedience (its meaning is thus internal), and the consequences of eating it are again rationalized and internalized, in the rebellion of the passions and the act of lust. For Pope's age, and Pope as poet, whatever may have been the case for Pope as a man, even this story had lost, perhaps, its full imaginative availability. It is certainly an exaggeration in a recent writer to say that it would have been "unthinkable" in Pope's time for a serious poet to have used the Scriptural story,[1] but the comment has the virtue of forcing on our attention Pope's further conceptualization of Milton's theme. In the *Essay*, the narrative that served Milton to vindicate God and account for the nature of man has been replaced by the chain of being; the Garden of Eden by the garden of temptations in the world at large; the hero Adam by the honest man; and the paradise to be regained is not, as in Milton, partly inward and partly objective through the actual coming of Christ at the end of the world, but, so far as the poem is concerned, wholly inward. Pope's instinctive transliteration of this theme into rationalistic terms made it available, possibly to himself and certainly to his age, as nothing else could have done; and it may not be going too far afield to suggest that there is between his poem and Milton's greater one a relation something like that which Werner Jaeger posits for Archilochus and Homer. The poetry of Archilochus, Jaeger says, "and that of his age, was born of the need of the free individual to see and solve the problem of human life outside the mystic content of epic poetry, which had hitherto been the only sphere in which it could be posed or answered".[2] So Pope can be said to have tried to give a poetic definition to the problems of man's nature and God's justice outside the sphere of religious allegory, heroic drama,

---

1. Basil Willey, *The Seventeenth-Century Background* (1934), p. 296.
2. *Paideia* (tr. Highet), I (1939) 124.

and scriptural story, where they had for the most part been confined before.

On the other hand, it is equally important for understanding the poem to recognize that it reacts with vigour—whether consciously or unconsciously—against certain contemporary tendencies of a sort that poets are likely to protest against in any age and that later poets have felt the effects of with some distress. One such group of tendencies was that which eventuated in the scientific myth (it has been called in our day both "the fallacy of misplaced concreteness" and "the postulate [i.e. fallacy] of impoverished reality") that reality in its essence is somehow simpler, barer, more mechanical, and in general less exciting than our experience of it—e.g., that the "primary" qualities of matter, mass, figure, extension, are more "real" than the attributes matter presents to us—and accordingly that the elements in our experience which declare that reality is more than this are to be received as fraudulent.[1] The result of this has been the imprisonment of mind at solipsistic casements, opening on the foam of appearances that are subjective, moral standards that are merely customs, ends and purposes that are only socio-psychological folklore. "The real is what it is, and there remains no valid reason [on the above hypothesis] why it should be otherwise."[2]

Though the *Essay on Man*, in its conceptual mutation of a mystic theme, perhaps itself reflects the movement of the modern mind toward this self-extinction, within its conceptual limits the poem is a massive rebuttal. Reflecting the traditional beliefs in the purposefulness of all realms, natural, moral, and metaphysical, Pope has housed these doctrines in a poetic universe and developing theme that assert nothing so strongly as the life, quality, design, direction, and objective meaning of man's experienced world. The concept of the chain of being, and the sense of God as living down into His Creation, which is its corollary, obviously

---

1. The first of the quoted phrases is from Whitehead's *Science and the Modern World* (Cambridge, 1926), p. 74; the second, from Iredell Jenkins's "The Postulate of an Impoverished Reality", *Journ. of Philos.*, xxix (1942) 533ff. For the same general criticism, see E. A. Burtt, *The Metaphysical Foundations of Modern Science*, 1932.

2. Iredell Jenkins, *op. cit.*, pp. 538–9.

E

contain for Pope something like the combination of objective truth with imaginative adaptability that the story of Eden had for Milton; for this reason he is able to clothe these abstractions with concrete circumstances and to endow them, in his poem, with what amounts to a kind of personality, distinguishing his treatment of them from that of others. The intensity, power, and speciality of Pope's handling can be best appreciated if one compares his vision of the chain of being with some other—say, Thomson's,[1] or such a passage as that on the One and Many with the relevant lines in Wordsworth's "Tintern Abbey".[2] In the latter instance, the question is not superiority but difference. For Pope the immanent power is unmistakable divinity; its immensity is paradoxical but sharply known, delineated in terms that ages have defined; there is a thunder in its presence as well as a stiller voice—and it is declared in categorical indicatives as a cosmic fact that no man dare ignore. In "Tintern Abbey", on the other hand, it is hard to say at first whether the presence is divine or an emanation from natural objects, whether it is outside and known to all, or inside and only available to poets: the lines are tentative, muted like the thing described.[3] Wordsworth's "presence" is much more naturalistic than Pope's, and it is clear that the Romantic poet is having a harder time of it doctrinally; in "Tintern Abbey" Pope's objective reality is threatening to disappear entirely inward, to the point at which Coleridge will exclaim:

1. *Essay on Man*, I 207*ff*; *Summer* (1727), 283*ff*.

2. Ll. 93*ff*.

3. One obvious preoccupation of Romantic poetry is so to enmesh and substantiate "Spirit" in particulars of landscape that it can be taken both in quasi-religious terms as an objective mystery and in naturalistic terms as a product of poetic imagination. Hence in part, one suspects, the double Romantic concern with natural objects faithfully observed (guarantee of realistic substantiation) and with esemplastic imagination—"a repetition in the finite mind of the eternal act of creation in the infinite I Am" (guarantee of something to be substantiated). Wordsworth's famous comment on English poetry from *Paradise Lost* to Thomson (scarcely an image of nature "from which it can be inferred that the eye of the Poet had been steadily fixed upon his object, much less that his feelings had urged him to act upon it in the spirit of genuine imagination") illustrates this double concern—and also its irrelevance to the markedly different preoccupations of the Augustans.

O Lady! we receive but what we give,
And in our life alone does Nature live.

But in Wordsworth reality never quite recedes to this point; and
from the testimony of men like Arnold and Leslie Stephen it would
appear that he performed a prime service for the nineteenth
century in finding poetic ways of embodying the conviction that
Coleridge's mood of dejection is not the whole truth. Wordsworth's
"presence" may be tentative, but "Tintern Abbey" and *The
Prelude* stand as monuments—not, I think, burial monuments—
to one version of the Ciceronian sentiment that there is some kind
of objective order beyond man, and that he who does not obey it
abandons his better self. Pope's *Essay* also is such a monument.

There is another set of tendencies in Pope's age, not entirely
unrelated to the scientific myth, which the *Essay* also repudiates,
or perhaps, better, reorients. It has been argued with some justice
by students of the Renaissance that besides the accepted and
therefore not too disturbing conflict between the perfection of the
universal order and man as sinner, the Renaissance intelligence
was troubled far more seriously by contemporary inroads upon the
very notion of such an order, in all its phases. Copernicus and
Galileo were about to cause some notable readjustments in man's
cosmological situation; Montaigne was contending that man was
not precisely creation's crown or set apart so far from the animals
as he conceived himself to be; and Machiavelli asserted flatly that
man's morality, viz. his political morality, had no relation to any
natural law or nature except the kind that Edmund found it
expedient to invoke in *King Lear*. Without putting too much stress
on these or any particular influences, one might fairly say that the
characteristic development of modern thought has been in these
directions and that by Pope's time the development was considerably advanced. The implications of Hobbes and Mandeville in
politics and morals have their affinities with those of Machiavelli;
seventeenth-century "theriophily" and scepticism, Restoration
Epicureanism in men like Rochester, and eighteenth-century sentimentalism all undermine in one way or other the complacency of
anthropocentrism; and the ultimate tendency of Newtonianism,
though not at once apparent, was of course to widen the gap
between man and a universe whose "real" attributes were

mechanical and mathematical. In short, the emphatically descriptive trends of modern learning had begun, and were calling attention to certain "irreducible and stubborn facts"[1] that either had to be accepted at face value or accommodated to some less exclusive scheme.

Men of religious and poetic temperament preferred the attempt to accommodate these facts, and this is also Pope's procedure in the *Essay on Man*. The vastness and impersonality of Newton's universe everywhere permeates the poem, but it is reoriented, in a way that it is not by Bolingbroke, for instance, to personality and the uses of religion. Mechanical images from the Newtonian world are woven into the tissue of images from older and more humane conceptions. God is an Eternal and Universal Cause, an abstract "Heaven", an impartial and disposing power, but He is also the Psalmist's God who is present in the clouds and winds, who directs the lightning, ocean, and the storms, who has made us a little lower than the angels and who laughs at terrestrial power; He is also Aaron's God, who revealed himself in the metamorphosis of the rod; Isaiah's God, whose footstool is earth; the God of Job, who cannot by searching be found out but in whose hand is the soul of every living thing; the God of Matthew, whose care embraces man and sparrows, and whose law and prophets are all summed up in love of Him and other men; the God of Paul, in whose being all are members. By the same token, while magnifying Newton's knowledge as the sort which unfolds all nature's law, Pope promptly puts it back into perspective against the knowledge of the angels.[2]

---

1. William James's phrase. *Letters* (ed. H. James, 1920), I 225.
2. Other accommodations of old and new can be noticed at the level of technique. The texture of the passage on the chain of being, for instance (and of several others: cf. I 23 *ff*, III 7 *ff*, etc.) results in part from the complex interactions of a traditional concept with particulars either derived from or reorganized in the light of the new sciences; these particulars being then presented in language that purports to offer the spare exactitudes of scientific discourse while actually generating a maximum of suggestion: cf. "the green myriads in the peopled grass", "the life that fills the flood", the bee's "sense so subtly true" ("true" is the crucial epithet), or the famous couplet about the spider—in all of which the kind of description one might expect to get from a sensitive Newtonian naturalist brims over into something that Pope, to judge from his poem and his com-

Similar procedures, taming new descriptive facts to a more familiar and normative scheme of things, can be seen in Pope's handling of anthropocentrism and of the political and moral propositions adduced by Hobbes and Mandeville. Pope's poem passionately opposes anthropocentrism in the usual senses of the term, and unmistakably draws on Montaigne's delineation of human arrogance in supposing the universe only made for man; but it notably rejects Montaigne's central argument that the powers of man and animal are different but in degree, refers animal wisdom as in traditional doctrine to the direct action of God, distinguishes its own position from Epicurean as well as Stoic views, readjusts the anthropocentric conception to include the animals and the animal element in man, and perhaps rests its theme, as earlier suggested, on the recognition that man must not arrogantly ignore these facts of his situation, but by taking account of his limitations discover his potentialities. So too with the ethics of individualistic egoism and political theory unrelated to higher law. It needs no emphasis that the types of method and theory represented by men like Machiavelli, Hobbes, and Mandeville, particularly the former two, have been of the first importance in the history of thought, that the old patterns badly needed the ventilation such thinking gave them, and that the urge to go behind fancy pictures to the real truth of things, as Machiavelli phrased it, is a founding principle of modern civilization. Rightly or wrongly, nevertheless, poets from Sophocles to Eliot have generally been disinclined to accept as final the fragmentations of man and universe that usually present themselves when one has got behind the poetic and religious pictures—one of the virtues of such pictures, as they might define it, being precisely to keep these fragments ordered into wholes. It has long been noticed that the Machiavellian of the Elizabethan drama is the villain, and it has likewise been pointed out that there are respects in which *Paradise*

---

ment on Newton in it, found wanting in Newtonianism. It is perhaps worth stressing that Pope's poetry in general (not the *Essay* alone) makes out of uncanny precisions in word-choice and word-order the kinds of value that other poetries achieve through a richer or warmer language: "Bare the mean Heart that lurks beneath a Star" (*Sat.*, II i 108); "I have not yet forgot my self to stone" (*Eloisa*, 24); "Light dies before thy uncreating word" (*Dunc.*, IV 654); etc.

Lost may be regarded as the greatest of seventeenth-century replies to Hobbes.[1]

So with Pope, in his own way and his own time. His *Essay* takes account of the power of egoism, of the rooting of the virtues in the same soil as the vices, and the social goods that may accrue from a-social motives ("private vices, public benefits"), as well as of the urge to power that for Hobbes could only be stabilized in the totalitarian state; but all these are comprehended in a frankly normative view. Hobbes's war of all on all appears in the poem, but it is no longer the state of nature, as it was for him; it is an "enormous", i.e. abnormal, condition, a distortion of the steady light of right reason by wit oblique, an antithesis to a thesis from which results the synthesis of a well-mixed state mirroring a higher order and a higher law. This is not to say that we are to expect of Shakespeare, Milton, or Pope effective refutation of ethical propositions on the plane of logic and discursive reason. Poetry's habit is to take the argument to another plane altogether, where, as by the author of the Book of Job, the problem is for the moment at any rate not resolved but dissolved because the context in which we look at it has been transfigured and enlarged. Nor is it to say that Pope, in seeking to tame the new conceptions to older patterns, was original: like Milton, if we may assume that *Paradise Lost* has some reference to Hobbist doctrine, Pope was only doing what a host of his contemporaries were trying or had tried to do, but being a poet, did it in a more memorable way. Here again we may legitimately see a "meaning" that the poem may have had for its author and his contemporaries, and has for us.

We may see another in the central theme itself. One way of stating this, as we have seen, would be to call it the theme of constructive renunciation. By renouncing the exterior false Paradises the true one within is won; by acknowledging his weaknesses man learns his strengths; by subordinating himself to the whole he finds his real importance in it. Renunciation in this sense, conceived not as stagnation of the spirit but redirection toward its truest ends,

---

1. Marjorie Nicolson, "Milton and Hobbes", *Stud. in Philol.*, XXIII (1926) 405–33. The attitude of the older English poets toward untramelled individualism is worth observing: in Shakespeare's Edmund and Iago and other villains, in Milton's rebel angels, and in Pope's *Essay on Man*.

is a ruling principle with Pope. It appears in the *Essay on Criticism*, where it is the foundation of all the qualifications specified for critics: we excel by giving up—not only what is inappropriate to the individual self but what is inappropriate to man as man. It appears again in the *Dunciad*, where the indictment of the indivi- dual dunces, hard nowadays to accept with our less rigorous understanding of the rôle of will, rests squarely on their failure to achieve individual self-knowledge, and the indictment of Dulness as a principle on the fact (emphasized by the imagery of the famous closing lines) that it diverts man to pursuits and interests that negate his human ends. [1] And the same principle appears in poems as widely different from these as the *Characters of Women* and the *Rape of the Lock*—the very method of the former, one might say, being a defoliation leaf by leaf of glittering false forms of womanli- ness, to unfold the true; while in the latter the complex tone is generated out of the poet's consciousness that illusion, though as bright and beautiful as Belinda's petticoat, exists to be laid aside. Once we sense the currency of other versions of this theme in Pope's poetry, we may be less likely than we have been to suppose the *Essay* an accident or excrescence in his career; and more likely to see in it, as we should, a further effort to explore, this time in its widest terms, what Pope, in common with other poets, had long since recognized as a fundamental fact about the nature of experience. As Santayana says in discussing Lucretius, Dante, and Goethe, the deepest insights of poets, in spite of differences in the mode of apprehension determined by the devices and desires of a given age, tend to show a family resemblance.

The maxim of Lucretius, that nothing arises save by the death of something else, meets us still in our crawling immortality. And his art of accepting and enjoying what the conditions of our being afford also has a perennial application. Dante, the poet of faith, will tell us that we must find our peace in the will that gives us

---

1. As Simplicius put it, "If you take upon you a character above your capacity, you fall into this twofold inconvenience, first to miscarry in what you have undertaken, and then to lose the opportunity of undertaking somewhat else, more proportionable to your ability, in which you might have come off with Honour." *Epictetus His Morals With Simplicius His Comment*, tr. Stanhope (2nd ed., 1700), pp. 371-2.

our limited portion. Goethe, the poet of romantic experience, will tell us that we must renounce, renounce perpetually. Thus wisdom clothes the same moral truths in many cosmic parables. The doctrines of philosophers disagree where they are literal and arbitrary—mere guesses about the unknown; but they agree or complete one another where they are expressive or symbolic, thoughts wrung by experience from the hearts of poets.[1]

IV

The primary advantage of grasping the *Essay on Man* as a thematic whole, keeping alive in its own time and with its own emphases one of the great religious and moral themes, is that this illuminates the work in its character and quality as a poem. So much has been said in the preceding pages that bears directly or indirectly on this topic that it will suffice in concluding to underline three points.

The first is the magnitude and range of Pope's subject. It has been easy for the twentieth century to overlook this because, as a critic of Milton has recently observed,[2] in fundamental outlook Milton is nearer to Shakespeare—and he might have added, Pope is nearer to Milton—than either is to us. The worlds of all three poets, if we limit the statement to their conceptual worlds, are more alike than unlike, their assumptions and beliefs sharing an inherited spaciousness, and the issues with which they deal, once we understand them, centrality and permanence. Whatever the *Essay* may have owed in its biographical origins to Bolingbroke, speculative deism, Augustan fashions of philosophical poetry, or other contemporary stimuli, Pope has incorporated materials in it and handled them with a largeness that enable the poem to transcend its origins and establish contact with the collective religious and moral past. Between *Paradise Lost* and *The Prelude*, there is no other English poem of which this can be said. Not that great subjects, by themselves, produce great poems. But great subjects being one of the conditions of great poems, it is worth

1. *Three Philosophical Poets* (1910), pp. 69–70.
2. Douglas Bush, *Paradise Lost in Our Time* (1945), p. 31.

reminding ourselves that this is a condition the *Essay on Man* fulfils. The habits that have blinded us to Pope's achievement in this respect are the habit of fragmenting the ideas of the *Essay* out in individual passages (Pope would have called it "a love to parts") for praise or blame irrespective of their relation to the whole; and the further habit of putting a genetic interest in the poem above our critical interest. Thus—to illustrate both—a recent critic dismisses the *Essay on Man*, in view of the contrast of Epistles II and IV, as amounting to nothing but an illustration of the contemporary muddle of sentimentalism and anti-sentimentalism, "reflected in the eclectic mind of a great artist".[1] Fragmentarily and biographically speaking, such an analysis may be true or false, but in either case it has no manner of relevance to the *Essay*, where, whatever his private muddle, "the great artist" makes dramatic use of conflicts, just as Milton in *Paradise Lost* and elsewhere makes dramatic use of analogous conflicts that may have been troublesome for his private thought.

This is not of course to compare Pope's poem with Milton's. Pope's is distinctly a poem of the middle flight, as its opening lines assure us; a conversation (this is its effect, though strictly it has but one speaker) between cultivated men, rather than—what *Paradise Lost* has been aptly called—a ceremonial. Furthermore, though his theme is analogous to Milton's, Pope cannot and does not probe it to Milton's depth, one reason being that he has no characters involved in dramatic action. The imaginative virtue of a Satan is that though he may represent fallen pride, or evil, or any similar set of cognitive realities, and so call out attitudes long agreed on by collective racial reason, he may simultaneously call out others that he generates uniquely as agent and patient in the context of action that the poem supplies—becoming thus a means of exploring values that lie outside a rationally accepted scheme, extending the intellectual configurations of the poem without shattering them, in a manner perhaps analogous, in the religious life, to the extension of dogma by devotion. However this may be, Pope has had to find his own means of declaring the multivalence of experience where most poets since the seventeenth century have had to find them, in paradox, metaphor, shifts of tone, allusion,

---

1. H. N. Fairchild, *Religious Trends in English Poetry*, I (1939) 505, 507.

clashes of statement—means that the epic or dramatic poet can
add to his already great advantage—and the attenuation that
results is notable. Likewise, there is the absence of Magnificence.
Milton, sometimes Spenser, Shakespeare in his own way, are all
"Magnificent" poets in a sense that Donne and Pope and Keats are
not, a sense that has little to do with matter and everything to do
with manner. The ages that produced this quality may have paid a
high price for it, as they did for palaces and great churches, but it
has a virtue for poetry and Pope lacks it.

A second point that needs some emphasis is that the *Essay on Man*
is a public, social, and classical poem. Readers will come from it
disappointed if they go to it looking for the meditative vein of
Vaughan and Herbert and some poems of Donne, or the brooding
wonder of Wordsworth when he grapples with the problems of
man's destiny and mind. The difference between Pope's world
and Donne's is handsomely illustrated in the way in which the
Essay on Man (IV 40) echoes Donne's image of the compasses. In
Donne's world, this image is typically the symbol of an exclusion:
the union of two lovers, two individuals, two souls fortifying a
metaphysical mystery (almost a kind of Grace) against the laity
of the world. In Pope's, the image is just as typically the symbol of
inclusion: the union of the individual, not with another individual,
but with the kind. This change expresses in miniature not only the
philosophical shift from the seventeenth-century ideal of *pélerinage
de l'âme* to the eighteenth-century ideal of cosmopolitanism and
sociality (a shift further reflected in the fact that Pope's poems are
characteristically organized around a friend-to-friend and not
a lover-to-mistress relation). It possibly expresses also one religious difference between a Protestant and Roman Catholic
outlook—despite the fact that Donne was not always Protestant
nor Pope the devoutest sort of Roman Catholic. In the Roman
church, man may be and indeed is a pilgrim working out his own
salvation, but he works it out in terms of a vast and authoritative
social and religious whole in which his own individual experiences,
even if he is one of the greatest mystics, are always subject to
correction by the collective wisdom embodied in the whole. And
this may indeed be one reason why there are few poems, if any, in
the English tradition which body forth the sense of corporateness
so vigorously as Pope's. In the *Essay on Man*, attitudes generated by

deism, eighteenth-century sociality, and Roman Catholicism come together.

In the same way, there are fundamental differences between Pope's world and Wordsworth's. In Wordsworth, a student of his vocabulary observes, though a great deal of the subject-matter and diction stem from the eighteenth century, the quality we think of as characteristically Wordsworthian is the new complication introduced by the presence of the poet as a sensibility.[1] Wordsworth's experience is likely to be charted in terms of its sensory, almost physiological influences: "sensations sweet, Felt in the blood, and felt along the heart,—And passing even into my purer mind—With tranquil restoration"; and it is his own individual experience, felt in *his* blood, along *his* heart, passing into *his* mind. The objects that are absorbed into "Tintern Abbey" (the same could be said of *The Prelude*)—"these hedgerows", "these pastoral farms", these "wreaths of smoke", "the sounding cataract", "the tall rock, The mountain, and the deep and gloomy wood"—are held in place, justified, by their relation and their meaning to Wordsworth the experiencer. In the *Essay on Man*, the objects that Pope assimilates—weeds, oaks, spiders, bees, halcyons, lawns, floods, roses, rills—are held in place by their relation and meaning to a divine and universal plan. This difference is partly owing to the cause already noted, the fading by Wordsworth's time of the sense of metaphysical order in the world. In Ruskin's memorable words, "exactly in proportion as the idea of definite spiritual presence in material nature was lost, the mysterious sense of *unaccountable* life in the things themselves would be increased."[2] But it is partly owing also to a change in the centre of poetic interest. It is typical of Pope, when he is describing an inward happiness, to call it "The soul's calm sun-shine, and the heart-felt joy".[3] Feeling is denominated, but it is not traced, "in the blood, along the heart"; it is dealt with not as Pope's feeling but as any man's, and not at the level of discovery but of recognition. Simi-

---

1. Josephine Miles, *The Vocabulary of Poetry* (1946), p. 137. In this sensitive and suggestive study, the reader will find much to corroborate the suggestions of the following two paragraphs.

2. "Of Mediaeval Landscape", *Modern Painters*, III iv, ch. XIV, sec. 7.

3. *Essay*, IV 168.

larly, where Wordsworth's interest in a lake is that "oh, then, the calm And dead still water lay upon my mind Even with a weight of pleasure," Pope's interest is that "Self-love but serves the virtuous mind to wake, As the small pebble stirs the peaceful lake."[1] Wordsworth, like romantic poets in general, is engaged in exploring a new experience; there was nothing in English poetry quite like what Wordsworth there describes until Wordsworth described it. Pope, like classical poets in general, is ordering, shaping, giving form to the familiar. Pope's insight is as fine as Wordsworth's; it would be hard to exaggerate the quiet felicity of the comparison of virtuous happiness to the sun: bright, serene, predictable, out-going, life-giving, etc.; or of the repetition in the lake and pebble passage of the *Essay*'s pervading theme that the self is the dynamic or principle of "becoming" in the moral world, and yet exists, as the mystics would say, only to be swallowed up in being. But these are truths the world has always known; Pope's task is simply to refine our understanding of them.

This contrast explains in part the difference of Pope's and Wordsworth's styles. The hushed and at moments almost trance-like quality of Wordsworth's verse is appropriate to Wordsworth's theme. It is the rightful language of a poetry which seeks com-munion with nature, seeks to be operated on in a condition of wise passiveness, seeks to elaborate the harmonies of outer world and inner (tranquil lakes and tranquil thoughts, dancing daffodils and dancing hearts, beauties born of murmuring sound), seeks to relate all this, with precise and delicate definitions, to the curve of the author's sensibility—analysing and painstakingly recording what is found there. With this subject-matter, the mode of Words-worth's poetry is naturally descriptive, brooding, hesitant. In Pope's world, on the contrary, the emphasis is not on communion with nature or wise passiveness, but on wise activity: man is to operate on nature (in much the way that "art" does in classical aesthetics), co-operate with it, put it to work. Similarly, Pope's world, while it contains an ideal potential harmony of man and an *ordre naturel*, is bristlingly aware of all the actual disharmonies between them: in this respect, Pope's vision if not so probing as Wordsworth's is more adult and wide. Furthermore, Pope is

---

1. *Prelude*, II 170–2; *Essay*, IV 363–4.

interested not at all in the curve of his own but in the curve of the communal sensibility; his bond with the social audience is very close. All these facts combine to produce a style in the *Essay on Man* that is anything but tentative or trance-like, a style hortatory, cajoling, persuasive, imperative—"Then say not Man's imperfect," "Hope humbly," "Know then thyself," "Take Nature's path"—in which the sense characteristically called on is the sight, a more "public" sense than feeling: "Mark how it mounts," "See through this air," "See some strange comfort," "Look round our world," "See him from Nature," "See the sole bliss." The speaker is not Pope, but Everyman; the audience is Everyman too; and so is the subject. We should not expect to find in poems by, for, and about Everyman—which is to say, in classical poems—many attitudes of brooding wonder. Classical poets do not wonder at man: they may admire him at his best:

> Two of far nobler shape, erect and tall,
> Godlike erect, with native honour clad,
> In naked majesty seemed lords of all;

or they may regard him with mixed pity and laughter at his worst:

> Such of late
> Columbus found the American so girt
> With feather'd cincture, naked else and wild;

but they do not make him a subject of reverential awe. There is no more revealing passage (revealing of significant shifts in point of view) in all of nineteenth-century poetry than the lines in the *Recluse*[1] where Wordsworth applies to his theme—man's mind—the same panoply of venerative terms that Milton applies to God. For the romantic poet, divinity and mystery exist in man; for the classical poet, they exist in God.[2] It is no accident that the passages in Pope's *Essay* which have been credited with "sublimity" refer to God.

As one must go to the *Essay on Man* expecting a particular kind of speech and outlook (and not other kinds), one must go to it also expecting a particular balance of the concrete and universal. If

---

1. Ll. 777–93.
2. See on this point Martin Turnell, "Dryden and the Religious Elements in the Classical Tradition", *Englische Studien* (1935–6), LXX 244–61.

one were to draw a line, representing degrees of particularity, between such a poem as Hopkins's "Wreck of the Deutschland" and such a poem as Dryden's *Religio Laici*, Pope's *Essay* would fall somewhere about the middle, with a slight inclination toward Dryden. Compared with Hopkins, the *Essay on Man* is a poem conducted on a high level of abstraction; it states as often as it images (its images, as we have seen, are spare of sensory detail), it images less often than it names (this is a characteristic it shares with Wordsworth), and it names in a special way. Here we are in the presence of a fact of decorum. Pope could be lingeringly particular when this was relevant to his meaning—Belinda's dressing-table, Eloisa's landscape, Cotta's "lone Chartreux", the fop's Grand Tour in *Dunciad* IV. But the aspect of objects that is mainly decorous to his theme in the *Essay* is their relation to, their place in, the cosmic order, and it is this that much of his naming stresses. The spider's touch, the nice bee, the flowery lawn, man's imperial race, are limited to their essential and generic qualities in a poetic world of kinds for the same reason that everything else in this world is spoken of as "assigned", "measured", "proportioned", "placed": Pope's subject is not the visible universe but the intelligible manifested in the visible; the concreteness that he is concerned with is not of objects as individuals but of conceptual wholes in which objects are arranged—and where Keats's "coming musk-rose filled with dewy wine" would be as out of place as "Die of a rose in aromatic pain" would be out of place in the "Ode to a Nightingale". It is safe to say that whenever a reader of poetry thinks of such large abstractions as the scale of being, the cycle of life, or human "middleness", his mind is bound to turn to Pope.[1]

Pope was profoundly gifted at this task of bestowing *Dinglichkeit* on concepts. The measure of his success can be best appreciated by contrasting his poem with one to which it is often erroneously compared, Dryden's *Religio Laici*, already cited. Leaving aside the

1. It is of course important not to ignore the sensory qualities of the *Essay*. To take one instance, such a list of adjectives as the following (I borrow it from Miss Miles's study, cited above, p. lxxv, *n.* 1)—giddy, vast, argent, fiery, dull, watery, nectareous, balmy, livid, cloudless, aromatic, green, dim, vernal, thin, mazy, sour, wild, golden, cool, fresh, fine, iron, yellow, peaceful, boundless, gay —points to an element in the poem that modern readers are likely to forget.

question of ultimate merit, one can easily see that the two poems differ enormously in their methods. Dryden's poem is genuinely ratiocinative, genuinely an argument, and everything about it accords with this: its tone is thoughtful, dispassionate, expository, like that of a man recounting what he has seen at a play; its arrangement is a series of propositions leading up to conclusions, each proposition to be phrased as vividly as may be, but having no other relation to the whole than as a stage in a logical sequence. Pope's tone in the *Essay* is different. It is that of an actor in the play, shifting with the situation, not only from grave to gay and lively to severe, but from scorn to pity, humour to outrage, colloquialism to formality, persiflage to affirmation, all these moods conspiring to enact the experience that Dryden's speaker is recollecting. And Pope's arrangement is also different. Propositions occur in the poem, as they do in an actor's speeches, but less as theorems than as formulations and definitions of states of mind which are to accumulate finally in inclusions, not conclusions—in an imaginatively ordered world. The nub of all the differences can be grasped by contrasting the following quotations, two among many in which the contrast remains the same. Speaking of human incapacity to grasp the divine nature of God, Dryden says:

> In this wild maze their vain endeavours end:
> How can the less the greater comprehend?
> Or finite reason reach Infinity?
> For what could fathom God were more than He.

and Pope:

> He, who thro' vast immensity can pierce,
> See worlds on worlds compose one universe,
> Observe how system into system runs,
> What other planets circle other suns,
> What vary'd being peoples ev'ry star,
> May tell why Heav'n has made us as we are.
> But of this frame the bearings, and the ties,
> The strong connections, nice dependencies,
> Gradations just, has thy pervading soul
> Look'd thro'? or can a part contain the whole?[1]

---

1. *Religio Laici*, 38–41; *Essay*, I 23–32.

The "proposition" of both these passages is that a part cannot contain its whole. Yet without going into them in detail, it is clear that Dryden uses it as an axiom whose appeal is to the intellect while Pope translates it into a crescendo of images of cosmic grandeur and intricacy, shrinking the proud soul that is not, like God's, pervasive but would nevertheless pervade.

In sum, then, Pope's *Essay on Man* is a poem of abstractions, but of abstractions put to work in an artistic whole. The ideas that Pope calls into play are precisely the ideas most relevant to the theme of constructive renunciation—theodicy and ethics. The movement of thought which without being a linear progression determines the poem's general structure—from metaphysics to psychology, morals, politics, and thence to the happiness of the individual—corresponds to and helps compose the development from acceptance to discrimination and commitment. And the variety of images and allusions, the shifting tones, the juxtapositions of passages that suggest empathic living into the sum of things with passages that suggest standing aloof and critical, the paradoxes that give notice (by the only means possible to philosophical poetry) of the rational passing over into mystery—all these combine to dramatize the central meaning in the very texture of the verse: there is a fecundity and comprehensiveness in the Creation and in man himself which man cannot do justice to otherwise than by trusting it for what it is, and simultaneously an ideal order, unity, harmony, and purpose which man must both support and help to realize by disciplining himself.

It is ironical that the poem of Pope's which is most perfect in its formal unity and most impressive in its theme should be the one least known in our age, as we grow increasingly aware of the value of his other works.

CHRONOLOGICAL TABLE

The standard biographies are G. Sherburn's *The Early Career of Alexander Pope*, 1934, and W. J. Courthope's life in vol. v of the Elwin-Courthope edition of Pope's works, 1871–89. Sherburn's account stops in 1727.

1688 (May 21) Alexander Pope born in London of elderly parents.

*c.*1700 Pope's family moved to Binfield, in Windsor Forest, [?] to comply with anti-Catholic regulations.
Death of Dryden.

*c.*1705 Pope started to make acquaintance with the literary society of London.

1709 (May) The *Pastorals* published in the sixth part of Tonson's *Miscellanies*.

1711 (May) *An Essay on Criticism* published; praised in *The Spectator* by Addison, and damned by Dennis.

1712 (May) The *Messiah* published by Steele in *The Spectator*. Lintot's *Miscellany* published, containing the first version of *The Rape of the Lock*, and other poems by Pope. Pope was becoming acquainted with Swift, Gay, Parnell, and Arbuthnot, who together formed the Scriblerus Club.

1713 (March) *Windsor Forest*.
(April) Addison's *Cato* first acted, with a prologue by Pope. Pope was contributing to Steele's *Guardian*.
(October) Proposals issued for a translation of the *Iliad*.

1714 (March) The enlarged version of *The Rape of the Lock*.
(August) Death of Queen Anne.

1715 (February) *The Temple of Fame*.
(June 6) The *Iliad*, Books I–IV, published; followed two days later by Tickell's translation of *Iliad* I. During this year [?], Pope wrote his character of Addison, and became acquainted with Lady Mary Wortley Montagu.

1716 (March) *Iliad*, vol. II.
Pope's revenge by poison on Curll the publisher [Sherburn, ch. VI; N. Ault, *Pope's Prose*, pp. xciv ff.].
(April) Pope's family sold the house at Binfield, and settled at Chiswick, where their neighbour was Lord Burlington.

1717 (January) *Three Hours after Marriage* by Pope, Gay, and Arbuthnot, first acted.
(June) *Iliad*, vol. III.
The collected volume of Pope's *Works*, containing *Verses to the Memory of an Unfortunate Lady* and *Eloisa to Abelard*.
(October) Pope's father died.

1718 (June) *Iliad*, vol. IV.
Death of Parnell. Pope and his mother moved to Twickenham late in the year.

1719 Death of Addison.

1720 (May) *Iliad*, vols. V and VI.

1721 (September) The *Epistle to Addison* prefixed to Tickell's edition of Addison's *Works*.
(December) The *Epistle to Oxford* prefixed to Pope's edition of Parnell's *Poems*.

1723 (January) Pope's edition of John Sheffield, Duke of Buckingham's *Works* published, and seized by the Government on suspicion of Jacobitish passages.
(May) Pope called before the House of Lords as a witness at Atterbury's trial.

1725 (March) Pope's edition of Shakespeare published in six volumes.
(April) *Odyssey*, vols. I–III.
Bolingbroke returned from exile, and settled near Pope at Dawley Farm, Uxbridge.

1726 (March) Theobald's *Shakespeare Restored: or, a Specimen of the Many Errors . . . Committed . . . by Mr Pope.*
(June) *Odyssey*, vols. IV–V.
Pope visited by Swift. *Gulliver's Travels* published in October.

1727 (June) Pope-Swift *Miscellanies*, vols. I and II.
Swift's second visit to Pope.

1728 (March) Pope-Swift *Miscellanies*, "last" volume.
(May) *The Dunciad*, in three books, with Theobald as hero.

1729 (April) *The Dunciad Variorum.*

1731 (December) *Epistle to Burlington* [Moral Essay IV].

1732 (October) Pope-Swift *Miscellanies*, "third" volume.
(December) Death of Gay.

1733 (January) *Epistle to Bathurst* [Moral Essay III].
(February) The first *Imitation of Horace* [Sat. II i].
(February–May) *An Essay on Man*, Epistles I–III.
(June) Death of Pope's mother.

1734 (January) *Epistle to Cobham* [Moral Essay I].
An Essay on Man, Epistle IV.
(July) *Imitation of Horace* [Sat. II ii].
(December) *Sober Advice from Horace.*

1735 (January) *Epistle to Dr Arbuthnot.*
(February) *Of the Characters of Women* [Moral Essay II].
Death of Arbuthnot.
(April) The *Works*, vol. II.
(May) Curll's edition of Pope's letters.
Bolingbroke returned to France.

1737 (April) *Imitation of Horace* [Ep. II ii].
      (May) Pope's edition of his letters.
      Imitation of Horace [Ep. II i].
      An Essay on Man attacked by Crousaz, Professor of Mathematics and Philosophy at Lausanne.

1738 (January–March) *Imitations of Horace* [Eps. I vi and I i].
      (May–July) *Epilogue to the Satires.*
      Warburton commenced his replies to Crousaz.
      Pope visited by Bolingbroke.

1740 (April) Pope's first meeting with Warburton.

1742 (March) *The New Dunciad* [i.e. Book IV].

1743 (October) *The Dunciad* in four books with Cibber enthroned in the place of Theobald.

1744 (May 30) Death of Pope.

LIST OF THE PRINCIPAL POEMS
of Pope to be found in the other volumes

The translation of Homer is not included in this edition. The remaining poems will be found in volume vi.

ABBREVIATIONS
used in the Notes to the Introduction and to the Poem

ADVENTURER=Analogues of passages in the *Essay on Man*, collected by Joseph Warton in *Adventurer*, No. 63.

AITKEN="Notes on the Bibliography of Pope", by G. A. Aitken. *Transactions of the* [London] *Bibliographical Society*, xii (1911–13), 113–43.

AQUINAS=Translation by the English Dominican Fathers (*Summa contra gentiles*, 4 vols. in 6, 1923–9; *Summa theologica*, 20 vols., 1911–35).

ARISTOTLE, ETH. NICH.=W. D. Ross's translation of the Nichomachean Ethics, in the Oxford Aristotle (11 vols., 1908–31), vol. IX.

AUDRA=*L'Influence française dans l'œuvre de Pope*, par E. Audra. Paris, 1931.

AURELIUS=*The Emperor Marcus Antoninus His Conversation With Himself*. Tr. J. Collier. 1701.

BACON=*The Advancement of Learning*. W. A. Wright's edition, with numbered sections and paragraphs. 2nd ed. Oxford, 1876.

BAILEY=*Dictionarium Britannicum: or . . . Universal Etymological English Dictionary*. Rev. by N. Bailey. 1730.

BELLARMINE=Cardinal Robert Bellarmine's *De ascensione mentis in Deum*, tr. 1705, as *The Soul's Ascention to God*.

BLS=Boyle Lecture Sermons, i.e. *A Defence of Natural and Revealed Religion: Being . . . Sermons Preached at the Lecture founded by the Hon. Robert Boyle, . . . From 1691 to . . . 1732*. 3 vols., 1739.

BOWLES=Bowles's notes on the *Essay on Man* in his edition of Pope's *Works* (9 vols., 1806), vol. III.

BOYLE=Robert Boyle's collected *Works*. 6 vols., 1772.

BURTON=*Several Discourses*. By Hezekiah Burton. 1684.

CARRUTHERS=Carruthers's notes on the *Essay on Man* in his edition of Pope's *Poetical Works* (4 vols., 1853), vol. III.

CHAMBERS=*Cyclopaedia: or, An Universal Dictionary of Arts and Sciences*. By E. Chambers. 5th ed., 2 vols., 1741.

CHARLETON= *The Natural History of the Passions.* By Walter Charleton. 1674.

CHARRON= Pierre Charron's *Of Wisdom.* Tr. Stanhope. 3rd ed. 1729. 3 vols.

CHUDLEIGH, Ess.= *Essays upon Several Subjects. In Prose and Verse.* By Mary Chudleigh. 1710.

COEFFETEAU= *A Table of Humane Passions.* By Nicolas Coeffeteau. Tr. E. Grimeston. 1621.

CUMBERLAND= *A Treatise of the Laws of Nature.* By Richard Cumberland. Tr. and ed. J. Maxwell. 1727.

DU BARTAS= Joshua Sylvester's translation of Du Bartas's *Deuine Weekes and Workes.* In *The Complete Works of Joshua Sylvester.* Ed. Grosart. 1880. 2 vols.

EC= Pope's *Works.* Ed. W. Elwin and W. J. Courthope. 10 vols., 1871–89.

ERASMUS= *The Praise of Folly.* Tr. J. Wilson (1668), ed. P. S. Allen. Oxford, 1925.

ESPRIT= *Discourses on the Deceitfulness of Humane Virtues.* By Jacques Esprit. Tr. W. Beauvoir. 1706.

GREVILLE= Fulke Greville.

GRIFFITH= *Alexander Pope. A Bibliography.* By R. H. Griffith. 1 vol. in two parts, 1922, 1927.

HARVARD MS.= Autograph manuscript of the *Essay on Man,* Epistles I–III, in the possession of the Harvard University library.

HOOKER= *The Laws of Ecclesiastical Polity.* Ed. J. Keble. 3rd ed., 3 vols. Oxford, 1845.

HURD= Richard Hurd's essay "On the Marks of Imitation", in his edition of two of Horace's epistles. 1768.

HUTCHESON= *An Essay on the Nature and Conduct of the Passions and Affections.* By Francis Hutcheson. 1728.

KING= *An Essay on the Origin of Evil.* By William King. Tr. and ed. Edmund Law. 1731.

LA BRUYÈRE= *Works.* Engl. tr. 2 vols. 1776.

LA ROCHEFOUCAULD= *Moral Maxims and Reflections.* In four parts. Engl. tr. 1694.

MONTAIGNE= Montaigne's *Essays.* Tr. Charles Cotton. 3 vols., ed. 1693.

MORGAN MS.=Autograph manuscript of the *Essay on Man*, Epistles I–III and considerable parts of Epistle IV, in the possession of the Morgan Library, New York City.

MORRIS=E. E. Morris's notes in his edition of the *Essay on Man* (1895), ed. 1924.

OED=*Oxford English Dictionary*.

P=Note by Pope; usually followed by dates of the editions in which it was printed.

PALINGENIUS=*Zodiacus vitae; sive, De hominis vita libri xii*. Ed. Basle, 1621.

PASCAL=*Thoughts on Religion, and Other Curious Subjects*. Tr. B. Kennet, 3rd ed. 1731.

PATTISON=Mark Pattison's notes in his edition of the *Essay on Man*. Oxford, 1875.

PLUTARCH=Plutarch's *Morals*. Translated by several hands. Corr. and rev. W. W. Goodwin. 5 vols., Boston, Mass., 1870.

PRIOR=Prior's *Solomon*. 1718.

PUBLISHER=A collection of analogues between Palingenius's *Zodiacus vitae* and the *Essay on Man*, published in *The Publisher: Containing Miscellanies in Prose and Verse*. No. 2. 1745.

ROSCOE=Roscoe's notes on the *Essay on Man* in his edition of Pope's *Works* (10 vols. 1824), vol. v.

SENAULT=*The Use of Passions*. By J. F. Senault. Tr. Henry, Earl of Monmouth. 1671.

SHAFTESBURY=Shaftesbury's *Characteristicks*. 3 vols., 5th ed., 1732.

SHEFFIELD=John Sheffield, Earl of Mulgrave, Duke of Buckinghamshire.

SPENCE=*Anecdotes, Observations, and Characters of Books and Men. Collected by Joseph Spence*. Ed. S. W. Singer. 1820.

STANLEY=*The History of Philosophy*. By Thomas Stanley. 3rd ed., 1701.

SWIFT=*Prose Works*. Ed. Temple Scott. 12 vols., 1897–1908.

TEMPLE=*Works of Sir William Temple*. 2 vols., 1720.

THOMPSON=A. H. Thompson's notes in his edition of the *Essay on Man*. Cambridge, 1913.

TOPSELL=*The History of Four-footed Beasts and Serpents . . . Collected . . . by Edward Topsel . . . The whole rev., cor., and inl. . . . by J[ohn] R[owland]*. 1658.

WAKEFIELD = *Observations on Pope*. By Gilbert Wakefield. 1796.

WARBURTON = William Warburton's notes on the *Essay on Man* in the quarto edition dated 1743.

WARD = A. W. Ward's notes on the *Essay on Man* in his edition of Pope's *Poetical Works*. 1869.

WARTON = Joseph Warton's notes on the *Essay on Man* in his edition of Pope's *Works*. 9 vols., 1797. Vol. III.

WOLLASTON = *The Religion of Nature Delineated*. By William Wollaston. 7th ed., 1750.

NOTE ON THE ILLUSTRATIONS

Plate I (frontispiece). A sepia ink drawing by Pope, evidently the original from which was engraved the traditional frontispiece to the *Essay on Man*. This frontispiece first appeared in the editions of 1745 (Griffith, Nos. 607, 608), with a note by Warburton explicating its allegorical significance and stating that it had been "designed and drawn by Mr *Pope* himself". The drawing is mounted as frontispiece in a copy of the earlier of these editions (No. 607) which is now the property of Mr Wilmarth S. Lewis of Farmington, Connecticut. By his courtesy, it is here reproduced.

Plate II (facing p. 3). A painting of the same allegorical scene as that pictured in Plate I, but with an added central figure: an emaciated rake, obviously out at elbow (and knee), holding an engraving which depicts the Prodigal Son in an attitude of prayer beside the trough where he has just fed the swine. One or two details in the engraving are curiously reminiscent of Dürer's treatment of this subject, but the engraving is not a copy of Dürer, nor have I been able to establish any original for it—if indeed it had one.

The painting was first described in 1857 by Carruthers (*Life of Pope*, 2nd ed., pp. 90, 462–3) from information in a letter sent him by the then owner, the Rev. Thompson Stoneham, of Ketley parsonage, Wellington, Shropshire, in whose family it was said to have been long cherished as a specimen of Pope's work. Its next owner was the late A. Edward Newton, who purchased it in the early nineteen-thirties as a self-portrait by Pope (see his privately printed brochure entitled *Pope, Poetry and Portrait*, 1936), and it is now in the possession of his daughter, Miss Caroline Newton, of Berwyn, Pennsylvania. With her kind permission, I reproduce it here as an object of great association interest, however its relation to Pope and to Pope's work as a painter may ultimately be assessed.

AN
ESSAY on MAN

Or the FIRST BOOK of
ETHIC EPISTLES
TO
H. ST. JOHN L. BOLINGBROKE

II Sepia drawing probably by Pope: another
version of the frontispiece to the ESSAY ON MAN

See note on page XC

NOTE ON THE TEXT

The four epistles of the *Essay on Man* were published successively on 20 February, 29 March, 8 May[1] 1733, and 24 January 1734. Of Epistles I–III there were other folio issues,[2] but none of textual interest except Griffith's "Issue I" of Epistle I,[3] which shows extensive revision and rearrangement. Pope went on correcting the poem till he died; first in the collected editions, folio and quarto, of 1734[4]; then in editions of the *Works*, vol. II, of 1735,[5] 1736, and 1739; and finally in the Pope-Warburton quarto dated 1743, where several passages were inserted. Though no variants are found in the *Works*, vol. II, part i, of 1740[6] and 1743, or the *Works* of 1751, I have included these editions in the collations to complete the history of the text.

The text printed in this volume is in most respects[7] (including typography) that of the Pope-Warburton quarto, prepared during 1743 by Warburton under Pope's direction and published early in

---

1. Griffith's date, from Aitken, is 17 May, but the epistle is advertised as "this day published" in the *Daily Journal* of 8 May, and for "Monday next" in the *Post-Boy* of 5 May (Sat.). Where the daily newspapers yield dates of publication earlier or more precise than those in Griffith, I have recorded them in the ensuing notes.

2. Also at least one quarto issue of Epistle I, Griffith 305, published 22 March (*Daily Journal*). Griffith lists, on Aitken's authority, an earlier quarto issue (303); but so far as I know, this has never been recorded by any one but Aitken and may not exist. The quarto in the Brit. Mus. (Shelf-mark 11630.e.5(16)) that Griffith mentions as possibly a copy of this book is, I think, a copy of 305. It lacks title and half-title, but in other respects it is identical in collation with 305. I have not, however, been able to lay it beside a copy of 305 to verify this.

3. Advertised for "Monday" in both the *Daily Journal*, 19 April (Thurs.), and in *Hooker's Weekly Miscellany*, 21 April (Sat.).

4. *London Evening-Post*, 18–20 April.

5. The edition numbered *1735b* in the key to the critical apparatus was published 30 July (*Post-Boy*).

6. Advertised as "just published" in *Daily Advertiser*, 9 May.

7. For a trifling exception, see the textual note at II 99.

3

1744.[1] I have, however, silently corrected a few misprints, altered
the punctuation at II 99, and inserted consistently in the text (as
Pope's printer often failed to do) the section-numbers called for by
the "Arguments".

In listing the textual variants of the earlier editions and in reproducing Pope's notes to the poem, I have followed the typography of
the edition that first contains the variant or the note. Among the
notes I have included the summarizing glosses supplied at the foot
of the page in the octavo editions of the *Works*, vol. II, 1735–43; but
I have omitted the notes appended to the folio and quarto *Works*,
vol. II, of 1735 (under the title "Postscript"), which simply call
attention to revisions and hence duplicate the information provided in the critical apparatus.

The title of the poem in the early separate issues of Epistle I is:
AN/ESSAY/ON/MAN./Address'd to a FRIEND./. In later issues
of this epistle, and in all those of Epistles II–IV, this was changed to
AN/ESSAY/ON/MAN./IN *EPISTLES* to a *FRIEND.*/, and this
in turn became, in the collected editions of 1734: AN/ESSAY/on/
MAN, / Being the FIRST BOOK of / ETHIC EPISTLES. / TO
HENRY St. JOHN, L. BOLINGBROKE./, and in the quarto
Works, vol. II, of 1735: ETHIC EPISTLES,/TO/*HENRY St.
JOHN*/L. *BOLINGBROKE.*/—/Written in the Year 1732./—/.
The poem has no title in the first octavo edition of the *Works*,
vol. II, 1735, but the octavo editions thereafter revert to the title of
the 1734 editions and incorporate the line giving the date of com-
position from the 1735 quarto *Works*.

---

1. *London Evening-Post*, 21–3 February.

KEY TO THE CRITICAL APPARATUS

EPISTLE I
1733*a* = First edition, folio, Griffith 294.
1733*b* = Edition "Corrected by the Author", folio, Griffith 307.

EPISTLE II
1733 = First edition, folio, Griffith 300.

EPISTLE III
1733 = First edition, folio, Griffith 308.

EPISTLE IV
1734 = First edition, folio, Griffith 331.

EPISTLES I–IV
1734*a* = Collected edition, folio, Griffith 339–40.
1734*b* = Collected edition, quarto, Griffith 336–8.
1735*a* = Works, vol. II, quarto, Griffith 372.
1735*b* = Works, vol. II, octavo, Griffith 388.
1735*c* = Works, vol. II, octavo, Griffith 389.
1736 = Works, vol. II, octavo, Griffith 430.
1739 = Works, vol. II, octavo, Griffith 505.
1740 = Works, vol. II, part I, octavo, Griffith 523.
1743*a* = Works, vol. II, part I, octavo, Griffith 583.
1743*b* = Collected edition by Pope and Warburton, quarto, Griffith 589.
1751 = Works, ed. Warburton, octavo, vol. III, Griffith 645.

TO THE READER[1]

As the Epistolary Way of Writing hath prevailed much of late, we have ventured to publish this Piece composed some Time since, and whose Author chose this Manner, notwithstanding his Subject was high and of dignity, because of its being mixt with Argument, *which of its Nature approacheth to Prose.* This, which we first give the Reader, treats of the 5 Nature and State of MAN, *with Respect to the* UNIVERSAL SYSTEM; *the rest will treat of him with Respect to* his OWN SYSTEM, *as an* Individual, *and as a* Member of Society; *under one or other of which Heads all Ethicks are included.*

As he imitates *no Man, so he would be thought to vye with no Man in* 10 *these Epistles, particularly with the noted Author of* TWO *lately published*[2]: *But this he may most surely say, that the Matter of them is such, as is of* Importance *to* all in general, *and of* Offence *to* none in particular.

TO THE READER[3]

The Author was induced to publish these Epistles separately for two Reasons, The one, that he might not impose upon the Publick too much at 15 *once of what he thought incorrect; The other, that by this Method he might profit of its Judgement on the Parts, in order to make the Whole less unworthy.*

14 was] has been *300, 311, 313.*
16 thought] thinks *300, 311, 313.*
17 unworthy] unworthy of it *300, 311, 313.*

---

1. Prefixed to the early issues of Epistle I (Griffith 294, 296, 304, 305).

2. I.e. Pope's own acknowledged poems: *Mor. Ess.*, III, and *Imit. Hor.*, *Sat.*, II i.

3. Prefixed to Epistle II (Griffith 300, 311, 313) and late issues of Epistle I (Griffith 307, 409). The text here is that of 307 and 409.

THE DESIGN[1]

Having proposed to write some pieces on Human Life and
Manners, such as (to use my lord Bacon's expression) *come
home to Men's Business and Bosoms*, I thought it more satisfactory
to begin with considering *Man* in the abstract, his *Nature* and
his *State*: since, to prove any moral duty, to enforce any moral   5
precept, or to examine the perfection or imperfection of any
creature whatsoever, it is necessary first to know what *condition*
and *relation* it is placed in, and what is the proper *end* and *purpose*
of its *being*.

The science of Human Nature is, like all other sciences,   10
reduced to a *few clear points*: There are not *many certain truths* in
this world. It is therefore in the Anatomy of the Mind as in that
of the Body; more good will accrue to mankind by attending to
the large, open, and perceptible parts, than by studying too
much such finer nerves and vessels, the conformations and uses   15
of which will for ever escape our observation. The *disputes* are all
upon these last, and, I will venture to say, they have less sharp-
ened the *wits* than the *hearts* of men against each other, and have
diminished the practice, more than advanced the theory, of
Morality. If I could flatter myself that this Essay has any merit,   20
it is in steering betwixt the extremes of doctrines seemingly
opposite, in passing over terms utterly unintelligible, and in
forming a *temperate* yet not *inconsistent*, and a *short* yet not
imperfect system of Ethics.

This I might have done in prose; but I chose verse, and even   25
rhyme, for two reasons. The one will appear obvious; that principles, maxims, or precepts so written, both strike the reader
more strongly at first, and are more easily retained by him
afterwards: The other may seem odd, but is true, I found I

15–16 the conformation and uses of which] as *1734a–43a*.
21 the extremes of] *add. 1743b*.
23 forming a] forming out of all a *1734a–43a*.

1. Prefixed to all editions beginning with *1734a*.

could express them more *shortly* this way than in prose itself; and
nothing is more certain, than that much of the *force* as well as
grace of arguments or instructions, depends on their *conciseness*.
I was unable to treat this part of my subject more in detail,
without becoming dry and tedious; or more *poetically*, without   5
sacrificing perspicuity to ornament, without wandring from the
precision, or breaking the chain of reasoning: If any man can
unite all these without diminution of any of them, I freely confess he will compass a thing above my capacity.

What is now published, is only to be considered as a *general*   10
Map of MAN, marking out no more than the *greater parts*, their
extent, their *limits*, and their *connection*, but leaving the particular
to be more fully delineated in the charts which are to follow.
Consequently, these Epistles in their progress (if I have health
and leisure to make any progress) will be less dry, and more   15
susceptible of poetical ornament. I am here only opening the
fountains, and clearing the passage. To deduce the *rivers*, to
follow them in their course, and to observe their effects, may be
a task more agreeable.

2   more certain] truer *1735b–43a*.
12 *extent*] extents *1735c–43a*.
14–15 (if . . . progress)] *om. 1734a–35b*.
15 be] become *1734a–43a*.
16 poetical] *om.* 1735b–43a*.
18 may] will *1734a–35a*: would *1735c–43a*.

ARGUMENT of the FIRST EPISTLE[1]

Of the Nature and State of Man, with respect to the UNIVERSE.

OF Man *in the abstract.*—I. *That we can judge only with regard to* our own system, *being ignorant of the* relations *of systems and things*, VER. 17, &c. II. *That Man is not to be deemed* imperfect, *but a Being suited to his* place *and* rank *in the creation, agreeable to the* general Order *of things, and conformable to* Ends *and* Relations *to* 5 *him unknown,*VER. 35, &c. III. *That it is partly upon his* ignorance *of* future *events, and partly upon the* hope *of a* future *state, that all his happiness in the present depends*, VER. 77, &c. IV. *The* pride *of aiming at more knowledge, and pretending to more Perfection, the cause of Man's error and misery. The* impiety *of putting himself in the place* 10 *of* God, *and judging of the fitness or unfitness, perfection or imperfection, justice or injustice of his dispensations*, VER. 113, &c. V. *The* absurdity *of conceiving himself the* final cause *of the creation, or expecting that perfection in the* moral *world, which is not in the* natural, VER. 131, &c. VI. *The* unreasonableness *of his complaints* 15 *against* Providence, *while on the one hand he demands the Perfections of the Angels, and on the other the bodily qualifications of the Brutes; though, to possess any of the* sensitive faculties *in a higher degree, would render him miserable*, VER. 173, &c. VII. *That throughout the whole visible world, an* universal order *and* gradation *in the sen-* 20 *sual and mental faculties is observed, which causes a* subordination *of creature to creature, and of all creatures to Man. The gradations of* sense, instinct, thought, reflection, reason; *that Reason alone countervails all the other faculties*, VER. 207. VIII. *How much farther this* order *and* subordination *of living creatures may extend,* 25 *above and below us; were any part of which broken, not that part only,*

---

1. A table of contents for Epistles i–iii was first prefixed to *1733b*, and for Epistle iv to *1734*. Thereafter, "Contents" for i–iv appear in all editions. Alterations were made in the wording from edition to edition, but they are too trifling to be recorded. (For an exception see the note at the end of the "Argument" of Epistle iv.) The version given here is that of *1743b*.

9

but the whole connected creation *must be destroyed.* VER. 233. IX. *The* extravagance, madness, *and* pride *of such a desire,* VER. 259. X. *The consequence of all, the* absolute submission *due to Providence, both as to our* present *and* future state, VER. 281, &c. *to the end.*   5

EPISTLE I

A WAKE, my ST. JOHN! leave all meaner things
To low ambition, and the pride of Kings.
Let us (since Life can little more supply
Than just to look about us and to die)
Expatiate free o'er all this scene of Man;   5
A mighty maze! but not without a plan;

1 ST. JOHN] LÆLIUS *1733ab*.   6 but not] of walks *1733a*.

Epistle I. Of the NATURE and STATE of MAN with respect to the UNIVERSE.
[P. *1735b–43a*.]

1–5. W. Ewart (*N & Q*, 1 Ser. VII 570) cites Buchanan, *De Sphaera*, II 1–4:

> Iam mihi, Timoleon, animo majora capaci
> Concipe, nec terras semper mirare jacentes;
> Excute degeneres circum mortalia curas,
> Et mecum ingentes coeli spatiare per oras.

1. Pope tells Swift, 19 Dec. 1734, that Bolingbroke "is so taken up still, in spite of the monitory hint given in the first line of my essay, with particular men, that he neglects mankind, and is still a creature of this world, not of the universe . . ."
Laelius (cf. textual notes)] ". . . celebrated for his statesmanship, his philosophical pursuits, and his friendship, . . . described by Horace as delighting, on his retirement from public affairs, in the society of the poet Lucilius. Thus the name was fitted to the functions of Bolingbroke, and the relation in which he stood to Pope" [EC].
meaner] Meaner than philosophy: cf. *Imit. Hor., Ep.*, 1 i 17*ff*, 39*ff*, 73*ff*, 177*ff*.
3–4. Pattison compares Cicero (*Tusc. disp.*, III 28 [69]): "Querebatur [igitur] se tum, cum illa videre caepisset, exstingui"; and Wakefield cites Denham's *Of Prudence* [93–4]. Cf. also Ralegh, pref. to *Hist. of the World* (1736, I xxiii): "[Man] . . . hath so short a time in the world, as he no sooner begins to learn, than to die . . ."; Wollaston, p. 395, note u (quoting Democritus): "This world is a stage, life is the play; we come on, look about us, and go off again"; and Prior, III 528–9.
5. *Expatiate*] Used both figuratively (to speak or write at length) and literally (to wander at will) as part of the general metaphor of 5–14.
6–16. Pope's note beside this passage, on a fragment of paper tipped into the margin of the Harvard MS., shows that at some point he came to think of it as

applying to his larger plan (Introd., pp. xi–xii). "The 6th, 7th, and 8th lines allude to the Subjects of This Book, the General Order and Design of Providence; the Constitution of the human Mind, whose Passions cultivated are Virtues, neg[lected], Vices; the Temptations of misapplyd Selflove and wrong pursuits of Power, Pleasure and false Happiness. The 10th, 11th, 12th, etc. allude to the [sub]jects of the following books; the [various?] characters and capacities of Men, of Learning and Ignorance, [the?] Knowledge of mankind and the Manners [of the age?]. The last line sums up the moral and main Drift of the whole, [the?] Justification of the Ways of Provi[dence]." It is equally possible to interpret these lines (as perhaps they were originally composed) in the context of the *Essay* alone.

6–14. The editors of *The Explicator* (vol. 1, no. 2, Nov. 1942) observe the relevance of the garden figure to the *Essay's* theme ("as the seeming planlessness of the garden is planned . . . , so it might be with Man and his World; as the natural garden exhibits a wide range of diversity and prolific growth, so does the system of creation") and the further appropriateness of the language of the hunt into which this figure blends. Likewise suggestive of the poem's themes is the dramatic figure hinted at in *scene* of 5 and returned to in *manners* of 14.

6. *maze*] For the gardening sense, cf. T. Blount's *Glossogr.* (1661) s.v.: ". . . a device, like a Labyrinth, made in some Gardens in manner of a knot, with so many intricate turnings, wherein if one be once entred, it is hard getting out". For the figurative use to describe the intricacies of man, nature, and God, cf. Milton, *Par. Lost*, II 561; Dryden, *Relig. La.*, 38; R. Gould, *To the . . . Beaux Esprits*, sts. 4, 16; J. Sheffield, *Brutus*, 3rd chor., st.1; Garth, *Dispens.*, I 19–20; Thomson, *Winter* (1726), 380–3; A. Hill, *On Mr. Cowley's Introd. Pind. Verse*, st. 3; and Addison, *Cato*, I i 48–53:

> The ways of Heaven are dark and intricate,
> Puzzled in Mazes and perplex'd with errors:
> Our understanding traces 'em in vain,
> Lost and bewilder'd in the fruitless search;
> Nor sees with how much art the windings run,
> Nor where the regular confusion ends.

With Addison's "artful windings" and *regular confusion*, cf. *Ess.*, I 289.

but not without a plan] Either reading of this line (cf. textual notes) suggests that there is both intricacy and plan (cf. Addison, above, and *Par. Lost*, V 622–4). The earlier text placed the emphasis on man's not having a chart of the maze (*plan* as a drawing or sketch: *OED*, sense 1) and was misinterpreted (e.g. Johnson, *Lives of the Poets*, ed. Hill, III 162). The new reading placed the emphasis on there being an order in the maze (*plan* as a scheme of arrangement: *OED*, sense 2), even though, as the rest of the poem makes clear, man can obtain only glimmerings of its nature. For a further comment on this line, see W. Empson, *Seven Types of Ambiguity* (1930), pp. 258–60.

A Wild, where weeds and flow'rs promiscuous shoot,
Or Garden, tempting with forbidden fruit.
Together let us beat this ample field,
Try what the open, what the covert yield;   10
The latent tracts, the giddy heights explore
Of all who blindly creep, or sightless soar;

7 A] Or *1733a*.   11 the giddy] or giddy *1733a*, *1734ab*.

7–8. Cf. Shaftesbury, III 211: "Men must . . . explore the *interior Regions* and Recesses of the Mind, the *hollow Caverns* of deep *Thought*, the private Seats of *Fancy*, and the *Wastes* and *Wildernesses*, as well as the more fruitful and cultivated *Tracts* of this *obscure Climate*."

7. Milton, *Areop.* (ed. Hales, 1904), p. 17: "Good and evill . . . in the field of this World grow up together almost inseparably . . ."

Wild] Cf. Daniel, *To the Ladie Margaret*, 11: "The boundlesse wastes and wildes of man."

8. *Par. Lost*, I 1–2. Pope apprises us at the outset of the connection between his poem and Milton's. Cf. *Ess.*, I 16, and Introd., pp. liii, lxiv, lxx, lxxiii.

9–14. Pope to Gay, 2 Oct. 1732: "I advise you to make man your game, hunt and beat about here for coxcombs, and truss up rogues in satire." Pattison cites similar "serious" applications of the hunting figure from Quarles [*Iob Militant*, 13th meditation, 5–10] and from [Bp.] King [*The Labyrinth*, 39–40].

10. *open . . . covert*] Hunting terms for ground that does not afford shelter to the quarry and ground that does.

11. *Publisher* quotes Palingenius, I 66–7:
            . . . interdum, fretus ratione, latentes
        Naturae tentabo vias, atque abdita pandam.

tracts] Regions, territories, but also tracks. Cf. Sandys, *Paraphr. upon Job*, XXIII 21; Dryden's *Metam.*, XIII 36; and Pope's *Art of Sinking* (EC, x 345).

12. The force of the antithesis resides in the assumption that there is a mode of motion appropriate to man, which is neither creeping nor soaring, and that to depart from this is blindness in either case. "Those who *blindly creep* are the ignorant and indifferent; those who *sightless soar* are the presumptuous, who endeavour to transcend the bounds prescribed to the intellect of man" [EC]. Cf. Du Bartas's distinction (1st wk, 1st day, 138*ff*) between those who, soaring, "Climb . . . the battlements of Heav'n", those who, stooping, "th' Author's praise in Themselves eclipse", and his own "heedfull *Muse*", which, "trained in true Religion, Divinely-humane, keeps the middle Region". *Sightless soar* may allude to the belief (*Euphues*, ed. Arber, p. 87) that "no bird can look against the Sunne but those that be bredde of the Eagle". Cf. also Du Bartas, *loc. cit.*, 156–7. More specifically, the extremes may be those of virtuoso and metaphysician, as in *Dunc.* B., IV 449*ff*.

Eye Nature's walks, shoot Folly as it flies,
And catch the Manners living as they rise;
Laugh where we must, be candid where we can;   15
But vindicate the ways of God to Man.
    1. Say first, of God above, or Man below,
What can we reason, but from what we know?
Of Man what see we, but his station here,
From which to reason, or to which refer?   20

13. *walks*] Cf. besides the garden sense of this term its hunting sense as the haunt or resort of game.

shoot . . . flies] Bathurst to Pope, 19 Sept. 1730: ". . . you are perpetually roving, and one must shoot flying, to speak in the language of the country, to hit you." Cf. *Abs. and Achit.* [1032]: ". . . shoots their treasons as they fly" [Wakefield]; *Aureng-zebe*, III i: "Youth should . . . shoot [joys] as they fly" [EC].

14. Cf. *The Compleat Sportsman* (1718), p. 15: "And having pitch'd your Nets where you think the Game lies, beat the Ground, and make a Noise, and as the Fowl rise, they will be entangled in the Net."

Manners] Cf. Dryden (*Ess.*, ed. Ker, II 255): ". . . the manners; under which name I comprehend the passions, and, in a larger sense, the descriptions of persons, and their very habits"; Fielding, *Jos. Andrews*, III i: . . . "I describe not men but manners; not an individual but a species"; *Spectat.*, 273, and pref. to Pope's *Il.* (1715), leaves C1–C2.

15. *candid*] H. More, *Enchir. Eth.* (1690), p. 137: "Candor is that which guides us to interpret with Benignity the Words and Actions of all Men: But when they are such as cannot well be borne; then, with an honest and decent Liberty, to check and reprehend them."

16. *Par. Lost*, I 26; and *Ess.*, I 8n, above.

17ff. *He can reason only from* Things known, *and judge only with regard to his* own System. [P. *1735b–43a*.]

17–18. "The principle of analogical reasoning in theology is the assumption that the universe being regulated by uniform laws, those laws which we can trace in that part of it which falls under our observation, extend also to that part of it which we cannot see. Cf. Milton, *Par. Lost*, V 174" [Pattison].

19. *station*] Perhaps partly an astronomical term (cf. *OED*, s.v. 1 5, and Desaguliers, *Newt. Syst. of the World* (1728), nn. on pp. 8, 11–14), but chiefly a military and hierarchical one. In both cases the implied figure stresses man's limitedness of purview as compared with the power that assigned him to his post. See Introd., pp. lxxviii–lxxix.

Thro' worlds unnumber'd tho' the God be known,
'Tis ours to trace him only in our own.
He, who thro' vast immensity can pierce,

21 unnumber'd] unbounded *1733a*.
22 *Between ll. 22–3, 1733a has ll. 29–34, with the differences noted at
those lines, below.*

21–2. Cf. Montaigne, II 313–4: "Is . . . [God] oblig'd not to exceed the
Limits of our Knowledge? . . . Thou seest nothing but the Order and Revolution
of this little Vault, under which thou art lodged, if thou dost see so much:
Whereas his Divinity has an infinite Jurisdiction beyond: This Part is nothing in
comparison of the whole"; Browne, *Relig. Med.*, I xiii; Du Bartas, 1st wk, 1st day,
158–61; and Davenant, *To My Friend Mr. Ogilby*, 35–8.

23–32. Cf. Dennis, *Part of the Te Deum Paraphr.*, st. 6:
> Ten thousand Suns, prodigious Globes of Light
> At once in broad Dimensions strike our Sight;
> Millions behind in the remoter Skies,
> Appear but Spangles to our wearied Eyes:
> And when our wearied Eyes want further Strength,
> To pierce the Void's immeasurable Length,
> Our vigorous tow'ring Thoughts still further fly,
> And still remoter flaming Worlds descry.
> But ev'n an Angel's comprehensive Thought,
> Cannot extend so far as thou hast wrought;
> Our vast Conceptions are by swelling brought,
> Swallow'd and lost in Infinite, to nought.

23. *He*] This may be taken to mean "only that man" (with the ironical
implication that there is no such man) or to mean God or an angel. With the
latter interpretation, cf. *Tatler*, 119, where an angelic being is made to say:
". . . I rejoice when I strengthen my sight so as to make it pierce into the most
remote spaces . . . out of the reach of human eyes . . . While you are admiring
the sky in a starry night, I am entertained with a variety of worlds and suns
placed one above another, and rising up to such an immense distance, that no
created eye can see an end of them." Pope's passage is implicitly a reply to
Lucretius's celebration of Epicurus (I 62–79) as a mortal whose mind, defying
religion, did pierce through vast immensity (*omne immensum*, 74) and beyond the
universe (*flammantia moenia mundi*, 73) to reach a godlike knowledge of why we
are as we are. Pope's MS. version of 23–4 explicitly echoes the Lucretian
passage.

vast immensity] A phrase of special force in the age of the new sciences.
Cf. Wolseley, Pref. to *Valentinian* (*17th Cent. Crit. Ess.*, ed. Spingarn, III 16): "the
vast Immensity of Nature"; Hughes, *Ode to the Creator of the World*, st. 3.

See worlds on worlds compose one universe,
Observe how system into system runs,   25
What other planets circle other suns,
What vary'd being peoples ev'ry star,
May tell why Heav'n has made us as we are.
But of this frame the bearings, and the ties,

26 circle] and what *1733a–43a*.
28 has made us as we] made all things as they *1733b, 1735b–43a*.
After l. 28, 1733a has ll. 61–8, with the differences noted at those lines below.
29 But of this] Of this vast *1733a*.

24. *worlds on worlds*] Donne, *The good-morrow*, 13: "Let Maps to other, worlds on worlds have showne." The excitement of the phrase for Pope's age had moved from the geographical to the astronomical: cf. *Guardian*, 169: "How many fox-hunters and rural squires are to be found in Great Britain, who are ignorant that they have all this while lived on a Planet; . . . and that there are other worlds within our view greater and more glorious than our own."

26. Cf. *Dunc.* A, III 240: "And other planets circle other suns"; and Pope's note there referring the line to *Aen.*, VI [641]: "solemque suum, sua sidera norunt." Also, Prior, I 524.

27. A favourite hypothesis of scientists, divines, and poets, popularized especially by Fontenelle's *Pluralité des mondes*, and frequently used, as here, to humble human self-esteem: cf. Chudleigh, *Song of the Three Children*, st. 8, and pref. to the poem: "'Tis highly probable that as many of them are Suns, so others are habitable Worlds, and fill'd with Beings infinitely superior to us; such as may have greater Perfections both of Soul and Body . . ."

29–34. Cf. Thomson, *Summer* (1727), 271–4, 279–83:

> Shall little haughty Ignorance pronounce
> His Works unwise, of which the smallest Part
> Exceeds the narrow Vision of his Mind? . . .
> And lives the Man, whose universal Eye
> Has swept, at once, th' unbounded Scheme of Things;
> Mark'd their Dependence so, and firm Accord,
> As, with unfaultering Accent, to conclude
> That this availeth nought?

Cf. also Shaftesbury, II 289–90 [Warton].

29–31. The pervasive figure here seems to be blended of architectural, hierarchical, and astronomical allusions. *Frame* and *bearings* have architectural applications (cf. *OED*); *ties*, by its close connection in 29 with *bearings*, may have similar overtones, though its earliest use in this sense recorded by *OED* is dated 1793; and *gradation*, according to Chambers (art. Gradation) "in architecture

The strong connections, nice dependencies,   30
Gradations just, has thy pervading soul
Look'd thro'? or can a part contain the whole?
  Is the great chain, that draws all to agree,
And drawn supports, upheld by God, or thee?   34
    II. Presumptuous Man! the reason wouldst thou find,

31 Gradations] And Centres *1733a*.

signifies an artful disposition of parts, rising . . . by steps or degrees . . . ; so that
those placed before do not disservice, but rather service to those behind." At the
same time, *connexions, dependencies, gradations* (and cf. *centres just* in textual notes)
were key terms of the new sciences with respect to the hierarchies both of being
and the stellar systems.

  31–4. Bowles compares the apostrophes spoken to Job from the whirlwind.
The question formula (often with allusion to Job, xxxviii*f*) became a common
vehicle of physico-theological feeling: cf. L. de Beaufort, *Cosmopoea Divina*
(Leyden, 1656), pp. 126–7; N. A. Pluche, *Spectacle de la Nat.* (tr. 1760), 1 198–9;
and Sebon's *Theol. nat.* in Montaigne, *Œuvres* (Paris, 1924–32), ix 157.

  31. *pervading*] The earliest use of this word recorded by the *OED*.

  32. *or . . . whole*] Dryden, *Relig. La.*, 39–41:

> How can the less the greater comprehend?
> Or finite reason reach Infinity?
> For what could fathom God were more than He.

So Pascal exclaims, p. 288: "What Possibility is there, that the Part should
contain the whole?" the reason being, as for Pope, that "the Parts of the World
are so nicely interwoven, so exquisitely link'd and cased one within another,
that I look upon it as impossible to understand one without another, or even,
without All."

  33–4. Zeus's golden chain in the Iliad—"Whose strong Embrace holds
Heav'n, and Earth, and Main" (Pope's *Il.*, viii 26)—became identified (esp. in
neo-Platonism) with the chain of being. Hence Spenser (*F.Q.*, iv i 30) speaks of
"that great golden chaine" with which "blessed Concord hath together tide"
the world; as does also Stanley, p. 186: ". . . there is a Divine Chain, which . . .
maketh one of it self and those things which are united to it . . ."

  that draws . . . supports] i.e. the chain not only creatively effects order (cf.
Ess., iii 7*ff*), but continually sustains it when effected.

  35*ff*. *He is not therefore a Judge of his own perfection or imperfection, but is certainly
such a Being as is suited to his Place and Rank in the Creation.* [P. *1735b–43a*.]

  35. *Presumptuous Man*] Presumptuous not only because he aspires to such
knowledge as is not ordained for man (cf. 23–34), but because his question is
always the one in 36 and not the one in 38. For the phrase, see Quarles,
Hierogl., 1: ". . . that presumptuous thing, call'd man".

Why form'd so weak, so little, and so blind!
First, if thou canst, the harder reason guess,
Why form'd no weaker, blinder, and no less!
Ask of thy mother earth, why oaks are made
Taller or stronger than the weeds they shade?   40
Or ask of yonder argent fields above,
Why JOVE's Satellites are less than JOVE?
Of Systems possible, if 'tis confest

36 form'd] made *1733a*.   38 form'd] made *1733a*.

35-8. Cf. Shaftesbury, II 304-5: "'Why,' says one, 'was I not made by Nature strong as *a Horse?* Why not hardy and robust as this *Brute-Creature?* or nimble and active as that other?' . . . it were better . . . and more modest in him, to change the Expostulation, and ask, 'Why was I not made in good earnest *a very* Brute?'" (Cf. also *Ess.*, I 175-6.)

35-6. Rom. IX 20: "Nay but, O Man, who art thou that repliest against God? Shall the thing formed say to him that formed it, Why hast thou made me thus?"

37. *harder*] Harder in being a less congenial question for pride to resolve, and in view of man's unworthiness to have come off so well: Pope is stressing (cf. 23-32) a view like the psalmist's (Psa., VIII 3-4): "When I consider thy heavens, the work of thy fingers [I ask] What is man, that thou art mindful of him?"

39-42. Two instances of the hierarchical principle selected from the world that man does know.

39. *mother earth*] A reminder of the objector's limited state (cf. *Ess.*, IV 73), and perhaps an instance of the same principle of dependence (earth and man) as obtains between the shading oaks and weeds or between Jupiter and his satellites.

41-2. Voltaire's comment, "il n'y a point de mathématicien qui n'eût fait voir . . . à M. Pope que si Jupiter était plus petit que ses satellites, ils ne pourraient pas tourner autour de lui" (*Œuvres*, ed. Moland, IX 472), is beside the point. The question is why things are as they are and not otherwise; why God made the satellites satellites and not Jupiters, subsidiary bodies instead of primary; and, by analogy, why He made man man instead of angel or beast.

41. *argent fields*] Milton's phrase in *Par. Lost*, III 460. [Wakefield.]

42. *Satellites*] Here used as plural of the Latin *satelles* and syllabicated accordingly: cf. *OED*, s.v. *satelles*. Pattison cites a couplet from Desaguliers [*Newt. Syst. of the World* (1728), p. 27] rhyming the word with *race*.

43-50. The function of this passage is evidently to summarize a set of propositions common to theodicean thinking and thence narrow the argument to the single question whether the available evidence warrants criticism of God's ways in giving man the powers he has and not others. The propositions sum-

That Wisdom infinite must form the best,
Where all must full or not coherent be,   45
And all that rises, rise in due degree;
Then, in the scale of reas'ning life, 'tis plain
There must be, somewhere, such a rank as Man;
And all the question (wrangle e'er so long)
Is only this, if God has plac'd him wrong?   50
 Respecting Man, whatever wrong we call,⎤
May, must be right, as relative to all.   ⎦
In human works, tho' labour'd on with pain,

47 reas'ning life] Life and Sence *1733a–43a*.

---

marized are, (1) that a God of infinite wisdom exists; (2) that such a God will
necessarily have chosen to create, out of all possible systems, the best; (3) that
the best will necessarily have been that which actualizes the maximum number
of possible modes of being, and so is "full" of existents—a *plenum formarum*—
"cohering" because actualization of all the possibles leaves no gaps; (4) that the
plenum's structure is hierarchical, a ladder of beings of greater and greater com-
plexity of faculties, rising by even steps (*due degrees*) from nothingness (through,
among others, the vegetative, sensitive, and rational powers) to God. The conclusion is that in the part of the ladder which embraces rational existents (e.g.
man and angel) there could no more be a gap than elsewhere: there had to be
a creature which combined the rational nature with an animal one, for such
a creature (besides being an empirical fact) was certainly one of the conceivable
possibles. The argument then settles down to the important issue (49–50):
whether the powers of this hybrid creature are suited to the terrestrial and
mortal life assigned him. The epistle then tries to show, (1) that they must be
right with respect to the whole system of things, both *ex hypothesi* and on the
analogy that all visible creatures including man have a function though not
necessarily one known to them; (2) that they are right with respect to man himself, since they contribute to his well-being, which any alteration in them would
disturb. A hint of humour may lurk in l. 48.

51–2. A favourite thesis of physico-theological and scientific writings of the
day. For typical expressions, see Boyle, v 195–200, 217, 251–2; and Rich. Mead,
A Treatise conc. the Infl. of the Sun and Moon, 1704 (tr. Stack, 1748), pp. 32–3:
"The author of nature has certainly made all things to the greatest advantage
that could be, for the whole system of animals on our globe, altho' such a disposition might in some cases prove prejudicial to a few."

53–4. Shaks., *Hen. V*, I ii 211–12: "So may a thousand actions, once afoot,
End in one purpose."

works . . . movements] Metaphorical as well as literal (cf. *wheel*, 59). Work: "a

A thousand movements scarce one purpose gain;
In God's, one single can its end produce;   55
Yet serves to second too some other use.
So Man, who here seems principal alone,
Perhaps acts second to some sphere unknown,
Touches some wheel, or verges to some goal;
'Tis but a part we see, and not a whole.   60

58 some] a *1734a–35a*.

set of parts forming a machine or piece of mechanism" (*OED*); movement: "a
particular part or group of parts in a mechanism, serving some special purpose"
(*OED*). In man-made mechanisms many moving parts must be combined to
effect one end; in God's one part suffices for each end and also subserves
another.

56. Also a favourite thesis of divines and scientists. Cf. Boyle, v 137; and 414:
"And it is more, in the making so many and so various bodies act according to
their particular designations, and yet all of them conspire to the general ends of
the universe, that God's wisdom, and (if I may so speak) his skill is displayed,
than barely in the making bodies act appositely for ends to themselves unknown." Cf. also Dryden, *Eleonora*, 75–8, and Addison's remark (*Spectat.*, 565)
that, unlike God, "we ourselves cannot attend to many different objects at the
same time. If we are careful to inspect some things, we must of course neglect
others." Pattison cites Hooker, I ix 1.

57–9. The social instance of hierarchy, evoked in the relation of *principal* to
second, merges, at *sphere*, into an astronomical instance (cf. *wheel, verges*: *OED*),
whether the term alludes to the relationships of primary and secondary in the
Newtonian cosmology or to those of the concentric spheres in the Ptolemaic.

59. *wheel*] Above, 53–4*n*. Du Bartas, 1st wk, 7th day, 162–3:
God's the main spring, that maketh every way
All the small wheels of this great Engin play.

60. Cf. 1 Cor. XIII 12: "For now we see through a glass, darkly; but then face
to face: now I know in part; but then shall I know even as also I am known."
The idea is of course fundamental to theodicy: for contemporary statements,
cf. Hooker, I ii 5–6; Boyle, v 156–7, 251–2; Gastrell, *Cert. and Necess. of Relig. in
Gen.* (1697), pp. ix–xi; Needler, *Wks.* (1728), pp. viii–ix; *Reflexions on Man* (1733),
p. 38; and *Spectat.*, 237: ". . . we are not at present in a proper situation to judge
of the counsels by which Providence acts, since but little arrives at our knowledge, and even that little we discern imperfectly; or according to the elegant
figure in holy writ, 'We see but in part, and as in a glass darkly'."

When the proud steed shall know why Man restrains
His fiery course, or drives him o'er the plains;
When the dull Ox, why now he breaks the clod,
Is now a victim, and now Ægypt's God:
Then shall Man's pride and dulness comprehend   65
His actions', passions', being's, use and end;
Why doing, suff'ring, check'd, impell'd; and why
This hour a slave, the next a deity.

64 Now wears a Garland, an Ægyptian God *1733a–43a.*
66 actions', passions'] Action's, Passion's *1733a–43a.*

61–6. A similar point is made by Hooker, I iii 4: "The manner of this divine efficiency, being far above us, we are no more able to conceive by our reason than creatures unreasonable by their sense are able to apprehend after what manner we dispose and order the course of our affairs." While carrying on the analogical argument, the passage undertakes to dwarf man by stressing his kinship in pride and dulness with the animals: cf. the allusion in *Ess.*, I 12.

61–2. Pope to Martha Blount, 4 Sept. 1728: ". . . one circumstance . . . , as I travelled all alone, made me contemplative. I was drawn by a horse now employed by Lord C[obham] in rolling the gardens, which was the same in former days on which the Earl of Derwentwater rid at Preston. It made me reflect that man himself is as blind and unknowing of his fate, as the beast he bestrides: proud and prancing in his glory, and equally ignorant whither or to what he is running." Cf. *Ess.*, III 35.

63. Swift, *Tale of a Tub* (ed. Smith and Guthkelch), p. 16: ". . . Optat ephippia bos piger [Hor., *Ep.*, I xiv 43]. The dull, unwieldy, ill-shaped Ox would needs put on the Furniture of a Horse, not considering he was born to Labour, to plow the Ground for the Sake of Superior Beings . . ." For the phrasing, cf. Dryden's *Metam.*, xv 183: "(That neck with which the surly clods he broke)."

64. *Ægypt's God*] The sacred Memphian bull, worshipped under the name of Apis.

65–8. Cf. Plato, *Laws*, x 903b, which Cornford translates (*Gk. Relig. Thought*, 1923, pp. 220–1): ". . . the power who cares for the universe has disposed all things with a view to the preservation and excellence of the whole system, in which each part, according to the measure of its capacity, does and suffers what properly belongs to it . . . Your part in this system, stubborn man, is only one part, which, tiny as it is, contributes to the whole . . ."

67. The pairs of verbs pick up, respectively, the ideas in 63–4, 61–2, and suggest the duality of man's status in their active and passive forms.

Then say not Man's imperfect, Heav'n in fault;
Say rather, Man's as perfect as he ought;   70
His knowledge measur'd to his state and place,
His time a moment, and a point his space.
If to be perfect in a certain sphere,

69 *No new paragraph in Griffith Issue G.*
71 knowledge] Being *1733a–43a.*
73–6 *Om. here but used after l. 98, with the differences noted there, 1733a.*
     Om. altogether 1733b–43a.

69–70. A received opinion in apologetic thought: cf. *Ess.*, 1 65–8*n*; Regis, *Syst. de philos.* (1690), 1 260–1: ". . . il est très-facile de concevoir que Dieu a pu rendre l'homme plus parfait qu'il n'est; mais que si l'on veut considerer l'homme, non en luy-même, et séparément du reste des créatures, mais comme un membre de l'Univers, et une partie que est soûmise aux lois générales des mouvemens, on sera obligé de reconnoître que l'homme est aussi parfait qu'il l'a pu estre" [Pattison]; Boyle, v 200; *Spectat.*, 604; Hutcheson, pp. 186–7.

71. Again a received opinion of apologetics. See, for typical expressions, *Spectat.*, 237: ". . . as our faculties are narrow and our views imperfect, it is impossible but our curiosity must meet with many repulses. The business of mankind in this life being rather to act than to know, their portion of knowledge is dealt to them accordingly"; and J. Maxwell's remark in his translation of Cumberland, pp. 300–1: "It seems also probable, That the Degree of our Intellectual Capacity is very well suited to our Objects of Knowledge; and that, had we a greater Degree thereof, . . . we should be less Happy."

72. Cf. La Bruyère, II 137: ". . . all time is but an instant, compared with the duration of God, who is eternal: the extent of the whole universe is but a point, . . . compared with his immensity . . ."; S. Clarke, *Disc. Conc. . . . Nat. Relig.* (1716), p. 37; Aurelius [v xxiv]: "Remember what an *Atome* your Person stands for in respect of the *Universe*, what a Minute . . . of Time comes to your share . . ." [Pattison]; Seneca, *Ep.*, XLIX 4: "Punctum est quod vivimus . . ."

73–4. For the general attitude implied, cf. *Guardian*, 153: "A wise man will be contented that his glory be deferred until such time as he shall be truly glorified; when his understanding shall be cleared, his will rectified, and his happiness assured; or, in other words, when he shall be neither sinful, nor ignorant, nor miserable." Thompson cites Pope's letter to Caryll, 8 March 1733: "Nothing is so plain as that he [the author of the *Essay on Man*, as yet anonymous] quits his proper subject, this present world, to assert his belief of a future state, and yet there is an *if* instead of a *since* that would overthrow his meaning." But Pope could not have changed *if* to *since* without appealing to Revelation, which, as his remark to Caryll shows, he was determined not to do, and which lay outside the terms of his poem.

What matter, soon or late, or here or there?
The blest today is as completely so,   75
As who began a thousand years ago.
  III. Heav'n from all creatures hides the book of Fate,
All but the page prescrib'd, their present state;
From brutes what men, from men what spirits know:
Or who could suffer Being here below?   80
The lamb thy riot dooms to bleed to-day,

75-6. Reversed from Lucret. III 1087-94 (tr. Dryden, III 319-21) [Wake-field]:

> The man as much to all intents is dead,
> Who dies today, and will as long be so,
> As he who died a thousand years ago.

Pattison traces the idea to the Stoic paradoxes, and also cites Bayle, *Dict.*, art. Pauliciens, remarque E: ". . . si la douleur ou la joye nous étoient communiquées selon le même degré cent ans de suite, nous serions aussi malheureux ou aussi heureux la centième année que le premier jour."

The point of the passage is that, once transferred to beatitude in eternity, man loses nothing by not having been transferred there earlier, eternity being all "instant": cf. Waller, *To a Person of Honour*, 25-7:

> . . . eternity has neither past
> Nor future, authors say, nor first nor last,
> But is all instant.

77*ff.* *His happiness depends on his* Ignorance *to a certain degree.* [P. *1735b-43a.*]

77, 80. Cicero, *De divinat.*, II ix 22: "Quae enim vita fuisset Priamo, si ab adulescentia scisset, quos eventus senectutis esset habiturus"; Shaks., 2 *Hen. IV*, III i 45, 53-6:

> O God! that one might read the book of fate . . .
>   O! if this [its contents] were seen
> The happiest youth, viewing his progress through,
> What perils past, what crosses to ensue,
> Would shut the book, and sit him down and die;

77-8. *Publisher* compares Palingenius, v 55-6; Pattison suggests Horace, *Od.*, III xxix 29-30:

> Prudens futuri temporis exitum
> Caliginosa nocte premit deus.

79*ff.* See this pursued in Epist. 3. Vers. 66, &c. 79, &c. [P. *1735b-43a.*]

81-90. The force of this passage, and its relation to Pope's larger argument, come in part from man's being presented as the middle and least attractive term in the ratio: lamb is to man as man is to God. In his status as an inferior, man lacks the lamb's trustfulness; in his status as a superior, he lacks God's impartial thoughtfulness. Cf. the clash between the associations given to the

H

Had he thy Reason, would he skip and play?
Pleas'd to the last, he crops the flow'ry food,
And licks the hand just rais'd to shed his blood.
Oh blindness to the future! kindly giv'n,   85
That each may fill the circle mark'd by Heav'n;
Who sees with equal eye, as God of all,

---

lamb (*skip and play, pleased to the last, lick the hand*), those given to man (*bleed, shed his blood, riot*—the latter ironically emphasized by the judicial pretensions of *doom*), and those given to God (*kindly, equal eye, God of all*, etc.).

81–4. Pattison compares Dryden's *Metam.*, xv [648–90]; and cf. *Guardian*, 61 (by Pope), in which this passage of Ovid and Dryden's translation are quoted. D'Israeli, *Curios. of Lit.* (Boston, 1858, II 269) quotes from Dr William King's *Mully of Mountown*, and Wakefield refers to Phaedrus, *Fab.*, v i 4–5:

> Ipsi principes
> Illam osculantur, qua sunt oppressi, manum.

Cf. also Otway's lamb (*Ven. Pres.*, IV i 89–95), which, "in his fatal garlands Decked fine and pleased, . . . skips and plays".

85. *kindly*] Benevolently (as at I 283), but possibly with oblique allusion to "kinds" as species: cf. 79 and 86.

86. *circle . . . Heav'n*] Cf. *Par. Lost*, VII 224–31, where the Son marks out the bounds of the universe with his golden compasses, and cf. also the astronomical metaphor at *Ess.*, I 57–9.

87. Spenser, *F.Q.*, I viii 27:

> And he that high does sit, and all things see
> With equall eyes, their merites to restore;

and I ix 47:

> Is not he iust, that all this doth behold
> From highest heauen, and beares an equall eye?

In Pope's lines, God's vision (equal in its attention to all) has been placed in contrast with his creatures' blindness. *Equal* may also carry something of its Latin sense: *aequus*=propitious, benign. Cf. *OED*; Spenser, *Ruines of Time*, 80; *Amor.*, LXXXII 5; and *Par. Lost*, VIII 228.

87–90. Matt., x 29–31: "Are not two sparrows sold for a farthing? and one of them shall not fall on the ground without your Father. But the very hairs of your head are all numbered. Fear ye not, therefore, ye are of more value than many sparrows." Pope's passage says, like that in Matthew, that God's providence embraces both sparrow and man, and not (as Elwin supposed) that man and sparrow are of equal value. For the general idea, Pattison compares Plato, *Laws*, x 900c [tr. Jebb]: ". . . the Gods care about the small as well as about the great"; and see the whole discussion, 899–903. Cf. also Montaigne's retort (II 322–3) to the Ciceronian sentiment, *Magna di curant, parva neglegunt* (*De nat.*

A hero perish, or a sparrow fall,
Atoms or systems into ruin hurl'd,
And now a bubble burst, and now a world.   90
    Hope humbly then; with trembling pinions soar;
Wait the great teacher Death, and God adore!
What future bliss, he gives not thee to know,

93 future bliss] bliss above, *1733a*.

---

deor., II lxvi): "As if to that *King* of Kings it were more and less to subvert a Kingdom, or to move the Leaf of a Tree: Or as if his *Providence* acted after another manner in enclining the Event of a Battle, than in the leap of a Flea. The hand of his Government is laid upon every thing after the same manner, with the same Power and Order . . ."

91*ff*. *And on his* Hope *of a* Relation *to a future State.* [P. *1735b–43a*.] The syntax depends on Pope's note at 77*ff*.

"It has been objected to the sentiment of these lines that Pope has here represented man as enabled to bear the evils of life by aid of a visionary illusive fancy. The objection is unfounded. That we do not know in what happiness hereafter will consist, and yet that we are supported by that hope of an unknown future, is the position of Catholic theology. As faith is belief in the unproved, so hope is expectation of the unknown" [Pattison].

91–92. For the general attitude, cf. Hooker, I ii 5 (quoted above, p. xliv).

91. *Hope humbly*] With reference to the central position of hope and humility in religious thinking: cf. I Pet., v 6: "Humble yourselves therefore under the mighty hand of God, that he may exalt you in due time" (cf. *Ess.*, I 74).

with . . . soar] Cf. *Ess.* I 12, 173; II 23. Browne, *Relig. Med.*, I xiii:

Teach me to soar aloft, yet ever so,
When neer the Sun, to stoop again below.
Thus shall my humble Feathers safely hover,
And, though near Earth, more than the Heavens discover.

93. Cf. Is., LXIV 4, and I Cor., II 9: "Eye hath not seen, nor ear heard, neither have entered into the heart of man, the things which God hath prepared for them that love him." J. Hughes, *Ode to the Creator of the World*, st. 10.

Pope to Swift, 19 Dec. 1734: "I wish to God we could once meet again before that separation which yet, I would be glad to believe, shall reunite us: but he who made us, not for ours but his purposes, knows only whether it be for the better or the worse that the affections of this life should, or should not, continue into the other: and doubtless it is as it should be." Also, 12 Oct. 1738: "May the rest of you [what is not mortal], which is all, be as happy hereafter as honest men may expect, and need not doubt, while, knowing nothing more, they know that their Maker is merciful."

But gives that Hope to be thy blessing now.
Hope springs eternal in the human breast: 95
Man never Is, but always To be blest:
The soul, uneasy and confin'd from home,
Rests and expatiates in a life to come.

94 blessing now] bliss below. *1733a*.
97 from] at *1733a–43a*.
98 *Between ll. 98–9, 1733a has ll. 73–4, 287–8, 75–6 with the following
    differences:* 73 sphere] State; 74 soon or late, or here or there]
    here or there, or soon or late; 75 And he that's bless'd to day, as
    fully so; 76 a] ten.

---

94. Further open'd in Epist. 2. Vers. 283. Epist. 3. Vers. 74. Epist. 4. Vers.
346, &c. [P. *1735b–43a*.]
   Bacon, *De Augm*. VII i: ". . . a Christiana fide educti, debemus nos omnes
minorum et adolescentium loco statuere, ut non aliam foelicitatem cogitemus
quam quae in spe ita est." Cf. Rom., V 2; Heb., III 6. Thus Crashaw, *On Hope*,
51, refers to hope as "our earlier Heaven", and Pope, *El. to Abel*., 299, as "gay
daughter of the sky". Cf. also Suckling, *Against Fruition*, 23–4:
        'Tis expectation makes a blessing dear;
        Heaven were not heaven if we knew what it were.
   95. Ovid, *Heroid*., XVIII 178: "spes mihi semper adest"; Cicero, *Epist. ad Att*.,
IX 10: ". . . dum anima est, spes esse dicitur"; Terence, *Heaut. tim*., 981: "Modo
liceat vivere, est spes"; and cf. Gay, *The Sick Man and the Angel*, 49.
   96. Morris cites Johnson's observation on this line [*Life*, ed. Hill-Powell, II
350–1] that "the present was never a happy state . . .; but that, as every part of
life . . . was at some point of time a period yet to come, in which felicity was
expected, there was some happiness produced by hope." Hurd compares
Manil., *Astron*., [IV 5]: "Victuros agimus semper, nec vivimus umquam." Cf.
also Swift, I 282; Lucret., III 1082–3 (tr. Dryden, III 308–9):
        For still we think an absent blessing best,
        Which cloys, and is no blessing when possess'd;
Tibullus, *Eleg*., II vii 2: "Spes fovet, et melius cras fore semper ait"; and E.
Young, *Vindic. of Prov*. (1728), p. 58: ". . . I *was* Happy, a Few may possibly say,
I *shall* be Happy, Most say; I *am* Happy, None . . ."
   97–8. Pope's first figure (cf. textual notes) was that of the soul as house-
holder chafing under the restrictions of its narrow domain: cf. his *Elegy to . . . an
Unfort. Lady*, 18: "Dull sullen pris'ners in the body's cage", and his letter to
Caryll, 21 Dec. 1712 :". . . while my trembling body is cowering over a fire, my
mind is expatiating in an open sunshine"; and also, Donne, *2nd Anniv*., 221*ff*;
Dryden, *To . . . the Dss. of Ormond*, 118–9; Prior, III 19–36; Seneca, *Ep*., LXV

Lo! the poor Indian, whose untutor'd mind
Sees God in clouds, or hears him in the wind;   100
His soul proud Science never taught to stray
Far as the solar walk, or milky way;
Yet simple Nature to his hope has giv'n,
Behind the cloud-topt hill, an humbler heav'n;
Some safer world in depth of woods embrac'd,   105

16–17; and Gay, *Thought on Eternity*, 27–32. The phrase *at home* was apparently misinterpreted to imply a disbelief in immortality (e.g. by Warton), and was revised, possibly at the suggestion of Warburton. With the revised figure, cf. Drummond, *Flowres of Sion*, III 11–12 [Pattison], and Hen. More, *Psychathanasia*, I i 19: "Exil'd from our dear home, that heavenly soil".

99*ff.* There is irony directed against the Indian (cf. the naive materialism of his after-life, and *Ess.*, IV 177–8) as well as against proud Science. Both (being human) are incapable of understanding God's ways, though the Indian surpasses proud Science in trusting them.

100. Cf. Psa. CIV 3: ". . . who maketh the clouds his chariot: who walketh upon the wings of the wind" [Wakefield]. It is perhaps a part of the irony against proud Science that the Indian senses God's presence in the same places as the Psalmist.

102. See Cicero, *Tusc. disp.*, I xix; and F. Cumont, *After Life in Rom. Paganism* (1923), ch. III. For the phrasing, Hurd compares Dryden, *Thren. August.* [353]: "Out of the *solar* walk and heaven's high way".

milky way] Cf. Young, *The Last Day* (1713), II 369–70:
      Oh how divine! to tread the milky way
      To the bright palace of the lord of day.

103. *simple Nature*] Cf. *proud Science*, 101.

104. *Behind . . . hill*] *Relig. Ceremon. and Customs . . . of the World*, III (1731), 14: "The Brasilians . . . assure us, 'That the Souls of the Virtuous will go and meet those of their ancestors, beyond the high mountains . . .'" *Ibid.*, p. 113: ". . . paradise . . . they [the Virginians] . . . place towards that part where the sun sets, and behind the mountains."

an . . . heav'n] *Ibid.*, p. 89: "If after having . . . listend for a considerable time to what is objected with regard to that . . . uselessness of the senses after this life, we should ask, if they don't think our notions of paradise more conformable to reason than their own, they would answer that, *they have their paradise*, and *we ours*"; and cf. Hennepin's *Continuation of the New Discovery* (Engl. tr. 1698), p. 144, on which the foregoing passage is based: "'*That is very well for those of your Country, but we* Americans *do not go to Heaven after death: We only pass to the Country of Souls, where our People are employ'd in Hunting . . .*'"

105–8. The Indian is made to conceive his heaven in terms of isolation from the white man. Cf. *Winds. For.*, 407*ff.*

Some happier island in the watry waste,
Where slaves once more their native land behold,
No fiends torment, no Christians thirst for gold!
To Be, contents his natural desire,
He asks no Angel's wing, no Seraph's fire;   110
But thinks, admitted to that equal sky,
His faithful dog shall bear him company.

108 no Christians] nor Christians *1733a. Between ll. 108–109 1733a*
     has: But does he say, the Maker is not *good*,
                Till he's exalted to what state he wou'd?
                Himself *alone*, high Heav'ns peculiar care;
                Alone made happy, *when* he will, and *where*?
110 no Seraph's] or Seraph's *1733a–34b, 1735bc, 1739–43a;* nor
     Seraph's *1735a, 1736.*

---

108. *fiends, Christians*] The balanced structure of the line suggests an equation
of the two.

Christians . . . gold] Cf. Hennepin, *Continuation of the New Discovery* (Engl. tr.
1698), p. 115: ". . . there is no stratagem they will not make use of to get the
Furrs from the *Savages* at a Cheap Rate; they are stocked with Frauds and Lyes
to put off their effects with, and to gain double by them if they can; and this no
doubt is a great means to alienate the Minds of the *Savages* from a Religion,
which they see accompanied with so many Cheats and Artifices. . ."

thirst . . . gold] Possibly in ironic allusion to thirsts more suitable to Christians:
cf. Psa., XLII 2: "My soul thirsteth for God"; also, LXIII 1, CXLIII 6; and Matt.
v 6; John IV 13–15.

110–12. Cf. below, 1 125–8. Simple nature shows its humility both in not
aspiring to higher orders and in not excluding those lower.

110. *Seraph's fire*] An attribute traditionally assigned, owing to the "presumed derivation of the word from a Hebrew root sāraph to burn" (*OED*).
Cf. *Ess.,* 1 278.

111. *equal*] Cf. above, 87.

112. Cf. *Spectat.*, 56; Hennepin, *Continuation of the New Discovery* (Engl. tr.
1698), pp. 51, 110; Lafitau, *Moeurs des Sauvages* (Paris, 1724), 1 360; *Relig.
Ceremon. and Customs . . . of the World*, III (1731), 69, 89, esp. 153: ". . . they [the
Mexicans] threw the body into the fire with every thing that had been appointed for his use: they strangled a dog, who was to be his guide in the other
world . . ." Pope, *Il.,* XXIII 210–1 [Wakefield]:
                Of nine large Dogs, domestick at his Board,
                Fall two, selected to attend their Lord.

IV. Go, wiser thou! and in thy scale of sense
Weigh thy Opinion against Providence;
Call Imperfection what thou fancy'st such,   115
Say, here he gives too little, there too much;
Destroy all creatures for thy sport or gust,
Yet cry, If Man's unhappy, God's unjust;
If Man alone ingross not Heav'n's high care,

113 *No paragraph here 1733a–43a.*
116 Pronounce HE acts too little, or too much *1733a.*
118 Yet thou unhappy, think 'tis He's unjust *1733a.*
119–120 *Om. 1733a (but cf. textual note l. 108).*

113*ff.* *The* Pride *of aiming at more Knowledge and Perfection, and the* Impiety *of pretending to judge of the Dispensations of Providence, the causes of his* Error *and* Misery. [P. *1735b–43a.*]

Cf. Raphael's advice to Adam, *Par. Lost,* VIII 167–74.

113–15. *sense . . . Opinion . . . fancy'st*] The three terms stress the contrast of man's mind with God's: unlike God, man is dependent on sense, subject to opinion, and likely to be misled by fancy.

113–14. Prior, III 840–1:

> Stop thy inquiry then; and curb thy sense;
> Nor let dust argue with Omnipotence.

116. *here . . . there*] To man; to the other orders of being—and perhaps especially at this point, the higher orders of being, man's desire to trespass upwards being the subject of this section, as his desire to trespass downwards is of 173*ff.*

117. Pope treats this subject in some detail in *Guardian,* 61, instancing the destructiveness both of man's sports and of his gluttony.

gust] "In order to please your palate"—Morris, who cites Shakespeare (*Tim. of Ath.,* III v 54), and *Par. Lost,* x 565. And cf. Pythagoras' query in Dryden's *Metam.,* xv 202: "From whence, O mortal men, this gust of blood?"

118. Cf. La Rochefoucauld, IV lxxxvii: "The *Love* of our selves inclines us to look upon all the Pleasures, and Happinesses of Life, as Things that we have a Right to call Ours; and upon all the *Evils* and *Calamities,* as . . . Wrongs and Hardships upon us. This gives occasion to all the Complaints we hear against Humane Life." Cf. also, *Reflexions on Man* (1733), p. 72; and *Ess.,* I 186–8.

119–22. Cf. Abdiel's advice to Satan, *Par. Lost,* v 822*ff*:

> Shalt thou give law to God? shalt thou dispute
> With Him the points of liberty, who made
> Thee what thou art, and form'd the Powers of Heaven
> Such as he pleased, and circumscrib'd their being?

Alone made perfect here, immortal there: 120
Snatch from his hand the balance and the rod,
Re-judge his justice, be the GOD of GOD!
   In Pride, in reas'ning Pride, our error lies;
All quit their sphere, and rush into the skies.
Pride still is aiming at the blest abodes,   125

123 In Pride, in reas'ning Pride] In *Pride* (my Friend) in *Pride*
   1733a; In reas'ning *Pride* (my Friend) *1733b–36.*

121–2. Cf. Montaigne, II 314: "If he [God] has in some sort communicated
himself unto thee; 'tis not to debase himself to thy littleness, nor to make thee
Comptroler of his Power"; Dryden, *Relig. La.*, 93–5; *Pride and Discontent
Silenc'd*, 23–5, in Ralph's *Miscellany* (1729):
>   Dare puny Atoms, Heav'n's Decrees controul?
>   And counsel him, who guides the boundless Whole?
>   Laws to their Sovereign, and their Maker, give?
and Tickell, *Thoughts Occas. by the . . . Picture of K. Ch. I*, 35–8:
>   O power supreme! how secret are thy ways!
>   Yet man, vain man, would trace thy mystic maze,
>   With foolish wisdom, arguing, charge his God,
>   His balance hold and guide his angry rod.

122. Job, XL 2, 8: "Shall he that contendeth with the Almighty instruct
him?" "Wilt thou also disannul my judgment? wilt thou condemn me, that thou
mayest be righteous?"

123. Cf. *Ess.*, I 293 and textual note. Montaigne, II 313: "Nevertheless we
prescribe him Bounds, we keep his Power besieg'd by our Reasons (I call our
Ravings and Dreams *Reason*, with the Dispensation of *Philosophy*, which says,
that the wicked Man, and even the Fool, go mad by Reason . . .). We will
subject him to the feeble Appearances of our Understanding; him, who has
made both us and our Knowledge."

124. Cf. *Ess.*, I 57–9n; 247 ff, and 253. Wakefield notes that this is imagery
drawn "from an exorbitation of the celestial bodies" and cites Horace, *Od.*, I iii
38: "Coelum ipsum petimus stultitia," with Creech's translation [49–50]:
>   Grown Giants in Impiety
>   Our Impious Folly dares the Sky.
Cf. also, Montaigne, II 338: "For, as *Democritus* says, by the Mouth of *Cicero*,
*Quod est ante pedes, nemo spectat: Coeli scrutantur plagas. No Man regards what is
under his Feet, they are always prying towards Heaven.*"

125. *blest abodes*] Used here to discriminate the skies considered as the dwell-
ing-place of deity from the astronomical skies of the preceding line. For the
phrase and rhyme, cf. Dryden's *Metam.* (I 215) and his Persius (*Sat.*, II 112); and
Creech's Lucret. (I 1).

Men would be Angels, Angels would be Gods.
Aspiring to be Gods, if Angels fell,
Aspiring to be Angels, Men rebel;
And who but wishes to invert the laws
Of ORDER, sins against th' Eternal Cause.   130
    v. Ask for what end the heav'nly bodies shine,
Earth for whose use? Pride answers, " 'Tis for mine:

125-6. Cf. Shaks., *Hen. VIII*, III ii 441-3. Greville (*Treat. of Warres*, sts. 24-5)
has a passage to the same effect, ending with the line cited by Hurd: "Men
would be Tyrants, Tyrants would be Gods."

127-8. Cf. Chudleigh, *Ess.*, pp. 29-30:

> Accursed *Pride* taught Angels to rebel,
> Govern'd by That, immortal Spirits fell . . .
> This dang'rous Mischief I with Care will shun,
> Will never be by haughty Thoughts undone.

127. Cf. *Par. Lost*, VI 898-900:

> . . . the deep fall
> Of those too high aspiring who rebelled
> With Satan.

128. So Satan plans to destroy Adam and Eve (*Par. Lost*, IV 524-7) by per-
suading them to reject

> Envious commands, invented with design
> To keep them low, whom knowledge might exalt
> Equal with gods. Aspiring to be such,
> They taste and die;

and cf. Burton, p. 69: ". . . we desire Impossibles, when we seek after that . . .
which is proper to Angels or other Natures. These Desires ingage us in vain
Attempts: and the mischief is, that whilst we are in pursuit after that which is
unattainable, we neglect that which we might have, and is the proper Perfection
of our Nature".

129-30. E.g. man (cf. *Par. Lost*, IX 679*ff*) or Satan (*ibid.*, V 772-871). Milton's
God says (III 204-6) that man "affecting Godhead" sins

> Against the high supremacy of Heav'n.

131*ff*. *The* Absurdity *of conceiting himself the* Final Cause *of the Creation, or
expecting that Perfection in the* moral world *which is not in the* natural. [P. *1735b-43a*.]

Pope echoes in part Montaigne's attack (II 185*ff*, 189*ff*, 329) on anthropocentrism and cf. also Boileau, *Sat.*, VIII; Prior, I 549*ff*. The type of anthropocentric rapture Pope is replying to is illustrated philosophically in Sebon's *Theol.
nat.*, tr. Montaigne, *Œuvres* (Paris, 1924-32), IX 157; and poetically in Hill's
Creation (1720), st. 8, and Young's *Imper. Pelagi* (1729), str. III, sts. 7, 11. Cf. also
Death. A Poem. In Two Books (Dublin, 1731), p. 12, where Adam is apostro-
phized:

"For me kind Nature wakes her genial pow'r,
"Suckles each herb, and spreads out ev'ry flow'r;
"Annual for me, the grape, the rose renew   135
"The juice nectareous, and the balmy dew;
"For me, the mine a thousand treasures brings;
"For me, health gushes from a thousand springs;
"Seas roll to waft me, suns to light me rise;
"My foot-stool earth, my canopy the skies."   140
     But errs not Nature from this gracious end,
     From burning suns when livid deaths descend,

134 spreads] swells *1733b*.

> Say glorious Wretch, what Joys, what Pleasure grew,
> Produc'd by Nature, not design'd for you?
> For thee the purple Springs eternal Bloom;
> For thee the Trees project their awful Gloom;
> For thee the Plumb puts out its glossy Blue
> And blushing Roses shine with pearly Dew;
> For thee the Vines their purple Glories bear,
> And fraught with swelling Buds the Limbs appear,
> The Seasons laugh, and smiles the Buxom Year.

The "for thee" formula of such passages perhaps owes something to Lucretius' famous apostrophe: "te, dea, te . . . te" (1 6*ff*).

133. *genial*] Generative, as in *Par. Lost*, VII 282.

136. *juice nectareous*] Cf. Philips, *Cyder* (1708), p. 32: "nectareous Juice"— *OED*'s earliest use of the word *nectareous*.

balmy dew] For the phrase, cf. Rowe's Lucan (1718), IX 494.

139. *suns . . . rise*] So in Young's *Last Day* (1713), III 324–5, God is said to have hung the sun on high to light man to his pleasures.

140. EC and Pattison note and criticize the reference to Is., LXI 1—"Thus saith the Lord, The heaven is my throne, and the earth my footstool"— without observing its contribution to the crescendo by which the anthropocentrist becomes *the god of God* (122); and cf. the possibly similar implications of *nectareous* (136).

canopy] The canopy of a throne. Pope echoes in the last three words *Odyss.*, XI (tr. Broome) 237, and (as Wakefield notes) Garth, *Dispens.*, 1 175.

142. *burning suns*] Ancient attributions of the causes of plague to the sun and midsummer heats were continued through Pope's day. Cf. the citations of A. D. McKillop, *Background of Thomson's Seasons* (1942), pp. 166–8.

livid] The observed colour of plague victims. Cf. R. Bradley, *Plague at Marseilles Consider'd* (1721), p. vi; R. Crawfurd, *Plague and Pest. in Lit. and Art* (1914), pp. 28, 71.

When earthquakes swallow, or when tempests sweep
Towns to one grave, whole nations to the deep?
"No ('tis reply'd) the first Almighty Cause   145
"Acts not by partial, but by gen'ral laws;
"Th' exceptions few; some change since all began,

144 whole nations] a Nation *1733a*; and Nations *1733b–34b*; or
Nations *1735a–43a*.
145–146 *1733a reads:*
  Blame we for this the wise Almighty Cause?
  "No ('tis reply'd) he acts by *gen'ral Laws*;
*1733b–43a om. the quotation marks in front of 145, but 1739–43a
introduce them before the first.*

143–4. Pattison notes that "towns and districts swallowed by the sea" form
the subject of a chapter in Pliny's *Hist. nat.*, II xciv, and cites the Chilean earthquakes of February 1732, which swallowed up St Jago and caused inundation of
Concepción. For the language of Pope's description, cf. John Shower, *Practical
Refl. on Earthquakes* (1693, ed. 1750), p. 24: ". . . when the earth opens on a
sudden, and becomes the grave of whole families, streets, and cities"; p. 26
(quoting Seneca, *Nat. quaest.*, VI i [7]): ". . . for it does not only devour houses,
families, and single towns, but ruins whole countries and nations, either over-
turning or swallowing them up . . ."; p. 54: ". . . yea many hundred thousand
people may be swallowed up . . . , tumbling alive into one common grave . . ."

145–8. A highly elliptical passage, impacting in the mouth of the anthropocentrist stock explanations of physical evils: (1) that God's laws are calculated
for general good, not that of the part, though they may perhaps, on rare occasions, be suspended in the interest of the part; (2) that deteriorations in the
system (below, 147n) may account for the intrusion of some evils; (3) that the
Creation, as a thing created, is by definition imperfect, God alone being perfect.
Ll. 147–8 are crabbed in structure, but whether by oversight or whether by
mimesis (cf. *Rape of the Lock*, IV 126–9; *Dunc.* A, III 181ff), the rhetorical figure
which aims to satirize by mimicking an opponent's speech, is uncertain. Pope's
fluency, however, fails him oftener in the *Essay* than in any other poem—though
this does not mean it fails him very often. Pope's point (ll. 148–72) is that the
anthropocentrist has implicitly abandoned his position in the arguments used
to explain physical evils; ought to abandon it altogether; and if he does so, will
see that God's dispositions in the moral realm (likewise calculated for general
good) are as readily justified as His dispositions in the natural.

146–7. *Acts . . . few*] Standard doctrine of the schools: cf. Aquinas (*Sum. c.
gent.*, III lxxi [and cf. lxxii]), and Malebranche (*Entretiens metaphys.*, IX [ix–xi])
[Pattison].

147. *Th' . . . few*] In part, the question of particular providences. For Pope's

"And what created perfect?"—Why then Man?
If the great end be human Happiness,
Then Nature deviates; and can Man do less?   150
As much that end a constant course requires
Of show'rs and sun-shine, as of Man's desires;
As much eternal springs and cloudless skies,
As Men for ever temp'rate, calm, and wise.   154
If plagues or earthquakes break not Heav'n's design,

150 Then . . . and can] And . . . how can *1733a–34b*.
151 As much that end] Nature as much *1733a*.

own belief, see his letter to Broome, 14 Dec. [1730], discussing his mother's
escape from serious injury when she fell into the fire: "I think there are many
reasons to believe as well a particular as a general providence, and the effect of
such a belief is of singular use in our life and conduct"; and his statements on
the same occasion to Caryll and to Lord Oxford: 22 Oct. 1730, 3 Nov. 1730.

some . . . began] This may refer either to Newton's belief that irregularities
were gradually accruing in the system, as Warburton thought (see his note on
I 150), or to the traditional theory (revived in T. Burnet's *Sacred Theory of the
Earth*, 1681–9) that the world was less perfect since the Fall; or to both.

150. *deviates*] A further figure from "exorbitation" of bodies: cf. *Ess.*, I 124.
152. *desires*] I.e. passions.

151–64. Cf. Esprit, p. 364: "[Socrates taught] that Man is no less liable to
the Malice, and ill Nature of others, than to the injuries of the Air and the
malignity of the Stars; that he ought to bear as patiently the disorder of their
Mind and Actions, as that of the Seasons; and that as he is not in a Passion with
a Horse that kicks him, or with a Thunderbolt that falls upon his House, and
Burns it down, he ought neither to be angry with Furious Fellows that fall upon
him, and who with the violence of their Passions act with more liberty, but
with as much blindness as natural Causes, and with as much fierceness as
Brutes."

155–6. Cf. Introd., p. xxxiii. These lines are not necessarily fatalistic, though
often so interpreted. Judged in the light of the whole poem, their thesis appears
to be that as God has established general laws for the larger good of the whole
which sometimes bring about natural evils in particular instances, so—again in
accord with a larger scheme—God has given man passions which sometimes
result in moral evils. Taken in this sense, they constitute a reply to the conten-
tion, not uncommon in Pope's day (cf. Bayle, *Dict.*, arts. Pauliciens, Mani-
chéens) that a good God would have made man incapable of sinning. The doctrine of 157–60 that God uses both natural and moral forces to punish mankind
is likewise ancient and orthodox, and Pope may have added it—in 1743 (cf.
textual notes—to clarify his position.

Why then a Borgia, or a Catiline?
Who knows but he, whose hand the light'ning forms,
Who heaves old Ocean, and who wings the storms,
Pours fierce Ambition in a Cæsar's mind,
Or turns young Ammon loose to scourge mankind?   160
From pride, from pride, our very reas'ning springs;
Account for moral as for nat'ral things:
Why charge we Heav'n in those, in these acquit?
In both, to reason right is to submit.

    Better for Us, perhaps, it might appear,   165
Were there all harmony, all virtue here;

157–160 *Add. 1743b, 1751.*

157. *he . . . forms*] Cf. Psa. xcvii 4, cxxxv 7; Job xxviii 26, xxxvii 3. Pope's *Il.*, viii 95*n*, and his *Odyss.*, ix 75. The appropriateness of Pope's allusions to Scripture—for example, to the Old Testament God here and the New Testament God at i 88—should be noted throughout the poem.

158. *heaves . . . Ocean*] For the wording, cf. *Par. Lost*, xi 827.

wings . . . storms] Psa. civ 3, cvii 25.

159–60. Esprit, p. 8: "So that it may be said to all Conquerors: . . . 'You are the Ministers, whereby God executes the severe Decrees of his Justice, and the Arm which he makes use of to punish the proud Rebellion of Men . . .' "

160. Halifax compares the tyrannical ruler to "a Whip in God Almighty's hand, to be thrown into the Fire when the World hath been sufficiently scourged with it". *Wks.*, ed. Raleigh (1912), p. 64.

young Ammon] For the phrase, Wakefield cites Lee, *Alex. the Great*, ii i; Garth, *Dispens.*, i 45; Rowe, *Poem upon the Late Glor. Successes* [1707], 261.

163–72. A fairly common view in sermon literature. Cf. Wm. Clagett, *Seventeen Sermons* (1689), p. 435: "The Good we enjoy, and the Evil we suffer, are both from the hand of God. For his Providence always attends the working of second causes, either disposing them or permitting them to produce those things that happen in the World. When the Air is healthy or infectious; when the Seasons are Fruitful or unkindly; when the wind makes a Shipwrack, or when it brings the Ship safe into the Harbor; when we suffer by the malice and passions of others, or when they are taken in their own net and we escape; we are in all these and the like events to look further than the immediate causes of the Good or the Evil, and to acknowledge the over-ruling Providence of God."

164. Pascal, pp. 44–5: " 'Tis fit we should know, how to doubt where we ought, to rest assured where we ought, to submit where we ought. . . Reason, says St. *Austin*, would never be for submitting, if it did not judge that on some Occasions, Submission was its Duty."

That never air or ocean felt the wind;
That never passion discompos'd the mind:
But ALL subsists by elemental strife;
And Passions are the elements of Life.   170
The gen'ral ORDER, since the whole began,
Is kept in Nature, and is kept in Man.
    VI. What would this Man? Now upward will he soar,
And little less than Angel, would be more;
Now looking downwards, just as griev'd appears   175
To want the strength of bulls, the fur of bears.
Made for his use all creatures if he call,
Say what their use, had he the pow'rs of all?

175 downwards] downward, *1733a–43a.*

----

169. See Introd., pp. xxxiv*f.*

170. See this subject extended in Epist. 2 from Vers. 100, to 122, 165, &c. [P. *1735b–43a.*]

173*ff. The Unreasonableness of the Complaints against Providence, and that to possess more Faculties would make us miserable.* [P. *1735b–43a.*] Alluding to the kind of criticism of man's endowments registered by Lucret., v 222*ff*, Pliny, *Hist. nat.,* VII, *proem,* and summarized by Seneca, *De benef.,* II xxix (*Wks,* tr. Lodge, 1614, p. 36): "They complaine because wee equall not Elephants in bulke of bodie, Harts in swiftnesse, Birds in lightnesse, Bulls in force. They complaine that beasts have substantialler hides than we, that fallow Deere have a fairer haire, the Beare a thicker skinne, . . . And whereas nature permitteth not, that some properties should be united in one and the same creature (as that swiftnesse of bodie should be matched with mightinesse in strength) they suppose themselves iniured, because man was not composed of these diuers and dissident goods . . ." Cf. also Browne, *Relig. Med.,* I xviii; Shaftesbury, II 300*ff*; and Jos. Hall, *Solil.,* XXII (*Wks.,* 1662, III 432): "I admire thee O God, in all the workes of thy hands; and justly magnifie . . . thy mercy and wisdom in the equall distribution of all their powers and faculties, which thou hast so ordered, that every Creature hath some requisite helps, no Creature hath all . . . As for Man, the Lord of all the rest, him thou hast endued with Reason, to make his use of all these: whom yet thou hast so framed, as that in many qualities thou hast allowed the brute Creatures to exceed their Master: Some of them are stronger than he; some of them swifter than he . . .: he were no better than a mad man that should aske, why Man should not fly as well as the bird, and swim as well as the Fish, and run as fast as the Hart? Since that one faculty of Reason . . . is more worth than all the brutish excellencies of the world put together."

174. Psa. VIII 5.

Nature to these, without profusion kind,
The proper organs, proper pow'rs assign'd;   180
Each seeming want compensated of course,
Here with degrees of swiftness, there of force;
All in exact proportion to the state;
Nothing to add, and nothing to abate.
Each beast, each insect, happy in its own;   185
Is Heav'n unkind to Man, and Man alone?
Shall he alone, whom rational we call,

179 *New paragraph 1733a–35a;* these] each *1733a.*
182 with] due *1733a.*
183–6 *1733a prints these two couplets in reversed order and with the
       following differences:* 185 in its own] as it can. 186 Man, and
       Man alone] nothing but to Man. 183 So justly all proportion'd
       to each state.
183 the] their *1739–43a.*
187–8 *1733a reads:*
              Shall Man, shall reasonable Man, alone,
              Be, or endow'd with all, or pleas'd with none?

179–84. A favourite subject of the teleologists, expressed proverbially in
mediaeval and ancient science as "natura neque redundat in superfluis, neque
deficit in necessariis."

181. *compensated*] Pronounced *compénsated* in Pope's time, according to Bailey.
of course] In the normal course of events.

182. It is a certain Axiom in the Anatomy of Creatures, that in proportion as
they are form'd for Strength, their Swiftness is lessen'd; or as they are form'd for
Swiftness, their Strength is abated. [P. *1734a–51.*] On this, cf. I 173*ffn* (Seneca)
and Cicero, *De nat. deor.*, II xlviii: ". . . aut vires natura dedit aut celeritatem."

183–8. Cf. Erasmus, p. 67: "[Pythagoras] concluded that no Creature was
more miserable than man, for that all other Creatures are content with those
bounds that Nature set them, onely Man endeavours to exceed them"; Pomfret,
Upon the Div. Attrib., st. 3:
       By her [infinite wisdom] all Creatures have their Ends assign'd,
       Proportion'd to their Nature and their Kind; . . .
       Nothing, but Men, reject her sacred Rules,
       Who from the End of their Creation fly,
       And deviate into Misery.
The Auditor, 23 Jan. 1732: "'Oh! why (said I) must that Creature alone, for whose
Ease and Support all these Creatures were formed, be more unhappy than they?'".

185. Vid. Epist. 3 Vers 79, &c. and 110, &c. [P. *1735b–43a.*]

Be pleas'd with nothing, if not bless'd with all?
   The bliss of Man (could Pride that blessing find)
Is not to act or think beyond mankind;   190
No pow'rs of body or of soul to share,
But what his nature and his state can bear.
Why has not Man a microscopic eye?

188 *Between ll. 188–9, 1733a has ll. 207–32, with the differences noted at
     those lines, below.*
190 act] know *1733a;* act or think] think, or act, *1733b–34b.*
191–2 *1733a reads:*
          No self-confounding Faculties to share;
          No Senses stronger than his brain can bear.
193 eye] sight *1733b.*

189–92. Montaigne, II 450–1: "*What a vile and abject thing,* says he [Seneca]
is Man, if he do not raise himself above Humanity? 'Tis a good word and a profitable
desire, but withal absurd: For to make the handle bigger than the Hand, and
the Cubit longer than the Arm, and to hope to stride further than our Legs can
reach, is both impossible and monstrous; or that Man should rise above himself
and Humanity: for he cannot see but with his Eyes, nor seize but with his
Power."
   191–2. Aquinas, *Sum. c. gent.,* III V–VI: "In a substance, that is evil through its
lacking something natural and due to it, for that a man have not wings is not an
evil to him, because it is not natural for him to have them . . . But it is an evil if
he have no hands, which are natural and due to him, if he be perfect; and yet it
is not an evil to a bird."
   193. *microscopic] OED's* first use of the shortened form in place of *microscopical.*
   193–206. It was a point of constant emphasis in Pope's day that man's sensory powers had "that Degree of Perfection, which is most fit and suitable to our
Estate and Condition" (R. Bentley, *Eight Sermons,* in *BLS* I 25). Locke commented (*Ess. of Hum. Underst.,* II xxiii 12) on the propriety of human hearing and
sight, noting with respect to the latter that if man had "microscopical Eyes",
"he would not make any great Advantage by the Change." Others, including
Thomson (*Spring,* 1728, ll. 162*ff*), Fontenelle (*Dial. des morts,* tr. Hughes, 1708,
pp. 107–8), and Pope's friends Cheselden (*Anat. of the Hum. Body,* 1756, p. 310)
and George Cheyne (*Philos. Principles of Relig.,* 1715, I 353*ff*), commented on the
suitability of one or several of the senses. In a work praised by Bolingbroke
(*Wks.,* 1754, V 336, 339) and translated into English as *The Religious Philosopher*
(1730, I 313*ff*), the Dutch scientist Bernard Nieuwentyt remarked on all the
senses in turn, stressing (like Pope) the superiority of man's actual vision to
either microscopic or telescopic sight, the disadvantages that would accrue

For this plain reason, Man is not a Fly.
Say what the use, were finer optics giv'n,   195
T' inspect a mite, not comprehend the heav'n?
Or touch, if tremblingly alive all o'er,

---

194 Fly] Mite *1733b*.
195 What the advantage, if his finer eyes *1733a*; Say what th'
    advantage of so fine an Eye *1733b*.
196 Study a Mite, not comprehend the Skies? *1733a*; mite . . .
    heav'n] Mote . . . Sky *1733b*.
197 Or] His *1733a*; The *1735b–43a*; if] so *1733b*.

---

from either keener or duller hearing, the "Effluvia" that would offend if olfactory sensitivity were increased, the painfulness of life "if the Feeling were so tender and nice in all the Parts of the Body" as in some, etc. For a somewhat similar account, see Barrow's sermon, *The Being of God Proved from the Frame of the World*, Wks. (New York, 1845), II 237. Pope gives these materials an organization consonant with his theme: cf. 201–2n.

194. *Man . . . Fly*] The point of Pope's comparison is that the fly's eye was supposed to have microscopic powers. Cf. Cheselden, *Anat. of the Hum. Body* (1756), p. 299: "The larger animals having larger eyes, their organs of vision, like a microscope with a large lens, are fit to take in a greater view, but in that view things are not so much magnified; in lesser animals a small space is discerned, . . . but that greatly magnified"; Hen. Baker, *Microscope Made Easy* (3rd ed. 1744), p. 230: "There can be no doubt, that *Lice*, *Mites*, and multitudes of other *Animalcules* [he has been instancing flies] . . . have Eyes contriv'd . . . to discern Objects some thousands of times less than themselves. . . What a Power then of magnifying are such Eyes endued with!"

195–6. Cf. *Dunc.* B, IV 453*ff* and note.

196. The force of the antithesis rests on the common symbolical belief that man's sight, unlike the animals', was formed to look upwards: cf. Ovid, *Metam.*, I 76–86; *Par. Lost*, VII 505–16; K. E. Hartwell, *Lactantius and Milton* (1929), pp. 75 *ff*. Boyle makes an analogous point in saying (IV 26) that it is improper for men "to dispute anxiously about the properties of an atom, and be careless about the inquiry into the attributes of the great God, who formed all things . . ."; and cf. J. Leng, *Nat. Obligations to believe . . . Relig. and Div. Rev.*, *BLS* III (1719) 71: ". . . Men were . . . made . . . to be Spectators of Things above and in the Heavens, a Sight which no other Kind of Animals is concerned withal."

197–8. Wakefield cites Milton's question [*Sams. Ag.*, 93–7] why the sight was
                not, as feeling, through all parts diffused,
        That she [the soul] might look at will through every pore?

I

To smart and agonize at ev'ry pore?
Or quick effluvia darting thro' the brain,
Die of a rose in aromatic pain?   200
If nature thunder'd in his op'ning ears,
And stunn'd him with the music of the spheres,
How would he wish that Heav'n had left him still
The whisp'ring Zephyr, and the purling rill?
Who finds not Providence all good and wise,   205
Alike in what it gives, and what denies?

199 quick] keen *1734a–35a*; the] his *1733a*.
200 Die of a rose in] To sink opprest with *1733b*.
205 all good] all-good *1733a–43a*.

199–200. Ctess. of Winchelsea, *The Spleen* (1709), 40–41:
          Now the *Jonquil* o'ercomes the feeble Brain,
          We faint beneath the Aromatick pain.
Noted by Middleton Murry, *Countries of the Mind* (2nd ser., 1931), p. 174. Cf.
also Dryden, *Ann. Mirab.*, 116: "And some by aromatic splinters die." Wakefield compares "what Pliny fables of an ancient people, who subsisted by the
smell of flowers only, and aromatic plants; and were deprived of life by the more
violent effluvia of their odours: *Nat. Hist.*, VII 2." Professor G. R. Tracy suggests
to me that Pope's line may recall an old punishment by smothering in roses (cf.
textual notes); see John Webster (*Wks.*, ed. Lucas, I 210 and note).
     199. *effluvia*] Streams of invisible particles by which Epicurus and others
believed that odours communicated themselves to the brain. A copious history
of the theory is given by G. K. Chalmers, "Effluvia, the History of a Metaphor",
PMLA, LII (1937) 1031ff.
     201–4. Cf. Barrow, *The Being of God Proved from the Frame of the World* (*Wks.*,
New York, 1845, II 237): ". . . whence comes it to pass, that ordinarily in
nature nothing occurs noisome or troublesome to any sense . . .? . . . Where is it
that we meet with noises so violent, or so jarring, as to offend our ears? is there
not rather provided for us . . . some kind of harmony grateful to them; not only
. . . by rivers the soft warbling of the stream; but even the rude winds whistle in
a tune not unpleasant . . .?"
     201–2. Pope closes his instances with a comparison at the opposite end of the
scale—between man and angel (cf. man and fly, above)—alluding to the belief
that it was given to angels but not to mortals to hear the music of the spheres.
For references to this belief, see the poets cited by Wakefield, Pattison, and
Morris, esp. Shaks., *Merch. of Ven.*, v i 60ff.

VII. Far as Creation's ample range extends,
The scale of sensual, mental pow'rs ascends:
Mark how it mounts, to Man's imperial race,
From the green myriads in the peopled grass: 210
What modes of sight betwixt each wide extreme,
The mole's dim curtain, and the lynx's beam:
Of smell, the headlong lioness between,

207–10 *1733a reads:*

Thro' gen'ral Life, behold the Scale arise
Of *sensual,* and of *mental* Faculties.
Vast Range of Sense! from Man's imperial race
To [etc.]

207ff. *There is an universal* ORDER *and* GRADATION *thro' the whole visible world, of the* sensible *and* mental *Faculties, which causes the* Subordination *of Creature to Creature, and of all Creatures to Man, whose* Reason *alone countervails all the other Faculties.* [P. *1735b–43a. 1739–43a add as a second paragraph*]: The Extent, Limits, and Use of *Human Reason* and *Science*, the Author design'd as the subject of his next Book of Ethic Epistles.

209ff. "Pope has practised the great secret of Virgil's art, which was to discover the very single epithet that precisely suited each occasion" [Warton].

209. Man's . . . race] For the phrase, Wakefield cites *Rape of the Lock*, II 27, and Dryden's Virgil, *Geo.*, III 377.

212. The . . . curtain] It had only recently been recognized that contrary to ancient opinion moles had a degree of sight: cf. Boyle, v 407. In speaking of the curtain Pope may be drawing on the observation recorded in Chambers (art. Eye) that the mole, when above ground, "can protend" its eyes "forth beyond the skin, and again draw them back at pleasure", or on the fact that human eyelids and the special membrane in birds and frogs were often compared by natural philosophers to screens and curtains: cf. Boyle, v 436–7; Ray, *Wisd. of God in the Creation* (1714), pp. 338–40.

lynx] Traditionally supposed to possess "a more piercing sight than any creature in the world". John Swan, *Spec. Mundi* (1635), p. 451. *Beam* alludes to the old theory that sight depended on emission of rays from the eye: cf. Donne's *Extasie*, 7.

213. The manner of the Lions hunting their Prey in the Deserts of Africa is this; at their first going out in the night-time they set up a loud Roar, and then listen to the Noise made by the Beasts in their Flight, pursuing them by the Ear, and not by the Nostril. It is probable, the story of the Jackall's hunting for the Lion was occasion'd by observation of the Defect of Scent in that terrible Animal. [P. *1734a–51,* but *1735ac, 1736–43a have* observing *for* observation of *and 1739–43a* this terrible *for* that terrible.]

And hound sagacious on the tainted green:
Of hearing, from the life that fills the flood,   215
To that which warbles thro' the vernal wood:
The spider's touch, how exquisitely fine!
Feels at each thread, and lives along the line:
In the nice bee, what sense so subtly true
From pois'nous herbs extracts the healing dew: 220

216 *Between ll. 216–217, 1733a has ll. 219–220.*

On this line and Pope's note, cf. *A New Syst. of the Nat. Hist. of Quadrup.*, *Birds, Fishes, and Insects* (Edinburgh, 1791), I 346, 347: "The lion preys on all kinds of animals; as his scent is bad, he cannot hunt by the nose; but his peculiar and tremendous roar strikes terror into every beast . . . , and sets them in motion, in open view: he then selects his object, and takes it . . ." "The lion . . . has neither the senses of smelling nor of seeing, so acute as the other beasts of prey." Allusions to the lion's relatively imperfect smell and sight are also made by Buffon (*Hist. nat.*, tr. J. Wright, 1831, II 4), but I find nowhere the curious misinformation of Pope's note that lions hunt by ear. He may have owed it to his friend, the anatomist Cheselden, whose name he has placed beside this verse in the Harvard MS.

214. *sagacious*] "Acute in perception, esp. by the sense of smell" (*OED*). Dryden has "sagacious hounds" in *The Cock and the Fox*, 752.

tainted] "Imbued with the scent of an animal (usually a hunted animal)" (*OED*).

215. It was still a matter of debate in Pope's time and after whether fish had hearing or not. See the Royal Society's *Philos. Trans.*, XLV (1750) 149–55, 233–9; and R. Bradley, *Philos. Acct. of the Wks. of Nat.* (1721), p. 63: "But indeed I do not find that the curious Observers of *Fish* are of Opinion that they want any Sense but that of Hearing; and even they do not determine whether that Sense is absolutely wanting or not: But if I may be allow'd to judge from an Experiment I have made upon *Carps* in several Places, I believe it will be allow'd that they enjoy that Sense . . ."

217. Topsell, p. 778, applies the same epithet, remarking that the spider is "endued with the most exquisite sense of touching that possibly can be imagined."

219–20. Pliny, *Hist. nat.*, XXI xlv (I owe this reference to Professor R. H. Griffith). Cf. Erasmus, *Enchir.* (abr. and tr. in Coverdale's *Writings and Transl.*, Parker Soc., 1844), p. 449: ". . . and by the example of the bee refuse the poison, and suck out only the wholesome and sweet juice"; and Topsell, p. 910.

220. *healing dew*] The phrase reflects the common medicinal use of honey in Pope's day and the ancient belief that honey was a dew that fell on flowers.

How Instinct varies in the grov'ling swine,
Compar'd, half-reas'ning elephant, with thine:
'Twixt that, and Reason, what a nice barrier;
For ever sep'rate, yet for ever near!
Remembrance and Reflection how ally'd;   225
What thin partitions Sense from Thought divide:
And Middle natures, how they long to join,

221–2 *1733a reads:*

> How *Instinct* varies! what a Hog may want,
> Compar'd with thine, half-reas'ning Elephant!

221. *grov'ling swine*] Morris cites the same phrase from Milton, *Comus*, 53. Pope's choice of the swine as the lower term for the range of animal instinct is paralleled in Cumberland's remark (p. 99) that "the Soul of a Swine" has no higher function than, "instead of Salt, to preserve a Carcass from Rottenness".

223–4. Pope adopts regularly in the *Essay* (cf. III 83*ff*) the orthodox position, opposed by Montaigne and others, that man differs from animal in kind, not merely in degree.

223. *barrier*] Johnson, *Dict.* (1755): "It is sometimes pronounced with the accent on the last syllable, but it is placed more properly upon the first." Pope's usage varied: cf. his translation of Statius, 20: "And fix, O Muse! the barrier of thy song"; and *Dunc.* B, I 178.

224. Charleton, p. 46: "How neer so ever Brute Beasts may be allowed to approach to the Divine faculty of *Reason*, or *Discours*: yet most certain it is, no one of them hath ever been observed to *attain* thereunto."

225–6. Cf. Dryden, *Abs. and Achit.*, 163–4:

> Great wits are sure to madness near allied,
> And thin partitions do their bounds divide.

225. Cumberland, p. 112: "Shall I not reckon among the Perfections of the human Understanding, that it can *reflect* upon it self? . . . In this Power of the Mind, and the Actions thence arising, consists the whole force of *Conscience*, by which it *proposes* Laws to it self, *examines* its past, and regulates its future Conduct. Nor appear any Traces, in other Animals, of so noble a Faculty." The faculty allotted to beasts was remembrance—simple memory.

Pope expatiates on the functions of reflection at *Ess.*, III 133*f*.

226. Cf. Ovid's *Remed. amor.*, [I] 344 (tr. Tate): "Such thin Partitions Good and Ill divide" [Wakefield].

227. *Middle natures*] Natures transitional between the main steps of the scale, as in Geo. Herbert's *Providence*, 135–6:

> Frogs marry fish and flesh; bats, bird and beast;
> Sponges, non-sense and sense; mines, th' earth and plants.

And cf. Aristotle, *Hist. animal.*, VIII i and *De part. animal.*, IV xiii; Bacon, *Nov. Org.*, II xxx; Locke, *Ess. of Hum. Underst.*, III vi 12.

Yet never pass th' insuperable line!
Without this just gradation, could they be
Subjected these to those, or all to thee?   230
The pow'rs of all subdu'd by thee alone,
Is not thy Reason all these pow'rs in one?
    VIII. See, thro' this air, this ocean, and this earth,
All matter quick, and bursting into birth.
Above, how high progressive life may go!   235
Around, how wide! how deep extend below!
Vast chain of being, which from God began,
Natures æthereal, human, angel, man,
Beast, bird, fish, insect! what no eye can see,

232 these] those *1733a–43a.*
    Between ll. 232–233, 1733a has ll. 189–206, with the differences noted at those lines, above.
234 matter] Nature *1733a.*
238 Ethereal Essence, Spirit, Substance, Man, *1733a.*

231–2. Cf. note on *Ess.,* I 173*ff.*

233*ff. How much farther this* Gradation *and* Subordination *may extend? were any part of which broken, the* whole connected Creation *must be destroy'd.* [P. *1735b–43a.*]

233–41. On the imaginative excitement enkindled by discoveries through the microscope and telescope—to which the energy of these lines attests—see Marjorie Nicolson, "The Microscope and Engl. Imag." (*Smith College Studies in Mod. Lang.,* XVI (1935), no. 4); "The Telescope and Imag." (*MP* XXXII (1935) 233*ff*); "The New Astron. and Engl. Lit. Imag." (*SP,* XXXII (1935) 428*ff*).

233. *this air . . . earth*] The traditional classification of forms of life according to the three inhabited elements: cf. *Ess.,* III 116–20.

234. The populousness of matter as seen under the microscope fascinated Pope's contemporaries: cf. *Spectat.,* 519; Fontenelle, *Plural. des mondes* (tr. Glanvill, 1702), pp. 88–90; King, p. 102.

237–41. Cf. Thomson's *Summer* (1727), 283–6:
                            Has any seen
        The mighty Chain of Beings, lessening down
        From infinite Perfection to the Brink
        Of dreary *Nothing,* desolate Abyss!
Pascal's observation (p. 166) that man finds "himself hanging . . . between the two vast Abysses of Infinite and Nothing" [EC]; and La Bruyère, II 135: ". . . whose work are all these minute curiosities, so exceeding minute that no eye can perceive them, and, like the heavens, they border upon infinitude, though in the other extreme? Sure it can be no other than the same Being who made, and who moves, with so much facility, the heavens and the stars. . ."

No glass can reach! from Infinite to thee,   240
From thee to Nothing!—On superior pow'rs
Were we to press, inferior might on ours:
Or in the full creation leave a void,
Where, one step broken, the great scale's destroy'd:
From Nature's chain whatever link you strike,   245
Tenth or ten thousandth, breaks the chain alike.
   And if each system in gradation roll,
Alike essential to th' amazing whole;

241-2. *On . . . ours*] King, p. 125: ". . . you may wish that some other Place and Condition had fallen to your Lot; . . . but if you had taken up another's Place, that other, or some else, must have been put into yours, who, being alike ungrateful to the Divine Providence, would wish for the place which you now have occupied."

241. On this notion of the delicate interdependency of all things and man's crucial rôle in it, see Introd., pp. l–li. Also, Aurelius, v viii (cited by Warton and Pattison); G. Goodman, *Fall of Man* (1616), p. 17; Hooker, i ix 1.

243. Cf. *Ess.*, i 45. The ancient postulate that nature abhors a void.

244-6. Pattison quotes Lucan, vi 611–3. Disraeli, *Curios. of Lit.* (Boston 1858, ii 275), compares Waller *On the Danger His Majesty Escaped* [168–70]:

That chain that's fixed to the throne of Jove,
On which the fabric of our world depends;
One link dissolv'd, the whole creation ends.

Cf. also *Spectat.*, 404: ". . . the civil oeconomy is formed in a Chain as well as the natural: and in either case the breach but of one link puts the whole in some Disorder"; Thomson, *Spring* (1728), 155–8:

Even Animals subsist
On Animals, in infinite Descent
And all so fine adjusted, that the Loss
Of the least Species would disturb the whole;

and G. P. Marana, *Turkish Spy* (Engl. tr. 1702), vii 194; Kath. Philips, *Submission*, 17–20.

247-56. Cf. Copernicus's preface to *De Revolutionibus*, translated in D. Stimson's *Gradual Acceptance of the Copernican Theory* (New York, 1917), p. 112: ". . . I found at length . . . that if the motions of the other planets were added to the rotation of the earth and calculated as for the revolution of that planet, not only the phenomena of the others followed from this, but also it so bound together both the order and magnitude of all the planets and the spheres and the heaven itself, that in no single part could one thing be altered without confusion among the other parts and in all the universe."

248. *amazing*] A strong word in Pope's day (cf. *OED*, sense 1, and the citations there given), used perhaps with a glance back at i 6.

The least confusion but in one, not all
That system only, but the whole must fall. 250
Let Earth unbalanc'd from her orbit fly,
Planets and Suns run lawless thro' the sky,
Let ruling Angels from their spheres be hurl'd,
Being on being wreck'd, and world on world,
Heav'n's whole foundations to their centre nod, 255
And Nature tremble to the throne of God:
All this dread ORDER break—for whom? for thee?
Vile worm!—oh Madness, Pride, Impiety!
    IX. What if the foot, ordain'd the dust to tread,
Or hand to toil, aspir'd to be the head? 260
What if the head, the eye, or ear repin'd
To serve mere engines to the ruling Mind?

251–256 *Om. 1733a.*   252 run] rush *1733b–43a.*
257 break—for whom?] shall it break? *1733a*; thee?] thee, *1734a–*
1735a, 1740. 1736 (probably by error) lacks terminal punctuation.

   251–6. Pattison cites Manilius, *Astron.*, II [67*ff*].
   251. *unbalanc'd*] The antithesis of God's act of creation in *Par. Lost*, VII 242, whereby "Earth, self-balanc'd, on her centre hung."
   253. *ruling Angels*] A belief by no means wholly displaced in the Augustan age. Cf. Edm. Dickinson, *Physica Vetus et Vera* (Rotterdam, 1703), pp. 125–6, 224–7. According to Aquinas (*Sum. c. gent.*, III lxxx) the shaking of the ruling angels from their spheres is to be a sign of the end of the world.
   255–6. *Par. Lost*, VI 218–19, 832–4:
               . . . had Earth been then, all Earth
        Had to her centre shook . . .
                   Under his burning wheels
        The steadfast Empyrean shook throughout,
        All but the Throne itself of God.
   nod . . . tremble] Anti-climactic terms, after what has gone before; effecting a reminder that no destruction can destroy the uncreated.
   258. *The Extravagance, Impiety, and Pride of such a desire.* [P. *1735b–43a.*]
   Vile worm] Job, XXV 4–6: "How then can man be justified with God? . . . yea, the stars are not pure in his sight. How much less man, that is a worm?" Shaks., *Mer. Wives*, V v 87: "Vile worm, thou wast o'erlook'd even in thy birth." Dryden, *Relig. La.*, 93: "Dar'st thou, poor worm, offend Infinity?"
   259–66. "This fine illustration in defence of the System of Nature, is taken from St Paul, who employed it to defend the System of Grace (I Cor., XII 15–21)" [Ward]. Cf. Introd., pp. lvi–lvii.

Just as absurd for any part to claim
To be another, in this gen'ral frame:
Just as absurd, to mourn the tasks or pains   265
The great directing MIND of ALL ordains.
     All are but parts of one stupendous whole,
Whose body Nature is, and God the soul;
That, chang'd thro' all, and yet in all the same,

263-6. A favourite position in moral philosophy from the Stoics down. *Spectat.*, 404 supplies a typical statement of it, developing (as Pope does in *Ess.*, IV) its social implications: "Nature does nothing in vain; the Creator of the Universe has appointed every thing to a certain Use and Purpose, and determined it to a settled Course and Sphere of Action [cf. *Ess.*, I 124, *sphere*], from which, if it in the least deviates, it becomes unfit to answer those Ends for which it was designed. In like Manner it is in the Dispositions of Society . . ."

265. Vid. the prosecution and application of this in Epist. 4. Ver. 162. [P. *1735b-43a.*]

267-80. Cf. Introd., pp. lv-lvi. Note the correspondences (my italics) between Pope and Senault (p. 11): "For though this infinite essence depends not upon the world which he hath created, . . . yet is he *shed abroad in all the parts* thereof; there is *no inter-medium which he fills not up*. He applies himself to all Creatures, *in their operations, and without dividing his unity*, or *weakening his power;* he *gives light with the Sun*, he burneth with the fire, he *refresheth* with the water, and he *brings forth fruit with the trees*. He is *as great on earth as he is in Heaven* . . .; his power is alwaies equal, and *the stars* . . . cost him no more than the grass . . . So is the soul dispersed in the body, and penetrates all the parts thereof; It is *as noble in the hand as in the heart* . . ."

See Pope's letter to Caryll, written when the authorship of the *Essay* was still a secret [8 Mar. 1733], where Pope notes that despite the reference to God as soul of the world, "which at the first glance may be taken for heathenism", his whole paragraph proves the author "quite Christian in his system, from man up to seraphim".

267-8. Cf. Dryden, *Pal. and Arc.*, III 1042-3:
                    Parts of the whole are we; but God the whole,
                    Who gives us life and animating soul.

H. N. Fairchild (*Relig. Trends in 18th Cent. Poetry*, I (1939) 92) cites Toland's *Clito* (1700), [58-9]:
                    Or if . . . [God's] only but the World's great Soul;
                    Or parts the Creatures are, and God the whole.

269. So Augustine speaks of God as "immutabilis, mutans omnia" (*Conf.*, I iv); and cf. I Cor., XII 6: "And there are diversities of operations, but it is the same God which worketh all in all"; and Heb., I 10-12. Cf. also Spenser, *F.Q.*, VII vii 13: "Great nature Still moouing, yet vnmoued from her sted"; Prior, I 351: ". . . all is chang'd, though all is still the same."

Great in the earth, as in th' æthereal frame,   270
Warms in the sun, refreshes in the breeze,
Glows in the stars, and blossoms in the trees,
Lives thro' all life, extends thro' all extent,
Spreads undivided, operates unspent,
Breathes in our soul, informs our mortal part,   275
As full, as perfect, in a hair as heart;
As full, as perfect, in vile Man that mourns,

---

273. *Lives . . . life*] Cf. Augustine, *Conf.*, III vi: "sed tu vita es animarum, vita vitarum, vivens tu ipsa."

extends . . . extent] In opposition to Descartes, Henry More had recently stressed extension as well as indivisibility (cf. *Ess.*, I 274) as essential attributes of spirit (*Enchir. met.*, XXVII 5, XXVIII 3); and Newton had referred to space as God's "sensorium". *Opticks*, 2nd ed., 1718, pp. 345, 379.

274. Standard predications of God in catholic theology: cf. Bellarmine, p. 134: "For God is an indivisible spirit, and yet fills the whole world"; p. 179: ". . . God continually co-operates with all things which he hath made, and neither is, nor will be fatigu'd with his Co-operation." For *spreads*, cf. also J. Wilkins, *Nat. Relig.* (1705), pp. 117–18: "[God] doth spread himself to all places. . ."

275. Bellarmine, p. 135: "God is absolutely in all things, not only in corporeal, but also in spiritual. . ."

Breathes . . . soul] Gen., II 7: "[God] breathed into his nostrils the breath of life: and man became a living soul."

276–8. Bellarmine, p. 22: "But do not imagine, my Soul, that God doth so fill the World that a Part of him is in a certain Part of the World, and that he is whole in all the World, for God is without Parts, and is whole in the whole World, and whole in every a part of it." Cf. Aquinas, *Sum. c. gent.*, III lxix; Augustine, *Conf.*, I iii: "Sed quae imples omnia, te toto imples omnia"; *Spectat.*, 565: "His substance is within the substance of every living being whether material or immaterial. . ."

276. The point of the antithesis and the alliteration, on both of which the critics (e.g. Morris) have been severe, is the contrast of higher and lower in the hierarchy of the body (as of man with seraph in the hierarchy of beings)—the heart being traditionally thought of as the noblest organ and hair as an *excretum*: cf. Shaks., *K. Lear*, III ii 27*ff*; *Com. of Err.*, II ii 78.

For the theological bearings of the line, cf. Aquinas's argument (*Sum. theol.*, I lxxvi 8) that the soul is wholly in the whole body and at the same time wholly in each part of the body—which is also the position of Augustine, who instances the foot, eyes, tongue, and hands (*De immort. anim.*, XVI 25) and of Plotinus, who instances the eyes and ears (*Enn.*, IV iii 3; also IV ii 1).

As the rapt Seraph that adores and burns;
To him no high, no low, no great, no small;
He fills, he bounds, connects, and equals all.   280
   x. Cease then, nor ORDER Imperfection name:
Our proper bliss depends on what we blame.
Know thy own point: This kind, this due degree
Of blindness, weakness, Heav'n bestows on thee.

278 Seraph . . . adores] Seraphim . . . sings *1733a–34b*.
283 kind . . . due] just . . . kind *1733a*.

278. Above, I 110*n*. Aquinas, *Sum. c. gent.*, III lxxx: "The first and highest [of the angels] perceive the ordered scheme of providence in the last end itself which is the divine goodness . . .; and these are called Seraphim, i.e. fiery or setting on fire, because fire is used to designate intensity of love or desire, which is about the end." Cf. Spenser, *Hymn of Heav. Beauty*, 94–5 [Wakefield].

279. Cf. I 87–90. *Wisd. of Solom.*, VI 7: "He hath made the small and the great, and careth for all alike." *Spectat.*, 565: "There is nothing he has made, that is either so distant, so little, or so inconsiderable, which he does not essentially inhabit." Chudleigh, *The Offering*, 53–7:

        Nothing's so high nor yet so low,
        As to escape his Sight.

280. The four verbs epitomize much of the argument of *Ess.*, I, III, and IV. On *fills*, see the preceding lines and III 21–6, IV 61–2; on *bounds*, III 110 ￬nd 79*ff*; on *connects*, III 23 and 111*ff*; on *equals*, IV 53–62, esp. 61–2 and 326.

He . . . bounds] Cf. J. Davies of Hereford, *Mirum in Modum* (*Wks.*, ed. Grosart, 1878, i 18): ". . . [God] fills and bounds each place."

Equals is here transitive ("makes all equal"), as Morris rightly notes; and cf. Dryden, *Hind and Panth.*, 456: "Rebellion equals all". For the point that Pope is making with the word, compare Spenser's "Nature" (*F.Q.*, VII vii 14):

        Who Right to all dost deale indifferently,
        Damning all Wrong and tortious Iniurie,
        Which any of thy Creatures doe to other
        (Oppressing them with power, vnequally)
        Sith of them all thou art the equall mother
        And knittest each to each, as brother vnto brother.

281*ff*. *The Consequence of all, the* absolute Submission *due to Providence, both as to our* present *and* future *State.* [P. *1735b–43a*.]

281–4. *Par. Lost*, VIII 167–84, is the best commentary on this passage, and comes close to summarizing the argument of this Epistle.

Submit—In this, or any other sphere,   285
Secure to be as blest as thou canst bear:
Safe in the hand of one disposing Pow'r,
Or in the natal, or the mortal hour.
All Nature is but Art, unknown to thee;
All Chance, Direction, which thou canst not see;   290
All Discord, Harmony, not understood;

287–288 *Cf. textual note l. 98.*

285-8. Pope to Caryll, 3 Sept. [1718]: "I believe there is not in the whole
course of the Scripture any precept so often and so strongly inculcated, as the
trust and eternal dependence we ought to repose in that Supreme Being who is
our constant preserver and benefactor." Cf. also Wm. Clagett, *Seventeen
Sermons* (1689), pp. 447-8: "Let that which happens be of what kind it will, and
how great soever in the kind, yet from his Infinite Wisdom we ought to conclude
against all objections, That all things considered, it is the best for us. We perhaps do not see how it should be so, but we have not the less reason to believe it.
God's thoughts are above ours, and his ways above our ways; and we are not to
argue as if we understood ourselves as well as God understands us. Our business
is to submit to him patiently, and to depend upon him intirely, and to thank
him from our hearts for his continual Providence over us; . . . we cannot be
better than by being in God's Hands."

287-8. Cf. Pope, *Imit. Hor., Ep.*, I vi 7-10, and his letter to Martha Blount
[1726?] (EC, IX 307): "The separation of my soul and body is what I could
think of with less pain; for I am very sure he that made it will take care of it, and
in whatever state he pleases it shall be, that state must be right."

287. *disposing*] Possibly alluding to the phrase, "man proposes, God disposes," as reminder of the epistle's theme. And cf. Pope to Caryll, 20 June 1732:
"I am certain you . . . can resign . . . to the disposer of all men"; to Warburton,
21 Feb. 1744: "I would rest . . . in a full resignation of my being to be disposed
of by the Father of all mercy . . ."

289. A traditional conception in both pagan and Christian thought (like the
four which follow it). See Plato, *Soph.*, 265b; Augustine, *De civ. dei*, XI xxi;
Dante, *De Monar.*, I iii: ". . . deus aeternus, arte sua quae natura est"; Hobbes,
Leviath., pref., "Nature, the art whereby God hath made and governs the
world"; Browne, *Relig. Med.*, I xvi: ". . . Nature is the Art of God"; Isaac
Watts, *Philos. Ess.* (1733), pp. 199, 207.

290. A favourite topic of the Stoics; the theme of Boethius's *De cons. phil.*, and
cf. Matt., x 29-30, and Christian writing in general, e.g. Esprit, p. 13: ". . . unaccountable Events are only so to our Ignorance, but not to God's Providence,
which governs them all, and excludes all manner of Chance."

291. Cf. Introd., pp. xxxivf, xlviiif. The passage cited by Warton from Fell-

All partial Evil, universal Good:
And, spite of Pride, in erring Reason's spite,
One truth is clear, "Whatever IS, is RIGHT."

293 in erring] and in thy *1733a*.

---

tham's *Resolves* [3rd ed. (1628) 131] is typical: "The whole *world* is kept in order
by *discord*; and every part of it, is but a more particular *composed jarre*... And ...
it makes greatly for the *Maker's glory* that such an admirable *Harmony* should be
produced out of such an *infinite discord*."

293-4. Cf. *Against Chance and Fate*, 67-76, in the miscellany printed by John
Clarke, *Poems on Sev. Occas.* (1724), p. 42:

> Then, feeble Reason! thy Pursuit must cease:
> Implore the God of Knowledge, Truth, and Peace,
> To teach that Rebel Folly we call Wit,
> That 'tis her noblest Conquest to submit.
> Vain Man, whom Pride and Obstinacy sway,
> Persists disputing when he should obey:
> To Terms of Honour giv'n he scorns to yield:
> And strives, tho' vanquish'd, to maintain the Field.
> Here end thy Search; and fix thy lasting Trust
> On the most wise, most pow'rful, and most just.

293. *in ... spite*] Above, 1 123, 161, 164*n*. Milton, *Sams. Agon.*, 322: "Down,
Reason, then; at least vain reasonings down ..."

294. Gen., XVIII 25: "Shall not the Judge of all the Earth do right?" Hos.,
XIV 9: "... for the ways of the Lord are right"; Milton, *Sams. Agon.*, 1745-8:

> All is best, though we oft doubt
> What the unsearchable dispose
> Of Highest Wisdom brings about;

Dryden, *Oedip.*, III i: "Whatever is, is in its causes just." Pope to Swift, 2 Apr.
1733: "But it suffices me to know it [their abode beyond the grave] will be
exactly what region or state our Maker appoints, and that whatever is, is
right"; to Orrery, 10 Dec. 1740: "... in the disposition of this system, God has
been pleased, no doubt for good ends, though to us unseen, to unite [joys and
pains] too closely for the tender frame of human happiness... Whatever is, is
right. It was the saying of Socrates, and the firm faith of, my lord, your ...
servant"; and to Martha Blount [1726?], quoted above, 1 287-8*n*.

ARGUMENT of the SECOND EPISTLE[1]

Of the Nature and State of Man, *with respect to* Himself,
as an Individual.

I. THE *business of Man not to pry into* God, *but to study* himself. *His*
Middle Nature; *his Powers and Frailties,* VER. 1 to 18. *The Limits*
of his Capacity, VER. 19, &c. II. *The two Principles of Man,*
Self-love *and* Reason, *both necessary,* VER. 53, &c. Self-love *the*
stronger, and why, VER. 67, &c. *Their end the same,* VER. 81, &c. 5
III. *The* PASSIONS, *and their use,* VER. 93 to 130. *The* predominant Passion, *and its force,* VER. 131 to 160. *Its Necessity, in directing*
Men to different purposes, VER. 165, &c. *Its providential Use, in fixing*
our Principle, and ascertaining our Virtue, VER. 177. IV. Virtue
and Vice *joined in our* mixed Nature; *the limits near, yet the things* 10
separate *and* evident: *What is the office of* Reason, VER. 203 to 216.
V. *How odious* Vice *in itself, and how we deceive ourselves into it,*
VER. 217. VI. *That, however, the* Ends of Providence *and* general
Good *are answered in our Passions and Imperfections,* VER. 238, &c.
How usefully these are distributed to all Orders of Men, VER. 242. 15
How useful they are to Society, VER. 249. *And to the* Individuals,
VER. 261. *In every* state, *and every* age *of life,* VER. 271, &c.

---

1. See the note on the "Argument" of Epistle 1.

EPISTLE II

Know then thyself, presume not God to scan;
The proper study of Mankind is Man.
Plac'd on this isthmus of a middle state,
A being darkly wise, and rudely great:
With too much knowledge for the Sceptic side,   5
With too much weakness for the Stoic's pride,
He hangs between; in doubt to act, or rest,

2 proper study] only Science *1733*.   6 the] a *1733–35a*.

Epistle II. *Of the* Nature *and* State *of* Man *as an* Individual. [P. *1735b–43a*.]

1*ff*. *The business of Man not to pry into God, but to study himself. His* Middle
Nature, *his* Powers, Frailties, *and the* Limits *of his* Capacity. [P. *1735b–43a*.]

1–18. As has long been noted, this passage shows Pope's reading in Pascal.
Cf. Pope to Caryll, 6 Feb. 1731: "Your recommendation of Pascal's *Pensées* is a
good one, though I have been beforehand with you in it. . ."

1–2. "This is the oldest dictum of logic or philosophy on record. . . Its
original purport was to direct curiosity away from the phenomena of the universe . . . as inscrutable, towards life and human affairs. The contrast intended
by Pope is between the futility of metaphysical speculation on the attributes of
the Deity, and the more profitable employment of the study of man" [Pattison].
Cf. Xenophon, *Memor.*, I 11–13 (tr. Loeb, 1938): "[Socrates] did not even dis-
cuss that topic favoured by the talkers, 'the Nature of the Universe': and
avoided speculation on the so-called 'Cosmos' of the Professors, how it works,
and on the laws that govern the phenomena of the heavens: indeed he would
argue that to trouble one's mind with such problems is sheer folly. . . Did these
thinkers suppose that their knowledge of human affairs was so complete that
they must seek these new fields . . ., or that it was their duty to neglect human
affairs and consider only things divine? Moreover, he marvelled at their blindness in not seeing that man cannot solve these riddles. . ."

Pattison quotes Taine's comment (*Lit. angl.* [III vii 4]: "Le premier vers
résume tout le livre précédent, et le second résume tout le livre présent. . ."

1. *presume . . . scan*] A universal maxim in moral literature. Cf. above, 1–2*n*,
and Erasmus, p. 112; Montaigne, II 270; Job, XI 7; Hooker, I ii 2; R. Herrick,
What God Is and *Sobriety in Search*; *Par. Lost*, VIII 70*ff*, 119*ff*, 167*ff*, 188*ff*; Boileau,
Ep., v; Temple, I 172, 164.

scan] Often misread to imply the total exclusion of knowledge about God.

53

Pope's point is that God's dispensations are not to be presumptuously pried into and carped at by human reason: cf. *OED* (citing this line): "To criticize; . . . to judge by a certain rule or standard"—in Pope's case, as Epistle I shows, by purely rational rules. Compare Milton's use, *Par. Lost*, VIII 72–5:

> . . . the great Architect
> Did wisely to conceal, and not divulge
> His secrets to be scann'd by them who ought
> Rather admire.

The word appears in similar contexts in Gould, *To the . . . Beaux Esprits*, st. 12, and Pomfret, *Upon the Divine Attributes*, st. 4. The extra connotation added by the meaning of the Latin root is noticed in Hume's note on Milton's lines (*Par. Lost*, 1695 ed.): "Not declare and make common his Secrets, to be pryed into by Men, who ought to admire, and not hope to discover their unimaginable Springs and Contrivance. . . *To be scan'd*, to be measured; of *Scandere*, Lat. to climb up into, as Mankind would do, if possible, to measure the Heavenly Sphears and Bodies."

2. For the phrasing, EC cites Pascal, p. 248, who says "to study Man" is "the proper Employment and Exercise of Mankind"; and Charron [bk 1, introd.]: "La vraie science et le vrai étude de l'homme est l'homme." For the point Pope is making, see Quarles, *Hieroglyph.*, I 1–2 [Pattison]:

> Man is man's ABC: There is none that can
> Reade God aright, unlesse he first spell Man,

and Introd., pp. li–lii.

3. Warton cites Cowley, *Life and Fame* [10–11]:

> Vain, weak-built *Isthmus*, which dost proudly rise
> Up betwixt *two Eternities*.

Pattison adds Prior, III 613–4:

> Amid two seas on one small point of land
> Wearied, uncertain, and amaz'd we stand.

Cf. also, *ibid.*, 645–6; Pascal, pp. 166–7; *Spectat.*, 590: ". . . many witty authors compare the present time to an isthmus, or narrow neck of land, that rises in the midst of an ocean, immeasurably diffused on either side of it."; and Lillo, *Arden of Fev.*, III iii.

4. *A . . . wise*] 1 Cor. XIII 12 is relevant; and cf. *Ess.*, I 61*ff*, 91*ff*.

5. So for Pascal (p. 160) man has "an Idea of Truth, not to be effaced by all the Wiles of the Sceptick".

6. *Stoic's pride*] The traditional charge against the Stoics because of their belief that men could extirpate their passions and attain to impassivity, like God's. Cf. Pascal (p. 30), and Addison, *Cato*, I iv 83–4: " 'Tis pride, rank pride, . . . I think the *Romans* call it Stoicism."

7. *in . . . rest*] The contrast in this line and the next is between Stoic and Epicurean alternatives: cf. *Ess.*, IV 21–4 and notes. *Rest* is Stoic apathy, and *act* is apparently Epicurean hedonism, which Pope seems to have identified, à la Hobbes, with ceaseless appetitive agitation.

In doubt to deem himself a God, or Beast;
In doubt his Mind or Body to prefer,
Born but to die, and reas'ning but to err;   10
Alike in ignorance, his reason such,
Whether he thinks too little, or too much:
Chaos of Thought and Passion, all confus'd;
Still by himself abus'd, or disabus'd;
Created half to rise, and half to fall;   15
Great lord of all things, yet a prey to all;

8 To deem himself a Part of God, or Beast *1733*, *1735b*.

---

8. Cf. *Spectat.*, 408; St Evremond, *Sonnet* (1657), 15–17, in *Œuvres* (1740), I
148 (2nd ser.):

> Change l'état douteux dans lequel tu nous ranges,
> Nature, élève-nous a la clarté des Anges,
> Ou nous abaisse au sens des simples animaux;

Pascal, p. 30: "What then is to be the Fate of Man! Shall he be equal to God?
Or shall he not be superior to the Beasts?"

10. *Born . . . die*] Plutarch, I 328: "For a man that is in his wits cannot be
ignorant that he is . . . born to this very end that he must die." Cf. Sandys,
Paraphr. upon Job, ch. IV; Pascal, p. 8; *Odyss.*, III (tr. Pope) 116–17, 296.

reas'ning . . . err] Cf. Pascal, p. 151, Fontenelle, *Dial. des morts* (tr. Hughes,
1708), p. 21; Congreve, *Mourn. Bride*, III i 31–3; Cicero, *Philippicae*, XII ii 5:
"Cuiusvis hominis est errare."

11–12. I.e. man's proper reasoning should fall between these extremes in the
direction of self-knowledge, as in the remainder of this epistle. Cf. Pascal,
p. 180: "If we think too little of a Thing or too much, our Head turns giddy, and
we are at a loss to find out our Way to truth" [EC]; and Bezaleel Morrice, *On
Human Condition*, 7–10, in his *Miscell. or Amusements* (1712), p. 42:

> In Study be thy Care and Conduct such
> As not to think too little or too much;
> Try well the knowledge of thy self to find,
> And seek the useful Knowledge of thy Kind.

13. For the phrasing, see Pascal, p. 162: "What a Chimaera then is Man!
. . . What a confused Chaos! What a Subject of Contradiction!" [EC].

15. *Ibid.*, p. 162: "If he is too aspiring and lofty, we can lower and humble
him; if too mean and little, we can raise and swell him" [EC].

16. Sprat, *Plague of Athens*, st. 1:

> Unhappy man! by nature made to sway,
> And yet is every creature's prey;

R. Gould, *Satyr against Man* (*Wks.* 1709, II 149); Prior, I 237.

K

Sole judge of Truth, in endless Error hurl'd:
The glory, jest, and riddle of the world!
   Go, wond'rous creature! mount where Science guides,
Go, measure earth, weigh air, and state the tides;   20
Instruct the planets in what orbs to run,

21 Shew by what Laws the wand'ring Planets stray *1735a–43a*.

17–18. Cf. Pascal, p. 162: "A profess'd Judge of all Things, and yet a feeble
Worm of the Earth, the great Depositary and Guardian of Truth, and yet a
meer Huddle of Uncertainty; the Glory and the Scandal of the Universe . . ."
   19–30. See Pope's epitaph on John, Lord Caryll (vol. vi).
   19–22. Horace, *Od.*, i xxviii 1–6; Augustine, *Conf.*, v iii: ". . . nec inveniris
[i.e. Deus] a superbis, nec si illi curiosa peritia numerent stellas et harenam, et
dimetiantur sidereas plagas, et vestigent vias astrorum"; Erasmus, p. 112:
". . . how pleasantly do they dote while they frame in their heads innumerable
worlds; measure out the Sun, the Moon, the Stars, nay and Heaven it self . . .;
lay down the Causes of Lightning, Winds, Eclipses, and other the like Inexplic-
able matters; . . . as if they were . . . dropt down among us from the Council of
the Gods; while in the meantime Nature laughs at them and all their blind
conjectures. . . These . . . have not the least degree of knowledge, . . . neither
know themselves . . ."; Boileau, *Ep.*, v; *Spectat.*, 408: "Human nature I always
thought the most useful object of human reason. . . . enquiry into which as
much exceeds all other learning, as it is of more consequence to adjust the true
nature and measures of right and wrong, than to settle the distances of the
planets, and compute the times of their circumvolutions."
   20. Reminiscences of Scriptural passages where God not man is celebrated
as the proper "measurer" of the universe heighten the irony of this and the
succeeding lines; cf. Is. XL 12: "Who hath measured the waters in the hollow of
his hand, and meted out heaven with the span, and comprehended the dust of
the earth in a measure, and weighed the mountains in scales, and the hills in a
balance?" and cf. *Par. Lost*, IV 999–1001.
   measure earth] Job, XXVIII 24–6. Many calculations of the earth's measure-
ments were being made in Pope's time and earlier. Cf. Chambers, art. Earth.
   weigh air] Alluding to the experiments of Torricelli, Boyle, and others; and
cf. Job XXVIII 25, where God only is able to "make the weight for the winds".
The value of such information was much ridiculed—e.g., by Shadwell,
Virtuoso, v i.
   state . . . tides] With reference to the work of Newton, continued in Pope's
time by Euler, Bernouilli, and others, to determine the causes and operations of
the tides.
   21. Cf. the determinations of planetary motions by Newton, Halley, Flam-
steed, Cassini, etc.

Correct old Time, and regulate the Sun;
Go, soar with Plato to th' empyreal sphere,
22 regulate the Sun] teach the Sun his way *1735a–43a.*

---

22. *Correct . . . Time*] Pattison: "Said by Warburton to be an allusion to Sir I. Newton's Chronology [*Chron. of Antient Kingdoms, Amended* (1728), in which Newton sought to rectify by astronomical calculations the dates traditionally assigned to various events of ancient history]. Perhaps the reform of the Calendar ['Old style' to 'New style', finally introduced in 1752], which was then under discussion, is meant." A third, and perhaps likelier, alternative, is that Pope refers to some such "correction" as Newton describes in *Principia* (tr. Motte, 1729), 1 11: "Absolute time, in Astronomy, is distinguish'd from Relative, by the Equation or correction of vulgar time. For the natural days are truly unequal, though they are commonly consider'd as equal, and used for a measure of time: Astronomers correct this inequality for their more accurate deducing of the celestial motions."

regulate . . . Sun] Wakefield: ". . . we are to understand the ascertainment of true time from apparent time, resulting from the seeming progress of the sun in the ecliptic compared with the circle of the earth's diurnal revolution". The earlier reading (cf. textual notes) seems to have come to Pope via Prior, 1 651: "[God] set the moon, and taught the sun his way." The irony is perhaps enhanced by the frequent contemporary use of "correct" and "regulate" to describe the adjustment of mechanisms more appropriate to human powers, such as watches and clocks.

23. *empyreal sphere*] The outermost sphere of the universe, abode of God and (for Pope) of Plato's archetypes of Ideas.

23–30. Swift, *Tale of a Tub* (ed. Smith and Guthkelch), pp. 157–8: "And, whereas the mind of Man, when he gives the Spur and Bridle to his Thoughts, doth never stop, but naturally sallies out into both extreams of High and Low, of Good and Evil; His first Flight of Fancy, commonly transports Him to Ideas of what is most Perfect, finished, and exalted; till having soared out of his own Reach and Sight, not well perceiving how near the Frontiers of Height and Depth, border upon each other; With the same Course and Wing, he falls down plum into the lowest Bottom of Things. . ."

23–6. Cf. P. Shorey, *Platonism, Anc. and Mod.* (1938), p. 108: "The histories of philosophy in the 17th and 18th centuries presented a hard, matter-of-fact, unintelligent and unsympathetic view of Plato and Platonism. . ." Even by the Cambridge Platonists, as Tullock points out (*Rational Theol. in the 17th Cent.*, 11 pp. 478*ff*), Platonism was not discriminated from the extremes of neo-platonism, which seemed fanciful to many. For the opinion of an orthodox clergyman, see John Maxwell's introduction to his translation of Cumberland, pp. lxiv–lxvi. P. lxvi: "Such is their [the Platonists'] Divine Virtue as it is an Aversation from Terrestrial, Material, and Mortal, Nature, and an Affectation of being wholly incorporeal and immaterial; for this Affectation of Immaterial Intellectual

To the first good, first perfect, and first fair;
Or tread the mazy round his follow'rs trod,   25
And quitting sense call imitating God;
As Eastern priests in giddy circles run,
And turn their heads to imitate the Sun.

Nature, and to be mere intellectual Souls, is an irreligious *Philosophick* Vanity
and Extravagance, not intirely free from Magick." And cf. Halifax, *Wks.*, ed.
Raleigh (1912), p. 103: "the phrenzy of Platonick Visions".
   26. P. Shorey, *Platonism, Anc. and Mod.* (1938), p. 58: "But pure thought . . .
is dangerously akin in some of Plato's imitators to pure jargon. . . . As Pope put
it: 'And quitting sense call imitating God'. Unintelligibility is mistaken for
profundity." But the line refers, in addition, to the soul's leaving behind the
body ("sense") for neo-platonic trances, such as Plotinus is said to have enjoyed,
and to the characteristic teaching of neo-platonists that "he that dares soar
above the gross impediments of flesh, to converse with divine objects, will
become little less than a God" (G.-B. Gelli, *Circe*, tr. H. Layng, 1745, p. 225);
and cf. Castiglione's *Courtier*, bk iv.
   27–8. Cf. Pope's letter [Nov. 1716] (EC, ix 363) to Lady Mary Wortley
Montagu, who had gone to Constantinople: "How happy will it be, for a gay
young woman, to live in a country where it is a part of religious worship to be
giddy-headed!"—and to Lord Bathurst, 23 Sept. 1719: ". . . one may address to
you as to a very abstracted person, like Alexander Selkirk, or the self-taught
philosopher. . . I remember the latter of those I mentioned, gave himself up to
a devout exercise of making his head giddy with various circumrotations, to
imitate the motions of the celestial bodies." Pope's allusion in the second passage is to a book by Abu Bakr ibn al-Tufail, translated by Simon Ockley in 1708
as the *Improvement of Human Reason, Exhibited in the Life of Hai Ibn Yokdhan*. On
pp. 117–18, having reasoned that his soul must be of the nature of the celestial
bodies, Yokdhan presumes it his duty to imitate them in all their characteristics,
including their circular motion and their constant contemplation of God: "And
he us'd to help himself in this by violently turning himself round, in which
when he was very violently exercised, all manner of sensible Objects vanish'd
out of his Sight, . . . and he beheld . . . the necessarily self-existent Being. . ."
   Cf. also Lafitau, *Mœurs sauvages* (1724), i 201: "Les Indiens n'étoient pas
plûtôt levez le matin, que se tournant vers l'Orient ils saluoient le Soliel levant,
et trépignoient des pieds avec un mouvement qui sembloit imiter celui de ce
Dieu."
   28. EC cites Lady M. W. Montagu's description of the sacred dance of
the Mahometan monks [in her letter to the Ctess. of Bristol, 10 April 1718].
Wakefield notes an analogous Pythagorean practice described in Plutarch's life
of Numa.
   turn . . . heads] Figurative as well as literal.

Go, teach Eternal Wisdom how to rule—
Then drop into thyself, and be a fool!   30
Superior beings, when of late they saw

29–30. Cf. Chudleigh's remonstrance (*Ess.*, p. 34) against those "who think themselves capable of driving the Chariot of the Sun, of ordering the Affairs of the Universe, of managing the great Machine of Nature, and were the admirable Frame now to be set together, wou'd . . . be so arrogant, as to presume to advise the Almighty Architect, and think Themselves wise enough to assist him in the Government of the World. 'Tis wonderful that Men should be so little acquainted with themselves, be such Strangers to the Narrowness of their Faculties, to the Limitedness of their Understandings!" Esprit also (p. 38) deplores "that haughty Disposition, wherewith Philosophers ascended to the Knowledge of God, to value themselves the more . . .; and so, as St Paul says [Rom. 1 22], Professing [themselves] to be wise . . . became Fools."

29. Job XL 1–2: "Moreover, the Lord answered Job, and said, Shall he that contendeth with the Almighty instruct him? he that reproveth God, let him answer it."

31–4. Though, as Pattison says, "critics have been divided as to the purport of this comparison," it is plainly both a compliment and something less—one phase in the pattern of paradoxical attitudes by which Pope elaborates his theme, as well as a reminder of that aspect of man which is to be the subject of this epistle: his dual nature, differentiating him from angels. Cf. Bellarmine, p. 142: ". . . Man . . . in point of Understanding, is not a little, but so far inferior to Angels, that be he never so ingenious, and never so inquisitive after Knowledge, if he be compared with an Angel, he deserves to be no more accounted of, than a Child not yet weaned"; Chudleigh, *Ess.*, pp. 23, 30; and *Spectat.*, 621, cited by D. F. Bond in *MLN*, XLIII (1928) 326. For the ape comparison, *Adventurer* suggests the fragment of Heracl.: "The wisest of men, in comparison with God, will appear an ape, in wisdom, in beauty, and in all things else" (F. M. Cornford's translation in *Gk. Relig. Thought*, 1923, p. 85), and *Publisher* cites Palingen., VI 181*ff*. Cf. also Shaks., *Meas. for Meas.*, II ii 117*ff*. Both the compliment and its qualification in Pope's case, rest on the hierarchical principle (noted by Aquinas, *Sum. c. Gent.*, III xci) that "the highest nature in its lowest degree touches the lower nature in its highest degree . . . ; just as the body that is perfected by the intellective soul is the highest in the genus of bodies, so the intellective soul that is united to the body is the lowest in the genus of intellective substances." The application to Newton had been foreshadowed in *Spectat.*, 635: "How doth such a genius as Sir Isaac Newton, from amidst the darkness that involves human understanding, break forth and appear like one of another species! . . . But alas! how narrow is the prospect even of such a mind! And how obscure to the compass that is taken in by the ken of an angel . . ." For Pope's disapproval of the Newtonians' idolatry of their master, see M. Nicolson in *Newton Demands the Muse* (1946), pp. 134*ff*.

A mortal Man unfold all Nature's law,
Admir'd such wisdom in an earthly shape,
And shew'd a NEWTON as we shew an Ape.
    Could he, whose rules the rapid Comet bind,   35
Describe or fix one movement of his Mind?
Who saw its fires here rise, and there descend,
Explain his own beginning, or his end?
Alas what wonder! Man's superior part
Uncheck'd may rise, and climb from art to art: 40
But when his own great work is but begun,
What Reason weaves, by Passion is undone.

35 whose rules the rapid Comet bind] who taught each Planet
    where to roll *1733–34b*; rapid] whirling *1735a–43a*.
36 his] the *1733–34b*, *1735b–43a*; Mind] Soul *1733–34b*.
37 Who mark'd their Points, to rise, and to descend *1733–34b*; its
    fires] the Stars *1735a–43a*.
38 his own] or his *1734a–35a*.

35–42. Seneca, *Ep.*, LXXXVIII; Montaigne, II 496–7: "Those People who ride
astride on the *Epicicle* of *Mercury*, who see so far into the Heavens . . . do not
know, how that moves which they themselves move nor how to give us a
Description of the Springs they themselves govern and make use of . . ."
    Ibid., I 242: "Every one ought to say . ., *Being assaulted, as I am, by Ambition,
Avarice, Temerity, and Superstition, and having within so many other Enemies of Life,
shall I go cudgel my Brains about the World's Revolutions?*"
    35–37. Wakefield sees an allusion to Newton's *Principia*, Bk III, prob. 21, which
"proposes to discover the trajectory of a comet from three given observations."
Cf. Desaguliers, *Newt. Syst. of the World* (1728), pp. 2–3n.
    37. "That is, saw, as it were, both the terminating points of such vast lines
as the greater axes of orbits, so immeasurably extended through pure space, and
of such eccentricity" [Wakefield].
    38. Cf. Prior, *On Exodus, III 14*, st. 1.
    39–42. K. Philips, *The Soul*, st. 1:
            How vain a thing is Man, whose noblest part,
            That soul which thro' the World doth rome,
            Traverses Heav'n, finds out the depth of Art,
            Yet is so ignorant at home?
    40. *climb . . . art*] Cf. Du Bartas, *La Seconde Sepmaine: Babylone*, 247–8, in
Wks. (1940), III 127: "montant d'art en art, Nous paruenions bientost au
sommet du rempart [of knowledge]."
    41–2. Cf. Prior, II 740–51.

Trace Science then, with Modesty thy guide;
First strip off all her equipage of Pride,
Deduct what is but Vanity, or Dress,   45
Or Learning's Luxury, or Idleness;
Or tricks to shew the stretch of human brain,
Mere curious pleasure, or ingenious pain:
Expunge the whole, or lop th'excrescent parts
Of all, our Vices have created Arts: 50

43–52 *Add. 1743b, 1751.*

43–52. Cf. Milton, *Par. Reg.*, IV 286*ff*; Montaigne, II 287*ff*; Greville, *Treat. of Hum. Learning*, sts. 66*ff*.

43. Cf. Greville, *Treat. of Hum. Learning*, st. 146:

Next that we doe not ouerbuild our states,
In searching secrets of the Deity, . . .
But measure first our own Humanity; . . .
And so seeke wisedom with sobriety.

45. Greville, *Treat. of Hum. Learning*, st. 77.

46. Ward: "I.e. what is done by learning after a fashion intended to make a show or to save trouble". Cf. Burton, p. 92: "Many of our Sciences are very remote from use, and 'tis of little Advantage either to the Man himself, or the rest of the World, that he's acquainted with such Theories, or Terms of Art. But the Knowledge of that which nearly concerns Man, is of himself, and the way to govern his Actions. . ."

47. *stretch . . . brain*] Cf. Browne, *Relig. Med.*, I ix: "As for those wingy Mysteries in Divinity, and airy subtleties in Religion, which have unhing'd the brains of better heads, they never stretched the *Pia Mater* of mine."

48. *Mere . . . pleasure*] Cf. Augustine, *Conf.*, x xxxv: "Vana et curiosa cupiditas, nomine cognitionis et scientiae palliata".

ingenious pain] Eccles., I 18: ". . . he that increaseth knowledge increaseth sorrow."

49. *lop . . . parts*] Cf. Swift, *Tale of a Tub* (ed. Smith and Guthlekch), p. 98 (quoting Pausanias): "*They were a Race of Men, who delighted to nibble at the Superfluities, and Excrescencies of Books; which the Learned at length observing, took warning of their own Accord, to lop the Luxuriant, the Rotten, the Dead, the Sapless, and the Overgrown Branches from their Works.*"

50. Cf. Seneca, *Ep.*, XC; Plutarch, I 85: ". . . all mechanic arts and trades, all vain and insignificant employments, such as regarded only curiosity or pleasure, were strictly prohibited them [the Spartans], as things that would make them degenerate . . ."; J. Collier, *Sev. Disc. upon Pract. Subjects* (1725), p. 336: "For, what's the Effect of many of these Contrivances [Arts] except the furnishing of Luxury and Pride, the assisting Ambition and Revenge . . . ?"

Then see how little the remaining sum,
Which serv'd the past, and must the times to come!
   II. Two Principles in human nature reign;
Self-love, to urge, and Reason, to restrain;
Nor this a good, nor that a bad we call,   55
Each works its end, to move or govern all:
And to their proper operation still,
Ascribe all Good; to their improper, Ill.
   Self-love, the spring of motion, acts the soul;

51-2. Cf. Milton's view (quoted from P. B. Tillyard, *Milton: Private Corr. and Acad. Exercises* (1932), 116-7): "If we disregard and curtail all those subjects [e.g. metaphysics] which can be of no use to us, as we should, we shall be surprised to find how many whole years we shall save." R. Gould, *Jack Pavy, Wks.* (1709), II 322:

> But having cast to what Account 'twill come [knowledge],
> *I find all* Cyphers *for the* Total Sum.

La Bruyère, II 38; Fontenelle, *Dial. des morts* (tr. Hughes, 1708), p. 88: "There is a certain Measure of useful Knowledge, which Men attain'd early, which has receiv'd but small Additions, and beyond which they shall never be able to advance much, if at all."

53ff. *The* TWO PRINCIPLES *of* MAN, SELF-LOVE *and* REASON, *both necessary*, 59. *Self-love the* stronger, *and why?*, 67. *their* End *the same*, 81. [P. *1735b-43a.*]

53. Alluding to the fundamental antithesis, in all the traditional psychologies, between regulatory and appetitive elements in man's nature (cf. for example, Cicero, *De off.*, I xxviii, cit. EC)—usually connected in one way or another with the doctrine of his two souls, rational and sensitive.

54. *Self-love*] John Laird, *Philos. Incurs. into Engl. Lit.* (1946), p. 43: "Self-love was an unfortunate name, dominant in Pope's time, for self-maintenance or self-fulfilment. It was meant to describe the fact that each natural being strives to keep going with its own particular go." Cf. J. Norris, *Theory and Reg. of Love* (1688), p. 51: ". . . that special sort of Benevolence [i.e. of well-wishing to oneself] that we call *self-love*".

57-8. La Rochefoucauld, IV i: "*Self-love*, according as it is rightly or otherwise, understood . . . is the cause of all the Moral *Vertues* and *Vices* in the World."

59-60. *spring . . . balance*] Terms from watch-making, widely applied, as here, to human psychology: see O. Barfield, *Hist. in Engl. Words* (1926), pp. 161ff. Cf. also, Suckling, *That None Beguiled Be*, st. 2:

> Hope is the main-spring on which moves Desire,
> And these do the less wheels, Fear, Joy, inspire;
> The balance is Thought . . .

59. *acts*] activates.

Reason's comparing balance rules the whole.   60
Man, but for that, no action could attend,
And, but for this, were active to no end;
Fix'd like a plant on his peculiar spot,
To draw nutrition, propagate, and rot;
Or, meteor-like, flame lawless thro' the void,   65
Destroying others, by himself destroy'd.
   Most strength the moving principle requires;
Active its task, it prompts, impels, inspires.
Sedate and quiet the comparing lies,
Form'd but to check, delib'rate, and advise.   70
Self-love still stronger, as its objects nigh;

71 still] yet *1734a–35a*.

61, 63–4. Burton, p. 82: "Were it not for these Desires, the Body of Animals, for ought I know, would stand as still as Trees; 'tis the *appetitio Boni*, and the *Fuga mali* that puts Animals into motion, and distinguishes them from Plants that always keep their station." Otway, *The Orphan*, I ii 24–6:

> I would be busy in the world and learn,
> Not like a coarse and useless dunghill weed,
> Fix'd to one spot, and rot just as I grow.

62, 65–6. Burton, p. 64: "Man's Desires and Passions, inflamed by imagination, if Reason did not quench the Fire, would burn up the World: When they are swell'd with Imagination and Phantasy they are so immoderate and violent, that they would destroy him whose they are, and undo other Men, and put the whole course of Nature into Disorder." Self-love is likened, in Pope's metaphor, to the tendency of heavenly bodies to keep moving (the modern physicist's *inertia*), and reason to the force of gravitation that is necessary to hold them in their orbits. The same metaphor, in different terms, concludes Epistle III. Newton's postulates for the physical universe were being increasingly applied in Pope's time to the moral and political worlds. See A. D. McKillop, *Background of Thomson's Seasons* (1942), pp. 34 *ff.*

64. Possibly a reminiscence of Hamlet's "fat weed" (I v 32–4): "That rots itself in ease on Lethe wharf".

69. *the comparing*] Burton, p. 72: "Reason compares one thing with another, the want of which is the great Cause of immoderate Affection: For Men do not so often fail in loving that which is not good, as in loving the less good . . ."

71–2. Cf. Coeffeteau, p. 261: "It is an infallible Maxime in Philosophy, that objects by their presence, make a more powerful impression in our soules, than when they are absent"; Hooker, I vii 6; Burton, p. 72; Tillotson, *Sermon Preached at the Morning Exercise, at Cripple-Gate . . . 1660* (1709), p. 5: "We are near to our

Reason's at distance, and in prospect lie:
That sees immediate good by present sense;
Reason, the future and the consequence.
Thicker than arguments, temptations throng,   75
At best more watchful this, but that more strong.
The action of the stronger to suspend
Reason still use, to Reason still attend:
Attention, habit and experience gains,
Each strengthens Reason, and Self-love restrains.   80
     Let subtle schoolmen teach these friends to fight,
More studious to divide than to unite,
And Grace and Virtue, Sense and Reason split,

---

selves, and our own interest is near to us, and we see it in its full proportions, and with all possible Advantages; other Men and their Interests are at a distance from us, and seem less to us than they are".

73-4. Cf. Cicero, *De off.*, 1 4; Bacon, *Adv. of Learning*, II xviii 4: "For the affections themselves carry ever an appetite to good, as reason doth, the difference is, that *the affection beholdeth merely the present; reason beholdeth the future and sum of time.* . ." Noted by Ruffhead, *Life of Pope* (1769), p. 232n.

77-80. Cf. Burton, p. 100: "Undoubtedly, as a Man doth in one case, he is disposed to do in others; for every Action leaves behind it a disposition to do the like. He that acts with Reason and Deliberation, and from Judgment in one particular, will be inclined to do so in another, and at last in all."

79. *Attention*] Bailey, *s.v.*: "Attention of Mind (with Moralists) [is] an Act of the Will by which it calls off the Understanding from the Consideration of other Objects, and directs it to the Thing in Hand." Cf. C. Spearman, *Psych. down the Ages* (1937), 1 133ff.

habit and experience] On the rôle of habit in ethics, see Aristotle, *Eth. Nic.*, 1103; Bacon, *Adv. of Learning*, II xxii 8ff. Pope to Fortescue, 8 Mar. [1733] (EC, IX 122-3): ". . . experience and habit (the two strongest of things)".

81. *subtle schoolmen*] Pattison: "Here it is to be taken in the wider sense, all who treat of morals in a technical way proper for the schools and not for the public." For the phrase, see Donne's *Elegie on the L.C.*, 20: "subtile Schoolmen".

82. Pattison cites Bacon, *Of Studies*: "If his wit be not apt to distinguish or find differences, let him study the schoolmen; for they are *cymini sectores*." And cf. the scholastic talents of Hudibras in Butler's poem (1 67-9).

83. The point here, and throughout the epistle, is that human goodness accrues from the "proper operation" (II 57) of the whole personality, instinctual and rational, natural and divine. "He may have thought that it was needless to try and settle the precise part which belonged to grace, since nature and grace are both gifts of the same Almighty Being" [EC]. This was precisely the

With all the rash dexterity of Wit:
Wits, just like fools, at war about a Name,   85
Have full as oft no meaning, or the same.
Self-love and Reason to one end aspire,
Pain their aversion, Pleasure their desire;
But greedy that its object would devour,
This taste the honey, and not wound the flow'r: 90
Pleasure, or wrong or rightly understood,

position of the Cambridge Platonists, e.g. Culverwell, *Light of Nature* (1652), p. 168: "Grace doth not come to pluck up nature as a weed, to root out the essences of men; but it comes to graft spirituals upon morals, that so by their mutual supplies and intercourse they may produce most noble and generous fruit." Cf. with Culverwell's figure, *Ess.*, II 175–6, 181*ff.*

split] With allusion to their abilities as *cymini sectores*: cf. above, 82*n*.

84. *dexterity of Wit*] Shaks., *Merry Wives*, IV v 121: "My admirable dexterity of wit".

88. Charleton, p. 82: ". . . all Affects which external objects can possibly excite in us . . . may be commodiously referred to two general heads, namely *Pleasure*, and *Pain*"; F. Gastrell, *Cert. and Necess. of Relig. in General* (1697), p. 11: "[Pleasure and pain] are the first and only Springs of *Action* which set all our Powers awork, . . . the obtaining the one and avoiding the other being the whole Employment of the Soul . . ."; *Civil Polity* (1703), p. 39.

89–90. St Evremond says of pleasure (*Wks.* tr. Des Maizeaux, 2nd ed., 1728, I 45): "There's a certain nick of time, a certain medium to be observ'd, with which few people are acquainted. We must enjoy the present Pleasures, without impairing the future." Cf. Herbert, *Providence*, 65–8:

> Bees work for man; and yet they never bruise
> Their master's flower, but leave it, having done,
> As fair as ever and as fit to use;
> So both the flow'r doth stay and honey run;

Ch. Sedley, *A Poem* (*Wks.* 1722, I 4); Topsell, leaf A 7r; Glanvill's translation of Horace, *Od.*, I xiii (*Odes and Sat. of Hor.*, 1715):

> Quickly they're glutted who so fierce devour;
> They suck the Nectar, and throw by the Flower.

For the explicit application of this image to self-love, see La Rochefoucauld, I ii: ". . . if for a little while it [self-love] dwell upon some other thing [than itself], 'tis only as *Bees* do, . . . with a Design to draw out all the *Virtue* there to their own advantage". Pope was always opposed (as perhaps here) to the extremism of La Rochefoucauld's views: see below, II 195–6*n*, and Introd., p. xii, *n*. 5.

91–2. Cf. Aristotle, *Eth. Nic.*, 1175b: "Now since activities differ in respect of goodness and badness, and some are worthy to be chosen, others to be avoided, and others neutral, so, too, are the pleasures: for to each activity there

Our greatest evil, or our greatest good.
III. Modes of Self-love the Passions we may call;
'Tis real good, or seeming, moves them all;
But since not every good we can divide,   95
And Reason bids us for our own provide;
Passions, tho' selfish, if their means be fair,
List under Reason, and deserve her care;
Those, that imparted, court a nobler aim,

99 Those, that imparted,] Those that *imparted, 1733, 1735c–43a*;
Those that imparted, *1734ab, 1743b*; Those that, imparted,
*1735a. I follow the punctuation of 1751, to clarify what I take to be
the sense.*

---

is a proper pleasure. The pleasure proper to a worthy activity is good and that
proper to an unworthy activity bad; just as the appetites for noble objects are
laudable, those for base objects culpable." Also *ibid.*, 1104b, 1105a.

93*ff. The* PASSIONS, *and their* Use. [P. *1735b–43a.*]

93. The traditional derivation of the passions from man's appetitive impulse,
i.e. self-love. Cf. La Rochefoucauld, I ii; and Glanvill, *Vanity of Dogmat.* (1661),
p. 119: ". . . each *passion* in us [is] no other but *self-love* sweetened by milder
Epithets."

94. Cf. Aristotle, *Eth. Nic.*, 1113a: "That *wish* is for the end has already been
stated; some think it is for the good, others for the apparent good"; Hooker,
I vii 6: ". . . if that be desired which is evil, the cause is the goodness which is
or seemeth to be joined with it."

95–6. I Tim. v 8: "But if any provide not for his own, and specially for those
of his own house, he . . . is worse than an infidel." This principle was taken over
into general moral doctrine: cf. More, *Utopia* (Everyman ed., p. 74): "These
lawes [of personal and social obligation] not offended, it is wysdome, that thou
looke to thine own wealthe"; Augustine, *De civ. dei*, XIX xiv; Hooker, I x 2;
Swift, I 286.

97–100. Cf. Montaigne, III 550: "Pain, Pleasure, Love and Hatred are the
first things that a Child is sensible of; if when his *Reason* comes to him, he apply
himself to it, that is Virtue"; Coeffeteau, p. 69: ". . . Passions considered as they
submit themselves unto the lawes of reason, are no infirmities of the soule, but
. . . instruments and obiects of vertue . . ."; Cumberland, p. 166; *Spectat.*, 224;
Wollaston, pp. 67–8; Swift, I 278.

98. *List*] Enlist.

99. *Those, that imparted*] Pattison: "I.e. the passions when reason is imparted
to them."

Exalt their kind, and take some Virtue's name.   100
    In lazy Apathy let Stoics boast
Their Virtue fix'd; 'tis fix'd as in a frost,
Contracted all, retiring to the breast;
But strength of mind is Exercise, not Rest:
The rising tempest puts in act the soul,   105
Parts it may ravage, but preserves the whole.
On life's vast ocean diversely we sail,

---

100. *Exalt their kind*] Cf. N. Lee: *To the Unknown Author of Abs. and Achit.*, 7–8:
            Like Angels' love to human seed inclin'd,
            It starts a giant and exalts the kind.

101–2. Cf. *Ess.*, II 6. For the bearing on Pope's theme (above, II 83*n*), cf.
Cicero, *De. fin.* (tr. S.P., rev. J. Collier, 1702, p. 243): ". . . *genuine* Vertue . . .
never neglects any Part of Human Nature, but consults for the Whole, whereas
the Vertue which the Stoicks patronize, takes one Part of Human Nature into
its Protection, and leaves the rest to shift for itself." The "boasting" of the
Stoics was regularly criticized, e.g. by Hutcheson, p. 117: ". . . the *Stoick Sect*,
. . . boasting of an undisturbed Happiness and Serenity"; and by Maxwell in
his introduction to Cumberland, pp. xlvi–xlviii. For phrasing cf. E. Young,
Imper. Pelagi, Strain 1, st. 17: "Their want and apathy let Stoics boast."

103–4. Cf. Milton, *Areop.* (ed. J. W. Hales, 1904, p. 18): "I cannot praise a
fugitive and cloister'd vertue, unexercis'd and unbreath'd, that never sallies out
and sees her adversary"; Montaigne, II 145–6; E. Young, *Vindic. of Prov.* (2nd ed.,
1728), p. 49: "Indolence, or Rest is inconsistent with our Nature, and not to be
found in Heaven itself. . . On the contrary, our Heaven will consist in a Pleasing
Motion, a Delightful Exertion . . ."

105–8. St Evremond (*Wks.* tr. des Maiseaux, 1728), I 48; *Spectat.*, 316; *ibid.*,
408: ". . . the passions, which are to the mind as the winds to a ship, . . . only
can move it, and they too often destroy it; if fair and gentle they guide it into the
harbour; if contrary and furious, they overset it in the waves . . . Reason must
then take the place of pilot, and can never fail of securing her charge if she be
not wanting to her self . . ." The force of the comparison between passions and
winds, a commonplace in moral writings [below, II 108*n*], was augmented by
the belief that winds also, by their movement, preserved the air from stagnation:
cf. Du Bartas, 1st wk, 7th day, 506–7; Dryden, *The Medal*, 254–5; Fontenelle,
Dial. des morts (tr. Hughes, 1708), pp. 31–2; *Spectat.*, 408.

105. *The . . . tempest*] Cf. Pope's *Il.* (I 258): "the rising Tempest of his Soul".

107. Wakefield cites Tate's paraphrase of Simonides [7] in Dryden's *Misc.*
[(1727) v 54]: "On Life's wide Ocean diversly launch'd out".

Reason the card, but Passion is the gale;
Nor God alone in the still calm we find,
He mounts the storm, and walks upon the wind.   110
    Passions, like Elements, tho' born to fight,
Yet, mix'd and soften'd, in his work unite:

---

108. *card*] *OED* (citing this line): "The circular piece of stiff paper on which the 32 points are marked in the mariner's compass". The meaning should probably include the mariner's chart or map: cf. Bailey, *s.v.*, the citations of Pattison and Morris, and Habington's *To Zephirus* (*Castara*, 1812, p. 178).

Passion . . . gale] Cf. above, 105-8n, and P. Le Moyne, *Peintures morales* (Paris, 1645) I 513-5; R. Burton, *Anat. of Mel.*, Part 1, sec. 3, mem. 3, subs. 1; Montaigne, II 393; Senault, p. 115; T. Wright, *Passions of the Minde* (1630), pp. 59, 71, 334; T. Nourse, *Discourse upon . . . Man* (1697), pp. 106-7.

109-10. Cf. the "great calm" of Matt. VIII 26, after which the disciples "marvelled, saying, What manner of man is this, that even the winds and the sea obey him!" Wakefield cites 1 Kings XIX 11-12: ". . . and after the wind an earthquake; . . . And after the earthquake a fire; . . . and after the fire a still small Voice"; Pattison cites Psa., XVIII 10: ". . . Yea, [God] did fly upon the wings of the wind."; Morris cites Addison, *Campaign*, 292, where an angel "Rides in the whirlwind and directs the storm". Cf. also, *Dunc.* A, III 260.

111-22. A further comparison between man and the exterior universe to emphasize the importance of utilizing his whole nature—in keeping with the implications in the preceding passage that the world outside man is inclusive, not exclusive: frost alone is not enough; tempests are as necessary as calms, gales as necessary as compasses or maps; God manifests himself in both the stillness and the storm; and cf. II 65-6n, and the remainder of this epistle, *passim*. The commencement of this passage with a reference to God's reconciling activity at the Creation (111-12) and its conclusion in the painting metaphor (121-2), underline the point that man's duty is to achieve by creative skill an inner harmony of all his powers, imposing order on the *chaos* indicated in II 13.

111-12. The traditional conception of personality as a blending of the four humours or elements in man, the application of which to the passions was regularly made. Cf. Tillyard, *Eliz. World Picture* (1944), 55-64; Miloyevitch, *La Théorie des passions de P. Senault et la Morale Chrétienne en France au XVII siècle* (Paris, 1934), p. 186; Senault, pp. 104-5; A. Le Grand, *Man without Passion* (tr. G. R., 1675), p. 105; and *The Government of the Passions* (2nd ed., 1704), p. 79: ". . . if [Man] has occasion for Love to unite him to those things he desires, he stands in no less need of Hatred, to preserve him from those that might annoy him. The whole Universe subsisteth but by the contrariety of the Elements . . ."

These 'tis enough to temper and employ;
But what composes Man, can Man destroy?
Suffice that Reason keep to Nature's road,   115
Subject, compound them, follow her and God.
Love, Hope, and Joy, fair pleasure's smiling train,
Hate, Fear, and Grief, the family of pain;
These mix'd with art, and to due bounds confin'd,
Make and maintain the balance of the mind: 120

113–16. Cf. Coeffeteau, p. 66: "For as health doth not consist in the ruine of contrary qualities which are found in man, but in the temperature which a good constitution giues them: And as to make a perfect musique, wee must not take away the diuersity of tunes, but reduce them to a good accord to make the harmony perfect [cf. *Ess.*, II 121]; so the striuings of vertue consistes not wholly to roote all naturall *Passions* out of the soule, but to moderate and gouern them by the rule of reason"; Charleton, pp. 168–9; Milton, *Areop.* (ed. J. W. Hales, 1904), pp. 25–6: "Wherefore did he creat passions within us, pleasures round about us, but that these rightly temper'd are the very ingredients of vertu?"; *Spectat.*, 224; *Plain Dealer*, 87.

117–18. The passions specified form one of the standard classifications. Cf. Hutcheson, pp. 58–9; Sir J. Davies, *Nosce Teip.* (*Poems*, ed. Grosart, 1876, I 73):

> The *motiue* vertue then begins to moue;
> Which in the heart below doth Passions cause,
> *Ioy, griefe*, and *feare*, and *hope*, and *hate*, and *loue*;

Mem. of Scribl. (EC, x 322). In the Morgan MS. Pope has written beside 111–22: "Arist. Eth. 1.7 reduces all ye Passions under Pleasure and Pain as their universal Principles. The mean between opposite Passions makes Virtue, ye Extremes Vice."

118. *the . . . pain*] For phrasing cf. Dryden, *State of Inn.*, v [i]: "the numerous family of death", and Garth, *Dispens.*, vi 138: "the faded family of Care" [Wakefield]. And cf. Dryden's Lucret., iv 127: "the meagre family of care".

119–22. The painting figure was a favourite in psychological and ethical contexts: cf. Senault, pp. 104–5; La Bruyère, I 51: "Modesty is to Merit as shades to figures in a picture, giving it strength and beauty"; E. Young, *Vindic. of Prov.* (2nd ed., 1728), p. 30: "The *Tempers* are, as I take it, lesser *Passions*, or, various fainter *Shades*, or *Blendings* of Those strong *Colours* of the Soul of Man"; Prior, II 234–5:

> Love? why 'tis joy or sorrow, peace or strife;
> 'Tis all the colour of remaining life.

119. *to . . . confin'd*] Cf. Coeffeteau, p. 74: ". . . [Reason's] duty is to prescribe them their bounds, and to reduce them to a mediocrity as vertue requires."

> The lights and shades, whose well accorded strife
> Gives all the strength and colour of our life.
>   Pleasures are ever in our hands or eyes,
> And when in act they cease, in prospect rise;
> Present to grasp, and future still to find,   125
> The whole employ of body and of mind.
> All spread their charms, but charm not all alike;
> On diff'rent senses diff'rent objects strike;
> Hence diff'rent Passions more or less inflame,
> As strong or weak, the organs of the frame;   130
> And hence one master Passion in the breast,

121–2. Wakefield: "Well-accorded strife is the *rerum concordia discors* of Ovid, *Met.*, I 433, or his own harmonious confusion in his *Windsor Forest*, 14"; and cf. above, II 111ff *n*. For the Augustan conception of paintings as composed "tensions" of light and shade, here applied to the composition of human personality, cf. *Ess. on Crit.*, 488ff; Dryden, *Ess.* (ed. Ker), II 147ff; Addison, *Letter from Italy*, 93ff; and Congreve, *To Sir Godfrey Kneller*, 25–7.

123–6. Cf. above, II 88n (Gastrell). Pattison cites Montaigne (I 93]: ". . . let the Philosophers all say what they will, the main thing at which we all aim, even in Virtue itself, is Pleasure."

127–30. Aristotle, *Eth. Nic.*, 1176a: ". . . [Pleasures] vary to no small extent, in the case of men at least; the same things delight some people and pain others . . . ," and *ibid.*, 1113a; Burton, *Anat. of Mel.*, Part 3, sec. 1, mem. 2, subs. 2: ". . . several pleasant objects diversely affect divers men"; Temple, I 273–4: ". . . there is no Mistake so gross . . . as to think Pleasures arise . . . from the Impression given us of Objects, rather than from the Disposition of the Organs that receive them. The various Effects of the same Objects upon different Persons, or upon the same Person at different times, makes the contrary most evident."

128–9. *Brit. Apollo*, 3: ". . . Diversity of Objects have the Power to excite various Passions in the Sensitive Soul, as they happen differently to strike upon it."

130. So in *Spectat.*, 224, every man is said to be more or less actuated by ambition "in proportion to the vigour of his complexion", and Burton observes (*Anat. of Mel.*, Part 1, sec. 2, mem. 5, subs. 1), that the soul's actions take a tincture from the body's organs: "Sanguine are merry, Melancholy sad, Phlegmatic dull, by reason of abundance of those humours, and they cannot resist such passions which are inflicted by them. . ."

131ff. On the theory of the ruling passion, cf. Introd., pp. xxxviff.

131–2. Cf. Montaigne, I 368: "And as they say, that in our Bodies there is a Congregation of divers Humours, of which, that is the Soveraign, which according to the Complexion we are of, is commonly most predominant in us:

Like Aaron's serpent, swallows up the rest.
 As Man, perhaps, the moment of his breath,
Receives the lurking principle of death;
The young disease, that must subdue at length, 135
Grows with his growth, and strengthens with his strength:
So, cast and mingled with his very frame,
The Mind's disease, its ruling Passion came;
Each vital humour which should feed the whole,
Soon flows to this, in body and in soul.   140
Whatever warms the heart, or fills the head,

So, though the Soul have in it divers motions to give it Agitation; yet must there of necessity be one to overrule all the rest . . ."; J. Norden, *Vicissitudo Rerum* (1600), st. 51. Pattison cites Bacon, *Adv. of Learning*, II xxiii 21.

 132. *Aaron's serpent*] As in Exod., VII 10–12. The ruling passion is a manifestation of God's power: cf. *Imit. Hor.*, *Ep.*, II ii 274 *ff*. Voltaire says (marginalia on the *Essay*—see G. R. Havens, MLN, XLIII (1928) 438) that the comparison is taken from Smalridge's sermons. I have not been able to verify this.

 133 *ff*. *The* PREDOMINANT PASSION, *and its* Force. The Use of this doctrine, as apply'd to the Knowledge of mankind, is one of the subjects of the second book. [P. *1735b–43a, but 1739–43a omit the second sentence.*]

 133–6. In *Gent. Mag.*, LXXXI (1811) 28, "W.P." notes a parallel in *Mirror for Magistrates* [ed. L. B. Campbell (1938), trag. 21, 733–6]:
    Strayght after byrth due is the fatall beere.
    By deathes permission the aged linger here.
    Euen in thy Swathebands out commision goeth
    To loose thy breath, that yet but yongly bloweth.
Pattison cites Manil., *Astron.*, IV 16: "Nascentes morimur, finisque ab origine pendet" [cf. the analogues supplied in A. E. Housman's edition] and Seneca, *Herc. Fur.*, III 874: "Prima quae vitam dedit hora, carpit".

 138. *ruling Passion*] The phrase appears in Pascal, p. 286, and Roscommon, *Ess. on Trans. Verse*, 92.

 139–46. Cf. Jonson, *Every Man Out*, Induction, 112–20:
    It may by Metaphore applie itself
    Unto the generall disposition:
    As when some one peculiar qualitie
    Doth so possesse a man, that it doth draw
    All his affects, his spirits, and his powers,
    In their confluctions, all to runne one way,
    This may be truly said to be a humour.

 139, 141. By vital humour Pope seems to signify the several sorts of "spirits" —natural, vital, animal—that in the old physiology were credited with nourishing the powers of body and soul: cf. M. Foster, *Lects. on the Hist. of Physiol.* (1901),

L

As the mind opens, and its functions spread,
Imagination plies her dang'rous art,
And pours it all upon the peccant part.
    Nature its mother, Habit is its nurse;   145
Wit, Spirit, Faculties, but make it worse;
Reason itself but gives it edge and pow'r;
As Heav'n's blest beam turns vinegar more sowr;

148 *Between ll. 148–9, 1734a–35a have:*
        The ruling Passion, be it what it will,
        The ruling Passion conquers Reason still.

---

pp. 12*ff*; and E. M. W. Tillyard, *Eliz. World Picture* (1944), pp. 63–4. Of these the vital spirits were manufactured in the *heart* and the animal spirits in the *head* (i.e. brain). P. A. Robin points out (*Old Physiol. in Engl. Lit.*, 1911, p. 150), that the "natural" or lowest of the three sorts of spirits usually go unmentioned in literary allusions—as here.

142. I.e. as the individual matures from infancy into manhood. Cf. Hooker, I vi 3; *Dunc.* B, IV 155–6. Quillet's *Callipaedia*, bk IV, gives a full account of contemporary doctrine on this point.

143–4. The traditional view of the dangerous force of imagination in man's moral life. Cf. M. W. Bundy, *Theory of Imag. in Classical and Mediaev. Thought,* Univ. of Ill. Studies, XII (1927); C. D. Thorpe, *Aesth. Theory of Hobbes* (1940); Charron, I 177*ff*; E. Young, *Vindic. of Prov.* (2nd ed. 1728), p. 8. For the physiological effects of imagination, see Charleton, p. 71, and Burton, *Anat. of Mel.*, Part I, sec. 2, mem. 3, subs. I.

144. *the peccant part*] Chambers art. Peccant: "Peccant, in medicine, an epithet given to the humours of the body, when they offend either in quantity or quality, i.e. when they are either morbid, or in too great abundance". Cf. Dryden's Juvenal, X 490 [Wakefield].

146. An ancient maxim when applied to the passions in general. Cf. Montaigne, II 258: "Great Wits are ruin'd by their own proper force and quickness"; W. Charleton, *Two Discourses* (1675), p. 59: "Passions are generally stronger in those men, who excell others in fineness of Wit and quickness of Imagination"; Charron, I 166; Cheyne, *Ess. of Health and Long Life* (1724), p. 171; and cf. R. Wallerstein, "Shaftesbury and his Place in . . . *Abs. and Achit.*", *Hunt. Libr. Quart.*, VI (1942–3) 445*ff*.

Faculties] Bailey, *s.v. faculty*, lists three sorts—natural, vital, and animal, corresponding to the kinds of spirits.

147. Warburton instances the character of Cotta in *Mor. Ess.*, III 177*ff*.

148. Bacon's *Nat. Hist.*, IX 898: ". . . in making of Vinegar, they use to set vessels of wine over against the noon-sun; which . . . leaveth the liquor more sour and hard."

We, wretched subjects tho' to lawful sway,
In this weak queen, some fav'rite still obey.   150
Ah! if she lend not arms, as well as rules,
What can she more than tell us we are fools?
Teach us to mourn our Nature, not to mend,
A sharp accuser, but a helpless friend!
Or from a judge turn pleader, to persuade   155
The choice we make, or justify it made;

149–50. Cf. Dryden, 1 *Conq. of Gran.*, III i:

> Ah, why did heaven leave man so weak defence,
> To trust frail Reason with the Rule of Sense! . . .
> . . . like a captive king, 'tis borne away,
> And forced to countenance its own rebels' sway.

Prior, II 959–62:

> Yet this great empress [reason] of the human soul
> Does only with imagin'd power control;
> If restless passion by rebellious sway
> Compels the weak usurper to obey.

Reason as "queen" appears in Cicero, *Tusc. disp.*, II xxi: "regina ratio". For the metaphor of the "favourite", cf. D.T., *Essais Politicke and Morall* (1608), leaf Div: ". . . like a weaker Prince, [the soul] suffers herselfe . . . to be led away by the suggestions of such her followers"; and Greville, *Treat. of Hum. Learning*, st. 11.

151–2. Erasmus, p. 31: ". . . how powerful Reason is, let common experience declare, inasmuch as she, which yet is all she can do, may call out to us till she be hoarse again, and tell us the Rules of Honesty and Virtue [without effect] . . ."

153. Pattison quotes Jer. Taylor's *Doctr. of Repentance*, ch. VIII, sec. 1: "The old philosophers . . . said that virtue was nothing else but 'a disposition and force of reason'; . . . yet this reason served to little other purposes, but to upbraid our follies and infelicities, and to make our actions punishable by representing them to be unreasonable . . ."

155–6. Daniel Dyke, *Mystery of Self-Deceiving* (1633), p. 295: "Our affections when they would have a thing, sharpen our wits and set them on worke to devise arguments to serve their turne. . . Surely our affections will plead mightily . . ."; Dryden, *Hind and Panther*, 1691–2:

> Where int'rest fortifies an argument
> Weak reason serves to gain the will's assent;

Applebee's Orig. Weekly, 12 May 1733: "The Reasons which Folk generally assign for doing what they do . . . are the *Defences* made by our *Reason* when our Passions are arraigned."

Proud of an easy conquest all along,
She but removes weak passions for the strong:
So, when small humors gather to a gout,
The doctor fancies he has driv'n them out.   160
    Yes, Nature's road must ever be prefer'd;
Reason is here no guide, but still a guard:
'Tis hers to rectify, not overthrow,
And treat this passion more as friend than foe:
A mightier Pow'r the strong direction sends,   165

157 an easy conquest] imagin'd Conquests *1734a–35a.*
160 them] 'em *1733, 1735b–43a.*
165–66 *Om. 1733.*

158. La Rochefoucauld, IV xxxi: "It is but very seldom, that *Reason* cures our *Passions,* but one *Passion* is commonly cured by another. *Reason* indeed often strikes in with the strongest side . . ."

159. Chambers, art. Gout, notes that the disease arises from "a redundancy of humours" and "may be considered as a . . . paroxysm, tending to free the body of an offensive . . . matter, by throwing it upon the extremities; . . . till by collecting again . . . it causes another paroxysm". For a somewhat similar illustration by medical analogy of the assimilative power of a ruling passion, see *Plain Dealer,* 4, where love is said to convert "all other Passions into itself, as the Plague does all other Distempers".

161–6. In *Imit. Hor., Ep.,* II ii 278*ff,* Pope observes that the reason why one individual is driven altogether by self-interest, another by benevolence,

> Is known alone to that Directing Pow'r,
> Who forms the Genius in the natal Hour;
> That God of Nature, who, within us still,
> Inclines our Action, not constrains our Will;
> Various of Temper, as of Face or Frame,
> Each Individual: His great End the same.

161. Juvenal, *Sat.,* XIV 321: "Nunquam aliud natura, aliud sapientia dicit"; *Spectat.,* 404: "Nature, if left to herself, leads us on in the best course . . ."

163. So Donne says of Elizabeth Drury (*2nd Anniv.,* 359–62) that "shee made warres" on her passions, yet her reason still "Did not o'rthrow, but rectifie her will"; and cf. *Spectat.,* 408.

165. Cicero, *De. fin.,* V xi: ". . . Maior aliqua causa atque divinior hanc vim ingenuit." In the context Cicero is discussing the inherence of self-love in all animate natures.

165*ff. Its* Necessity, *in directing men to different purposes.* The particular application of this to the *several Pursuits* of Men, and the *General Good* resulting thence,

And sev'ral Men impels to sev'ral ends.
Like varying winds, by other passions tost,
This drives them constant to a certain coast.
Let pow'r or knowledge, gold or glory, please,
Or (oft more strong than all) the love of ease;   170
Thro' life 'tis followed, ev'n at life's expence;
The merchant's toil, the sage's indolence,
The monk's humility, the hero's pride,
All, all alike, find Reason on their side.

174 All, all] And all *1733*.

falls also into the succeeding books. [P. *1735b–43a, but 1739–43a omit* also.]

165–8. As the two parts of the following illustration show (172–4, 169–71), two points are being made here: that ruling passions make men different; and that they make men constant (cf. 177 below).

165–6. The traditional view that God ensures the variety of dispositions and inclinations by which the world's work is enabled to be carried on. Cf. F. Garasse, *Somme théologique* (1625), pp. 167–75; Coeffeteau, pp. 85–6: "For wee see some loue painting naturally, others take delight in Geometry, some are passionatly affected to the Liberall Arts, others imbrace the Mechanicks; some loue Hunting, others burne with a desire of Play; some are borne to War; and others are inclined to Mildnes and Peace; some haue no contentment but in solitarinesse; and others cannot liue without the mannaging of affaires. And whence, say they, proceed these so different inclinations, but from the author of *nature?*"; *Reflexions on Man* (1733), p. 110; Pope's *Il.*, XVII 5*n* (speaking of Achilles and Patroclus): "Such Friendships are not uncommon, and I have often assign'd this Reason for them, that it is natural for Men to seek the Assistance of those Qualities in others, which they want themselves. That is still better if apply'd to Providence, that associates Men of different and contrary Qualities, in order to make a more perfect System."

167. Cf. *Plain Dealer*, 32:
           Passion's wild Influence ebb'd, and flow'd, my Mind;
           As Seas drive diff'rent, with the changing Wind.

170. *Guardian*, 22: "We seek happiness, in which ease is the principal ingredient, and the end proposed in our most restless pursuits is tranquillity". Cf. the extract from one of Pope's letters to Allen (EC, IX 199): "To be at ease is the greatest of happiness (at ease, I mean, both of mind and body), but to be *idle* is the greatest of unhappiness. . ."

174. Cf. La Rochefoucauld, IV xxxi, where it is observed that in the warfare of the passions, reason "often strikes in with the strongest side. And there is no *Passion* so Extravagant, but hath *Reason* ready to keep it in Countenance."

Th' Eternal Art educing good from ill,   175
Grafts on this Passion our best principle:
'Tis thus the Mercury of Man is fix'd,
Strong grows the Virtue with his nature mix'd;
The dross cements what else were too refin'd,
And in one interest body acts with mind.   180
   As fruits ungrateful to the planter's care

175ff. *Its* providential Use, *in fixing our* PRINCIPLE, *and ascertaining our* VIRTUE. [P. *1735b–43a.*]

175–6. Cf. above, II 83*n* (Culverwell). La Rochefoucauld, I cccciv: "Nature seems to have treasured up in every one of our Minds some secret *Talents*, and some particular faculty which we are not sensible of; it is the privilege of the *Passions* alone to bring these to light, and to direct us sometimes to surer and more excellent Aims than it is possible for Art to do."

175. Cf. Thomson's *Hymn*, 116 (*Seasons*, 1730), where he says that God "From seeming Evil still educes Good".

177. *Mercury . . . fix'd*] I.e. the dominion of a ruling passion "sets" or deter-mines the otherwise infinite variableness of man's emotional nature, as various "sulphurs" (according to the metallurgy of Pope's time) "fix", in the metallic substances as we know them, the primal mercury of which all of them are composed: cf. Chambers, art. Mercury of metals. The term *mercury* was fre-quently applied to volatility of character: e.g. Shadwell, *Sullen Lovers*, II i; and "Clio", *The Innocent Inconstant* in Savage's *Misc.* (1726), p. 100.

Mercury] W. Sichel (*Bolingbroke and his Times*, 1901–2, II 330) finds an allusion here to Bolingbroke, on the ground that he was sometimes nicknamed "Mer-cury" (*ibid.*, I 146 *n.* 3). If there is such an allusion it is a private *jeu* of the poet's in no way relevant to his poetic meaning.

179. Cf. Montaigne, III 2–3: "Our *Being* is cemented with sickly Qualities . . . Vices . . . help to make up the Seam in our piecing . . ."; and Shaks., *Meas. for Meas.*, V i 435–7:

> They say best men are moulded out of faults,
> And, for the most, become much more the better
> For being a little bad.

180. Pope's point is analogous to Donne's in *The Extasie*: neither body nor soul is dispensable.

181. *fruits*] Equivalent, as used here, to "grafts" or "scions".

ungrateful . . . care] Cf. Dryden, *Abs. and Achit.*, 12: "A soil ungrateful to the tiller's care".

ungrateful] *OED*: "Not responding to cultivation".

181–4. A different but related image appears in Plutarch's discussion of virtue (III 490–1): "For it is not the method and custom of reason . . . to destroy

On savage stocks inserted learn to bear;
The surest Virtues thus from Passions shoot,
Wild Nature's vigor working at the root.
What crops of wit and honesty appear   185
From spleen, from obstinacy, hate, or fear!
See anger, zeal and fortitude supply;
Ev'n av'rice, prudence; sloth, philosophy;
Lust, thro' some certain strainers well refin'd,

189–90   Om. 1733. Inserted between ll. 192–3, 1734a–35a.

and tear up all the passions and affections indifferently . . .; but rather—like some kind and careful Deity who has a tender regard to the growth and improvement of fruit-trees and plants—to cut away and clip off that which grows wild and rank and to dress and manage the rest that it may serve for use and profit."

185–92. *Govt. of the Passions* (2nd ed., 1704), p. 129: "From all these Discourses 'tis not easie to judge, that there is no Passion in our Souls, which may not be advantageously managed by Reason, as well as Grace. For, to summ up all what has been said in the whole Work; Love may be chang'd into a holy Amity, and Hatred may be brought to a just Indignation. Desires moderated are so many good Assistants, to acquire Virtue. Eschewing is the proper security of Chastity; Hope animates us to brave and generous Undertakings, and our Despair turns us from rash ones: Fear is serviceable to Prudence, and Boldness to Valour: As brutish as Anger seems, she sides with Justice: Joy is an innocent Antepast of Felicity: Grief a short Pain, that frees us from Eternal Torments: So that our Salvation depends only upon the good Use of our Passions, and Virtue it self, only subsisteth by the good Employment of these Motions of our Soul."

185–6. "Pope probably alluded to Swift [and if so, especially to the episode of the *Drapier's Letters*] when he spoke of the 'crops of wit and honesty' which were the product of 'spleen, obstinacy, and hate' " [EC]. On the good effects of fear, cf. Wycherley, *Upon the Boldness of Cowardice*; on those of spleen, cf. *The Lay Monastery*, 35; and on the relation of hatred to what Pope may mean here by *honesty*, cf. Plutarch, III 491: ". . . hatred and aversion for ill men promotes the execution of justice . . ."

187. *anger*] Generally accredited a useful passion when not in excess.

anger . . . fortitude] Senault, 127: "What must be added to Boldness, to make thereof true Fortitude?" Plutarch, III 491: ". . . moderate anger is of admirable use to . . . fortitude . . ."

188. *av'rice, prudence*] Montaigne, II 12: ". . . Avarice . . . does farther teach Discretion and Prudence . . ."

189–90. E.g., Cymon in Dryden's *Cymon and Iphig*. For the idea, cf. Hobbes,

Is gentle love, and charms all womankind: 190
Envy, to which th'ignoble mind's a slave,
Is emulation in the learn'd or brave:
Nor Virtue, male or female, can we name,
But what will grow on Pride, or grow on Shame.
 Thus Nature gives us (let it check our pride)   195

192 or] and *1734a–35a*.
194 will grow . . . grow} or grows . . . grows *1733*.

Humane Nature (1650), pp. 106–7; *Spectat.*, 224: "Love and the desire of glory, as
they are the most natural, so they are capable of being refined into the most
delicate and rational passions." Pattison compares for the phrasing (without
stating his source):

Ce qui épaisse paraît grossière

Bien coulée à tout femme sait plaire.

 189. *strainers*] "The image is from the clearing of a liquid, e.g. in decanting
wine . . ." [Morris].
 191–2. Cf. Bp. Butler, *Fifteen Sermons* (1726), I xi, note e: "Emulation is
merely the desire and hope of equality with, or superiority over others, with
whom we compare ourselves. . . To desire the attainment of this equality or
superiority by the *particular means* of others being brought down to our own
level, is, I think, the distinct notion of envy." Chudleigh, *Ess.*, p. 186: "That
which breeds Envy in narrow groveling Minds, begets Respect in brave and
generous Tempers . . ."
 193–4. Cf. Charleton, p. 140: "These two Passions, Glory and Shame, . . .
doe yet agree in their End, which is *to incite us to Virtue*; the first by *hope*, the
other by *fear* . . ."; La Rochefoucauld, I ccxxi; G.-B. Gelli, *Circe* (tr. T.
Brown, 1702), pp. 230–1; Mandeville, *Fable of the Bees* (ed. F. B. Kaye), 167,
213.
 195*ff*. VIRTUE *and* VICE *join'd in our* Mixt Nature; *the Limits* near, *yet the
things* separate, *and* evident. *The Office of* Reason. [P. *1735b–43a*.]
 195–6. An epigrammatic way of saying (in contradistinction to theories
that real virtue is the result of pure reason or pure grace) that we are indebted
to nature for a passional force that can be turned as readily into a characteristic
virtue as a characteristic vice. Cf. *Govt. of the Passions* (2nd ed., 1704), p. 61:
"Were it not then barbarous even to endeavour the stifling those Passions
which have so great an affinity with Virtue? or were it not high Ingratitude, not
to acknowledge those mighty Advantages we have received from Nature?"
Pride is not the passion named in l. 194, but the point of view of those who
subscribe to the Stoic notion that men can and should divest themselves of all
but reason (cf. II 6 and 101). The wording of the couplet is arranged to emphasize Pope's partial opposition to the school of La Rochefoucauld: cf.

The virtue nearest to our vice ally'd;
Reason the byass turns to good from ill,
And Nero reigns a Titus, if he will.
The fiery soul abhor'd in Catiline,
In Decius charms, in Curtius is divine.   200
The same ambition can destroy or save,
And make a patriot as it makes a knave.
    IV. This light and darkness in our chaos join'd,
What shall divide? The God within the mind.
    Extremes in Nature equal ends produce,   205

205–206 *Om. 1733.*

Spence, p. 11: "As l'Esprit, La Rochefoucauld, and that sort of people, prove that all virtues are disguised vices, I would engage to prove all vices to be disguised virtues. Neither, indeed, is true: but this would be a more agreeable subject; and would overturn their whole scheme."

197. *the byass*] Cf. Shadwell, *Humourists*, epilogue:

> A Humour is the Byas of the Mind,
> By which with violence 'tis one way inclin'd;

and Burton, pp. 87–8. The figure is from bowling.

198. *will*] Both "if he chooses" and "if he performs an act of will".

200. *Decius . . . Curtius*] Examples of patriotic self-abnegation. "Decius [cf. Livy, XIII ix], instructed by a vision . . . that the general on the one side and the army on the other was doomed, rushed into the thick of the fight to ensure by his own death the destruction of the enemy. . . Curtius [cf. Livy, VII vi], . . . when informed . . . that a chasm which had opened in the Roman forum could never be filled up till the basis of Roman greatness had been committed to it, was alleged to have mounted on horseback clad in armour, and to have leapt into the gulf" [EC]. Cf. *Dunc.* A, I 195–6.

201. Quintilian, *Inst. orat.*, I ii 22: ". . . licet ipsa vitium sit ambitio, frequenter tamen causa virtutum est". Cf. Aristotle, *Eth. Nich.*, 1107b.

203–4. Alludes to the creative act of God (Gen., I 4; *Par. Lost*, VII 249–51, 352) which man is to imitate in ordering his own "chaos": cf. II 111*ff n.* Also Quillet, *Callipaedia* (Engl. tr., 1701), IV 95–6:

> [Reason] searches far and near, with subtle light
> Dividing Vice and Virtue, Wrong and Right.

205. *Extremes in Nature*] Evidently the "reconciled extremes" of drought and rain, seedtime and harvest, life and death, change and permanence, to which Pope refers in *Mor. Ess.*, III 159*ff* and on which, in the traditional view, the well-being of the world is founded. Cf. the Hymn of Cleanthes. For an alternative but related meaning, cf. Chapman, *All Fools*, I i:

In Man they join to some mysterious use;
Tho' each by turns the other's bound invade,

207–10 *1734a–35a print these two couplets in reverse order and with the following changes:* 209 And . . . mix] Tho' . . . mix'd; 207 Now this, now that the other's bound invades; 208 light . . . shade] lights . . . shades.

> Extremes, tho' contrary, have the like effects;
> Extreme heat mortifies like extreme cold;
> Extreme love breeds satiety as well
> As extreme hatred; and too violent rigour
> Tempts chastity as much as too much licence;

and his *Byron's Conspiracy*, III i.

206. In *Mor. Ess.*, III 160, the analogue of this line applies to the reconciled social effects of the extremes represented in different men, e.g. the prodigal and the miser. Here the reference is evidently to the single individual in whom there is placed a tendency that can become either vice or virtue, as above in 195 ff: men with ambition have both a Nero and a Titus in them. The occasional obscurities of meaning in this part of the epistle seem to rise from Pope's use of the term *vice* to apply both to developed evil (such as Nero's) and to the potential evil that is always in a given passion. In the latter sense Pope's note at 195 ff states that "virtue and vice are joined in our mixed nature", and the poem states that "they join to some mysterious use"—e.g. like the good scion and the wild stock (above, 181 ff). So too (in 207 ff) virtue and vice mix so closely that it is impossible to determine which is the effect of the scion and which of the wild stock—i.e. in an ambitious statesman, how much is desire for self-aggrandizement and how much is public spirit. Pope is thus using *vice* both in a utilitarian sense for the bad effects of action (Nero) and in a rigoristic sense for a selfishly motivated action (Where ends the virtue and begins the vice?). In 212 and 217 *vice* seems again to be action in its effects; in 231 it may be either; and in 235–6 it is evidently both: if we follow ill (effects) we do so only in part, because self-interest (motivation) intervenes to restrain us (e.g. concern for reputation or health restrains us from thievery or lust); if we follow good (effects), we also do so only in part, because human motives are rooted in self-love with the result that the action, rigoristically speaking, is not a fully virtuous action; and this cannot be avoided because man is a creature compounded of self-love as well as of reason. On this whole problem, see Introd., pp. xxxvii–xxxix.

207–10. Cf. Plutarch, II 66: ". . . [Stoicism] will not admit any vice to come near where virtue is; . . . but affirms that he that is not a wise man can do nothing well, and that he that is so can do nothing amiss. . . But in human actions and the affairs of common life the judgement of Euripides is verified that

> Virtue and vice ne'er separately exist
> But in the same acts with each other twist";

As, in some well-wrought picture, light and shade,
And oft so mix, the diff'rence is too nice
Where ends the Virtue, or begins the Vice.   210
   Fools! who from hence into the notion fall,
That Vice or Virtue there is none at all.
If white and black blend, soften, and unite
A thousand ways, is there no black or white?
Ask your own heart, and nothing is so plain;   215
'Tis to mistake them, costs the time and pain.
   v. Vice is a monster of so frightful mien,

Milton, *Areop.* (ed. Hales, 1904), p. 17: ". . . the knowledge of good is . . . involv'd and interwoven with the knowledge of evill, and in . . . many cunning resemblances hardly to be discern'd"; Pope, *Il.*, 1 (1715), pref., leaf D2r: ". . . it is with great Parts as with great Virtues, they naturally border on some Imperfection; and it is often hard to distinguish exactly where the Virtue ends, or the Fault begins"; *Hypatia*, in the miscellany printed by John Clarke, *Poems on Sev. Occas.* (1724), p. 63:

     Of Vice and Virtue there the Bounds to fix
     Just where their fading Colours seem to mix.

211–15. I.e. good and evil are absolutes, and known intuitively. Pope is making the point of the Cambridge Platonists, e.g. Cudworth, *Immut. Morality* (1731), 1 ii 1: "Now things may as well be made white or black by mere will, without whiteness or blackness, . . . as morally good and evil, . . . Neither can omnipotence itself (to speak with reverence) by mere will make a thing white or black without whiteness or blackness; that is, without such certain natures . . . which beget those sensations or phantasms of white and black in us."
   217ff. VICE *odious in itself, and how we* deceive *ourselves into it.* [P. *1735b–43a.*]
   217–20. S. Daniel, *Complaint of Rosamond*, 461–2:

     . . . Nature checks a new offence with loathing,
     But use of sinne doth make it seeme as nothing;

Par. Lost, II 759–63:

     . . . back they recoiled afraid
     At first, and called me Sin, and for a sign
     Portentous held me; but familiar grown,
     I pleased, and with attractive graces won
     The most averse;

Dyke, *Myst. of Self-Deceiving* (1633), p. 182; Chudleigh, *Ess.*, pp. 73–4; *Spectat.*, 626: "What is it but novelty that . . . inspires horror? . . . hence, monsters by use, are beheld without loathing . . ."; *Spectat.*, 631: ". . . through the prevalence of custom, the most vicious actions lose their horror by being made familiar to us."

As, to be hated, needs but to be seen;
Yet seen too oft, familiar with her face,
We first endure, then pity, then embrace.　　220
But where th'Extreme of Vice, was ne'er agreed:
Ask where's the North? at York, 'tis on the Tweed;
In Scotland, at the Orcades; and there,
At Greenland, Zembla, or the Lord knows where:
No creature owns it in the first degree,　　225
But thinks his neighbour farther gone than he.

219　Yet] But *1733*.
220　*Between ll. 220–221, 1733 has:*
　　　　A *Cheat*! a *Whore*! who starts not at the Name,
　　　　In all the Inns of Court, or Drury Lane?
221　th'Extreme] the *Point 1733*.

---

218. Wakefield cites Dryden, *Hind and Panther* [33–4]:
　　　　For Truth has such a face and such a mien,
　　　　As to be lov'd needs only to be seen.

220. *pity*] Cf. Pope's version of Donne's 2nd satire, 3–5:
　　　　Yet here, as ev'n in Hell, there must be still
　　　　One Giant-Vice, so excellently ill,
　　　　That all beside one pities, not abhors.

221–30. Aristotle, *Eth. Nic.*, 1108b–9b: "For the brave man appears rash relatively to the coward, and cowardly relatively to the rash man; . . . the liberal man prodigal relatively to the mean man, mean relatively to the prodigal. Hence also the people at the extremes push the intermediate man each over to the other, and the brave man is called rash by the coward, cowardly by the rash man, and correspondingly in the other cases. . . But up to what point and to what extent a man must deviate before he becomes blameworthy it is not easy to determine by reasoning, any more than anything else that is perceived by the senses . . ."

222–30. For the image, cf. Montaigne, II 409; Pascal, pp. 182–3: "There is scarce any Thing, just or unjust, which does not change its Nature, upon changing its Climate. Three Degrees of Elevation in the Pole may ruin the whole Profession of Law. A meridian on the Globe . . . decides the most important Truths. . . Orthodoxy on one Side of the *Pyrenees*, may be Heresy on the other."

225. *degree*] An equivoque, sustaining both the usual sense and Pope's geographical image: cf. *zone* in 227.

225–6. Cf. Donne, *To Sir Hen. Wootton*, 7–9:
　　　　For here, no one is from the extremitie

Ev'n those who dwell beneath its very zone,
Or never feel the rage, or never own;
What happier natures shrink at with affright,
The hard inhabitant contends is right.   230
    VI. Virtuous and vicious ev'ry Man must be,
Few in th'extreme, but all in the degree;
The rogue and fool by fits is fair and wise,
And ev'n the best, by fits, what they despise.
'Tis but by parts we follow good or ill,   235

227 its] her *1733–34b*.

        Of vice, by any other reason free,
        But that the next to him, still, is worse than hee.

227–8. La Bruyère, II 27: "The same vices which are huge and insupportable in others we do not feel in ourselves . . ."; Chudleigh, *Ess.*, p. 90; Prior, *Ess. upon Opinion* (*Writings*, ed. Waller, II 202–3).

230. *hard*] "The man who lives in an atmosphere of vice becomes hardened to it, as the native of Greenland or Nova Zembla (l. 224) to cold" [Thompson].

231ff. *The* ENDS *of* PROVIDENCE *and* General Good *answer'd in our* Passions *and* Imperfections. *How usefully these are distributed to all* Orders *of men.* [P. *1735b–43a.*] The Morgan MS., where the phrase *passions and imperfections* in this note is replaced by the one word *imperfections*, suggests that *imperfections* is simply rigoristic language for the passions: as below, 241: *frailties*, and 247: *wants, defects.*

231–2. *Spectat.*, 183: ". . . there was no person so vicious who had not some good in him, nor any person so virtuous who had not in him some evil" [EC]. Cf. also *The Lay Monastery*, 14, 35. The lines are to be set against the Stoic paradox epitomized in Dryden's Persius, V 175–6:
        Virtue and Vice are never in one soul;
        A man is wholly wise, or wholly is a fool;
and cf. Plutarch, above, 207–10*n*.

234. Montaigne, II 556: ". . . I find that the best Vertue I have has in it some tincture of Vice. . ."; Dryden, *Aureng-Zebe*, III i:
        The best of men
        Some interest in their actions must confess;
        None merit, but in hope they may possess.

235–6. Cf. above, 206*n*, and for an analogous distinction, Hutcheson, p. 37: "An Action is *good, in a moral Sense*, when it flows from benevolent Affection, or Intention of absolute Good to others. Men of much Reflection may actually intend *universal absolute Good*; but with the common rate of Men their Virtue consists in intending and pursuing *particular absolute Good*, not inconsistent with universal Good.

> For, Vice or Virtue, Self directs it still;
> Each individual seeks a sev'ral goal;
> But HEAV'N's great view is One, and that the Whole:
> That counter-works each folly and caprice;
> That disappoints th'effect of ev'ry vice: 240
> That happy frailties to all ranks apply'd,
> Shame to the virgin, to the matron pride,
> Fear to the statesman, rashness to the chief,
> To kings presumption, and to crowds belief,

"An Action is *morally evil*, either from Intention of *absolute Evil*, universal, or particular, (which is seldom the case with Men, except in sudden Passions) or from pursuit of *private* or *particular relative Good*, which they might have known did tend to *universal absolute Evil*. For even the *want* of a just Degree of Benevolence renders an Action evil."

236. La Rochefoucauld, I ccliv: "Interest is the Thing that puts Men upon Exercising their *Vertues* and *Vices* of All Kinds."

237. Cf. above, 165*ff*; Temple, I 307: "Men have different Ends, according to their different Tempers"; R. Gould, *Satyr upon Man* (*Poems*, 1689, p. 214): "All [men are] ill, but then each takes a several way."

239–48. Cf. *The Lay Monastery*, II: "These Reflections [that most actions are motivated by vainglory] cannot but elevate our Conceptions, and engage the Mind in the Contemplation of the admirable Conduct of Providence, which makes use of culpable Passions and irregular Principles . . . to bring about Ends of the greatest Importance and Benefit to Mankind. If no great or illustrious Actions, in which the Common Good and the Happiness of Societies are concern'd, were to be perform'd by any but Disinterested Men who act from a Motive of real Vertue, How often would States and Kingdoms be involv'd in Confusion and Ruin, while no Warriors would be found to defend, nor Statesmen to direct and rule them? But when Principles of Vertue are wanting, as apparently they are in the Mass of Mankind, the desire of Popularity and false Glory, by the wise Administration of the Moderator of the World, in a great Measure supplies their Absence."

239–40. Cf. Augustine, *De civ. dei*, XI xvii: "Sicut naturarum bonarum optimus creator, ita voluntatum malarum justissimus ordinator".

240. Cf. S. Daniel, *To the Ladie Margaret*, 34–5 (speaking of vicious purposes): "the all-guiding Prouidence doth yet All disappoint . . ."

vice] "Real" or developed vice, as in Nero: cf. above, 206*n*.

242. This may refer either to the virgin's shame and the matron's pride as causes of chastity and fidelity, or to what Bayle called (*Œuvres diverses*, La Haye, 1737, II 272a) "la honte d'être vieille fille, la vanité d'être féconde" as causes of propagation of the species.

That Virtue's ends from Vanity can raise,   245
Which seeks no int'rest, no reward but praise;
And build on wants, and on defects of mind,
The joy, the peace, the glory of Mankind.
    Heav'n forming each on other to depend,
A master, or a servant, or a friend,   250
Bids each on other for assistance call,
'Till one Man's weakness grows the strength of all.
Wants, frailties, passions, closer still ally
247 build] builds *1733, 1735ab.*

245-6. La Rochefoucauld, III lxxi: "It is much better that great Persons should thirst after Honour; . . . for though the good they do, proceeds not from a principle of Vertue, yet the World however hath this Advantage, that their Vanity makes them do, what, if they were not vain, they would not have done"; La Bruyère, I 278: "Vanity and decency make us do the same things . . . to which inclination and duty should prompt us . . ."; *ibid.*, 292; and *Reflexions on Man* (1733), p. 119.

247-8. Bayle, *Œuvres diverses* (La Haye, 1737), II 284a, quotes approvingly an unnamed author's remark that "ce Dieu sage et prévoiant . . . qui vouloit . . . pourvoir à l'entretien de la Societé à laquelle il avoit destiné les hommes, et pour laquelle la vertu est nécessaire, . . . a mis dans leur esprit ces inclinations qui les portent naturellement au bien, et qui les poussent quasi malgré eux à faire de bonne actions, dans le temps même qu'ils croient n'agir que pour leur propre utilité."

249ff. *How useful these are to* SOCIETY *in general, and to* INDIVIDUALS *in particular, in every* STATE, *261, and ev'ry* AGE *of Life,* 271. [P. *1735b–43a.*]

249-52. A favourite thesis of traditional political theory, as Pattison notes. Warton contrasts the passage with Lucretius, v 222*ff*, and compares it with Shaftesbury [II 308-9]. Cf. also, *Ess.*, III 131*ff*, below, and J. Norris, *Poems and Discourses* (1684), p. 51: ". . . as Society is in its own nature an instrument of Happiness, so it is made much more so by the indigencies and infirmities of Men. Man, of all Creatures in the World, is least qualify'd to live alone, because there is no Creature that has so many necessities to be reliev'd. And this I take to be one of the great *Arts* of Providence, to secure mutual amity and the reciprocation of good turns in the World, it being the Nature of Indigency, like common danger, to indear men to one another . . ."

253-6. Cf. below, III 135-46. Erasmus (p. 39) voices a similar but more trifling insight: "In fine, I [Folly] am so necessary to the making of all society and manner of life both delightful and lasting, that neither would the people long endure their Governors, nor the Servant his Master, nor the Master his Footman, nor the Scholar his Tutor, nor one friend another, nor the Wife her Husband, nor

The common int'rest, or endear the tie:
To these we owe true friendship, love sincere,   255
Each home-felt joy that life inherits here:
Yet from the same we learn, in its decline,
Those joys, those loves, those int'rests to resign:
Taught half by Reason, half by mere decay,
To welcome death, and calmly pass away.   260
    Whate'er the Passion, knowledge, fame, or pelf,

the Usurer the Borrower, nor a souldier his Commander, nor one Companion another, unless all of them had their interchangeable failings, one while flattering, other while prudently conniving, and generally sweetning one another with some small relish of Folly."

255. *sincere*] Cf. IV 15*n*.

256. *home-felt joy*] Cf. Milton, *Comus*, 262: "home-felt delight"; and Pope's chorus for Sheffield's *Brutus*, 34: "home-felt rapture".

257-60. Cf. Seneca, *Ep.*, XXVI; Bacon, *Of Death*; Denham, *Of Old Age*, 895-12; Dryden's *Lucret.*, III 255-8; *Guardian*, 169; Bolingbroke to Swift, 20 Mar. 1731; Pope to Digby, 1 Sept. 1722; Pope to Knight, 8 Nov. 1729. Writing to Mrs Moore, 7 Dec. 1727, of the declines of age, Swift says, "yet they were intended by the author of our being to wean us gradually from our fondness of life, the nearer we approach toward the end of it". Cf. also, Dryden, *State of Innoc.*, V i:

> Thus, daily changing, with a duller taste
> Of lessening joys, I, by degrees, would waste:
> Still quitting ground, by unperceiv'd decay,
> And steal myself from life, and melt away.

260. *To . . . death*] Dryden's *Lucret.*, III 258: "[Democritus] Made haste to welcome death and met him half the race."

261-70. Cf. Sidney, *Apologie for Poetrie* (*Eliz. Crit. Ess.*, ed. G. Smith, I 150); Shaks., *Sonn.*, XCI 1-6:

> Some glory in their birth, some in their skill,
> Some in their wealth, some in their body's force,
> Some in their garments, though new-fangled ill;
> Some in their hawkes and hounds, some in their horse;
> And every humour hath his adjunct pleasure,
> Wherein it finds a joy above the rest;

S. Daniel, *Musophilus*, 406*ff*; Congreve, *Of Pleasing. An Epist. to Sir Rich. Temple*, 1-6; Chudleigh, *Ess.*, pp. 35-6; Neh. Grew, *Cosmol. Sacra* (1701), III ii 53, 56; *Spectat.*, 47; *Guardian*, 11; *Examen Miscellaneum* (1702), p. 119: "Providence has furnish'd every Condition with a Refuge of Satisfaction; the present Possession of Riches, and Honours, attones to the Fool for want of Sense; and the Man of Wit and Sense, pleases himself that he is no Fool in Cloath of Gold. The Thredbare Author is content to reflect, that the Rich Miser dies in a short

Not one will change his neighbor with himself.
The learn'd is happy nature to explore,
The fool is happy that he knows no more;
The rich is happy in the plenty giv'n,   265
The poor contents him with the care of Heav'n.
See the blind beggar dance, the cripple sing,
The sot a hero, lunatic a king;
The starving chemist in his golden views
Supremely blest, the poet in his muse.   270
      See some strange comfort ev'ry state attend,
And Pride bestow'd on all, a common friend;
See some fit Passion ev'ry age supply,

263 is] are *1733–34b*.   265 is] are *1733–34b*.
266 contents him] contented *1735c–43a*.

time, and that all his Honour and Glory is bury'd with him in the same
Grave, while he outlives Ages . . .; and so thro' other Conditions."
    262. Erasmus, *Ciceronianus* (*Opera*, Leyden, 1703, I 1022): ". . . haud scio an
si liceat ita permittente Deo multos inventuri simus, qui totam corporis sui
speciem velint cum aliena commutare, multo pauciores arbitror fore, qui
mentem et ingenium totum cum alterius ingenio sint permutaturi." Cf. G.-B.
Gelli, *Circe* (tr. T. Brown, 1702), p. 226.
    264. Prov. xv 21: "Folly is joy to him that is destitute of wisdom . . ."; Prior,
To . . . Charles Montague, 35–6.
    266. Psa., LXVIII 10, CXL 12; Matt., v 3; Jas., II 5; and cf. Swift, IV 209:
". . . your reward in Heaven is much more certain than it is to the rich, . . . for
yours is the Kingdom of Heaven."
    267–70. Cf. *Dunc.* A, III 7–12.
    272. Warton quotes La Rochefoucauld, I xxxvii: "It looks like an Indulgence
of Nature to give us pride, that . . . we might be delivered from the trouble of
knowing our own imperfections." Cf. also, Pascal, p. 174: "Our Pride is alone
a Counterpoise to all our Miseries; because it either conceals them, or glories in
their Discovery"; Edw. Young. *Love of Fame*, I 203–4:
          Pride, that impartial passion, reigns through all,
          Attends our glory, nor deserts our fall.
    273. A standard conception in the theory of passions. Cf. Coeffeteau,
pp. 654–5: ". . . there is not any age nor condition which doth not feele some
effects, and is not in some sort agitated [by passions]. Onely there is this difference, that the one haue a feeling of one sort, and the other of another. . . For
some are Passions befitting young men; others are incident to men of perfect
age; and some are those of olde men . . ."

M

Hope travels thro', nor quits us when we die.
   Behold the child, by Nature's kindly law,   275
Pleas'd with a rattle, tickled with a straw:
Some livelier play-thing gives his youth delight,
A little louder, but as empty quite:
Scarfs, garters, gold, amuse his riper stage;
And beads and pray'r-books are the toys of age: 280
Pleas'd with this bauble still, as that before;
'Till tir'd he sleeps, and Life's poor play is o'er!

275–82 *Add. 1743b, 1751.*

---

274. Wakefield cites Cato's *Distichs*, II 25: "Spem retine! spes una hominem nec morte relinquit"; cf. Coeffeteau, p. 514: ". . . most men liue by Hope, . . . this *Passion* never abandoning any man until he goes to the graue"; John Fletcher, *The Captain*, II i; J. Bodenham, *Politeuphia* (1674), p. 238; La Rochefoucauld, I clxix.

275–82. Cf. Horace, *Ars Poet.*, 158*ff*; Shaks., *As You Like It*, II vii 139*ff*. EC quotes Garth, *Dispens.*, v 101*ff*:

   Children at toys, as men at titles aim,
   And in effect both covet but the same.
   This Philip's son prov'd in revolving years,
   And first for rattles, then for worlds, shed tears.

Pattison compares Hutcheson, p. 131: "We once knew the time when an *Hobby-Horse*, a *Top*, a *Rattle*, was sufficient Pleasure to us. We grow up, we now relish *Friendships, Honour, good Offices, Marriage, Offspring*, serving a Community or a *Country*." Cf. also Jonson, *Timber*, ed. Schelling (Boston, 1892), pp. 46–7; Dryden, *All For Love*, IV i; *Spectat.*, 626; and Pope to Atterbury [May?] 1723 (EC IX 58): "What is every year of a wise man's life but a censure or critic on the past. Those whose date is the shortest, live long enough to laugh at one half of it: the boy despises the infant, the man the boy, the philosopher both, and the Christian all. You may now begin to think your manhood was too much a puerility: and you will never suffer your age to be but a second infancy. The toys and baubles of your childhood are hardly now more below you, than those toys of our riper and declining years, the drums and rattles of ambition, and the dirt and bubbles of avarice."

276. *Pleas'd . . . rattle*] R. Gould, *Satyr upon Man* (*Poems* (1689), p. 219): "Shake but a *Rattle* and the *Bratt* is pleas'd."

279. *Scarfs*] The badge of doctors of divinity [EC; Pattison].

280. In the "five acts" of life as seen by Sorbière (*Sorberiana, ou Bons Mots . . . de M. Sorbière*, Paris, 1694, p. 225), the fifth is "La Pieté et le Repos."

282. Temple, I 249: "When all is done, Human Life is, at the greatest, and

Mean-while Opinion gilds with varying rays
Those painted clouds that beautify our days;
Each want of happiness by Hope supply'd,   285
And each vacuity of sense by Pride:
These build as fast as knowledge can destroy;
In Folly's cup still laughs the bubble, joy;
One prospect lost, another still we gain;
And not a vanity is giv'n in vain;   290

---

283 Mean-while] 'Till then, *1733–43a*.
287 as fast as] up all that *1733–34b*.

---

the best but like a froward Child, that must be play'd with and humour'd a
little to keep it quiet till it falls asleep, and then the Care is over." Cf. Richardson Pack, *Miscell. in Pr. and Verse* (2nd ed., 1719), p. 29:

> Till tir'd, at length, with Change, and out of Breath,
> We close the *Scene*, and shut up all in *Death*;

and A. Hill, *Distinction of Ages*, 18.

Life's poor play] *Macbeth*, v v 25: "Life's but . . . a poor player."

283–4. Erasmus, pp. 91–2: ". . . the Happiness of men . . . onely depends
upon Opinion . . . ; the mind of man is so fram'd that it is rather taken with false
colours than truth . . ." Cf. Bacon, *Of Truth*; Esprit, p. 65; Waller, *On the Mis-
report of her being painted*, 21–2:

> With the same art wherewith [Heaven] gildeth so
> Those painted clouds which form Thaumantias' bow;

J. Hughes, *Ode to the Creator of the World*, st. 9: "Your clouds of painted bliss";
Sedley, *The Happy Pair* (*Wks.*, 1722, I 17); Edw. Young, *Love of Fame*, II 15–16.

285. Shaks., *Meas. for Meas.*, III i 2–3; Coeffeteau, p. 522; Cowley, *For Hope*,
1–2; *Examen Miscellaneum* (1702), p. 172; E. Young, *Vindic. of Prov.* (2nd ed.,
1728), pp. 23–4.

286. Cf. *E. on C.*, 209–10 and *Misc. Thoughts* (EC, x 551): "Every man has
just as much vanity as he wants understanding." Also, Temple, I 165:
". . . [Man's] Pride is greater than his Ignorance; and what he wants in Knowledge he supplies by Sufficiency."

288. *bubble*] The word takes on additional meaning from its common early
senses—"deceptive show" and "dupe".

289. Cf. *Ess.*, II 123–4.

290. Cf. Wollaston's *Design of Part of . . . Ecclesiastes* (1691), p. 25:

> To every thing some end does appertain
> (Not *Vanity* itself was made in *vain*).

Ev'n mean Self-love becomes, by force divine,
The scale to measure others wants by thine.
See! and confess, one comfort still must rise,
'Tis this, Tho' Man's a fool, yet GOD IS WISE.

291–2. See farther of the Use of this *Principle* in Man. Epist. 3. Ver. 121, 124, 134, 144, 199, &c. And Epist. 4. Ver. 358, and 368. [P. *1735b–43a.*]

Cf. Tillotson, *Sermon Preach'd . . . at Cripple-Gate, about . . . 1660* (1709), pp. 2–3: ". . . every Man can take his own Actions, and put them into the other Scale, and suppose, if this that I now do to another were to be done to me, should I like it? . . . And thus by changing the Scale, his own Self-Love, and Self-Interest, and other Passions, will add nothing to the weight; for that Self-Interest . . . makes him likewise (when the Scales are chang'd) unwilling that another Man should wrong him . . ."; *Reflexions on Man* (1733), pp. 116–17.

294. Cf. Rom. XVI 27: "To God only wise . . ."; and Erasmus, p. 158: "But more ingenuously does Jeremiah in his tenth chapter confess it, saying, 'Every man is made a fool through his own wisdome'; attributing wisedom to God alone, and leaving folly to all men else. . . Agen, that wise Preacher [in Ecclesiastes] that said, 'A fool changes as the Moon, but a wise man is permanent as the Sun', what else did he hint at in it, but that all mankind are fools, and the name of Wise onely proper to God? . . . with which agrees that which Christ himself in the Gospel denies, that any one is to be call'd good but one, and that is God."

ARGUMENT of the THIRD EPISTLE[1]

Of the Nature and State of Man, *with respect to* Society.

I. THE *whole Universe one system of Society,* VER. 7, &c. *Nothing made wholly for* itself, *nor yet wholly for* another, VER. 27. *The happiness of* Animals *mutual,* VER. 49. II. Reason *or* Instinct *operate alike to the good of each Individual,* VER. 79. Reason *or* Instinct *operate also to Society, in all animals,* VER. 109. III. *How   5 far* Society *carried by Instinct,* VER. 115. *How much farther by Reason,* VER. 131. IV. *Of that which is called the* State of Nature, VER. 147. *Reason instructed by Instinct in the invention of* Arts, VER. 171, *and in the Forms of* Society, VER. 179. V. *Origin of Political Societies,* VER. 199. *Origin of Monarchy,* VER. 209. 10 *Patriarchal government,* VER. 215. VI. *Origin of true Religion and Government, from the same principle, of Love,* VER. 231, &c. *Origin of Superstition and Tyranny, from the same principle, of Fear,* VER. 241, &c. *The Influence of Self-love operating to the* social *and* public *Good,* VER. 269. *Restoration of true Religion and Government on their* 15 *first principle,* VER. 283. *Mixt Government,* VER. 294. *Various Forms of each, and the true end of all,* VER. 303, &c.

---

1. See the note on the "Argument" of Epistle 1.

EPISTLE III

Here then we rest: "The Universal Cause
"Acts to one end, but acts by various laws."
In all the madness of superfluous health,
The trim of pride, the impudence of wealth,
Let this great truth be present night and day;   5
But most be present, if we preach or pray.
     Look round our World; behold the chain of Love
Combining all below and all above.

---

1 Here then we rest] Learn Dulness, learn! *1733–34b*.
4 the impudence] and Impudence *1733–35a*.
5 this] that *1733–34b*.
6 we] thou *1733–34b*.
7 Look round our] View thy own *1733–34b*.

Epistle III. Of the Nature and State of Man with respect to Society.
[P. *1735b–43a*.]
     1*ff*. The whole Universe one System of Society. [P. *1735b–43a*.]
     2. *one end*] The "gen'ral good", as in 14, below.
     4. *the . . . wealth*] Cf. *Imit. Hor.*, *Sat.*, ii ii 117, and *Donne*, ii 46.
     7–26. An influential group of concepts in traditional "poetic" metaphysics:
cf. for some of its best-known literary versions, Ovid, *Metam.*, xv 237*ff*; Boethius,
De cons. phil., ii m. 8, iv, pr. vi; Chaucer, *Knightes Tale*, 2129*ff*; and Dryden, *Pal.
and Arc.*, iii 1024–33:
> The Cause and Spring of motion, from above,
> Hung down on earth the golden chain of love.
> Great was th' effect, and high was his intent,
> When peace among the jarring seeds he sent.
> Fire, flood, and earth, and air by this were bound,
> And love, the common link, the new creation crown'd.
> The chain still holds; for tho' the forms decay,
> Eternal matter never wears away.
> The same First Mover certain bounds has plac'd,
> How long those perishable forms shall last.

     7. *Look . . . World*] Dryden's Juvenal, *Sat.*, x 1: "Look round the habitable
world . . ."

See plastic Nature working to this end,
The single atoms each to other tend,   10
Attract, attracted to, the next in place
Form'd and impell'd its neighbour to embrace.
See Matter next, with various life endu'd,
Press to one centre still, the gen'ral Good.
See dying vegetables life sustain,   15
See life dissolving vegetate again:
All forms that perish other forms supply,

 9 See, lifeless Matter moving to one End *1733.*
13 See Matter next] Behold it next *1733.*

9. *plastic Nature*] The informing and forming power of God, as manifested in
the creativity of nature: cf. the *natura naturans* of the Schools. The term was variously used in the 17th century, but usually to emphasize, in Tulloch's phrase
(*Rational Theol. in the 17th Cent.*, II 273), "the breath of the Divine in every part
of nature". Cf. Cudworth, *Intell. Syst. of the Univ.* (1678), III xxxvii 25; E. A.
Burtt, *Metaphys. Foundations of Physics* (1932), pp. 133*ff*; and J. W. Beach, *Concept of Nature in 19th Cent. Engl. Poetry* (1936), pp. 55*ff*.
   11–12. Cf. Dryden's Ovid, *Metam.*, I 29–30:
         Thus disembroil'd they [the elements] take their proper place;
         The next of kin contiguously embrace.
   12. *neighbour . . . embrace*] A locution emphasizing unity through love at the
inanimate level: cf. III 123. As McKillop notes (*Background of Thomson's
Seasons*, 1942, pp. 34*ff*), Augustan poets commonly interpreted Newtonian
"attractionism" in moral and human terms.
   13. Cf. *Par. Lost*, v 469–71:
                              . . . one first matter all,
         Endued with various forms, various degrees
         Of substance, and in things that live, of life.
   14. *Press . . . centre*] Alluding to the supposed movement of matter to earth's
centre.
   15–18. Warton quotes Shaftesbury, II 214: "Thus in the several Orders of
terrestrial Forms, *a Resignation* is requir'd, a Sacrifice and mutual yielding of
Natures one to another. The Vegetables by their Death sustain the Animals:
and Animal Bodys dissolv'd, enrich the Earth . . . Man . . . in his turn . . .
resigns his Form a Sacrifice in common to the rest of Things"; Pattison compares Lucretius, II 67*ff*.
   17. Cf. Sandys' Ovid, *Metam.*, xv 271–2:
         None holds his owne: for Nature euer ioyes
         In change, and with new formes the old supplies.

(By turns we catch the vital breath, and die)
Like bubbles on the sea of Matter born,
They rise, they break, and to that sea return.   20
Nothing is foreign: Parts relate to whole;
One all-extending, all-preserving Soul
Connects each being, greatest with the least;
Made Beast in aid of Man, and Man of Beast;
All serv'd, all serving! nothing stands alone;   25

---

18 we] they *1733-43a*. *1743b* is the first to place this line in brackets.
23 each] all *1733*.   24 Made] Makes *1739-43a*.
25 All serv'd, all] Each serv'd, and *1733*; All serv'd, and *1734a-35a*.

17-26. Cf. Ovid, *Metam.*, xv 237*ff*; Spenser, *F.Q.*, iii vi 37-8; Prior, i 349*ff*.
On the general social principle being stressed, cf. Burton, p. 58: ". . . how can
Man shut up himself within himself . . .? How can he do this, who considers the
World, and sees that the Universe it self subsists by reciprocation of Motions;
and there's nothing that receives, but makes returns; . . . if anything lose its own
Substance by Communication, yet it's found in something else; and by such
mutations the World continues."
    18. I.e. man is also subject to vicissitude.
    19-20. Pattison cites Leibniz [*Discours de la conformité de la foi avec la raison*]
viii; Hen. King, *Sic Vita*; and Young, *Love of Fame*, ii [285*ff*]:
                For what are men who grasp at fame sublime,
                But bubbles on the rapid stream of time.
                That rise, that fall, that swell, and are no more,
                Born and forgot, ten thousand in an hour?
Cf. also Lucian, *Charon* (*Wks.*, tr. Loeb, ii 435): "Let me tell you, Hermes,
what I think men and the whole life of man resemble. You have noticed bubbles
in water . . .? Some of them, being small, burst and are gone in an instant, while
some last longer . . . but in any case they all must burst"; Jer. Taylor's elabora-
tion of Lucian's figure in *Holy Dying*, i i; and Palingen., x 720*ff*; Beaumont and
Fletcher, *Mad Lover*, ii i; *Plain Dealer*, 114; Prior, iii 582.
    21-2. Thompson quotes Dryden's *Aen.*, vi 982-3: "one common soul Inspires
and feeds and animates the whole."
    23. Bowles cites Virgil, *Aen.*, vi [726-7].
    25. Cf. the quotation from Davies of Hereford in Introd., p. xlix; Tenison,
Sermon against Self-Love (1689), p. 19: "God hath disposed all things in mutual
subserviency to one another . . ."; *Reflexions on Man* (1733), p. 77: ". . . every
sort of creatures, according to the rank they obtain in nature, enjoys the useful-
ness of those below them, at the same time they are subservient to the happiness
of superior animals . . ."

The chain holds on, and where it ends, unknown.
    Has God, thou fool! work'd solely for thy good,
Thy joy, thy pastime, thy attire, thy food?
Who for thy table feeds the wanton fawn,
For him as kindly spread the flow'ry lawn.   30
Is it for thee the lark ascends and sings?
Joy tunes his voice, joy elevates his wings:
Is it for thee the linnet pours his throat?
Loves of his own and raptures swell the note:
The bounding steed you pompously bestride,   35
Shares with his lord the pleasure and the pride:

30 spread] spreads *1733–35a*.

---

26. Cf. Browne, *Relig. Med.*, I xxxiii.
    The . . . on] Cf. Dryden's phrasing in *Pal. and Arc.*, III 1030, quoted above at
III 7–26n.
    27*ff*. Nothing made wholly for *Itself*, nor yet wholly for *another*, but the
Happiness of all animals *mutual*. [P. *1735b–43a*.]
    Cf. Psa., CIV 10–30, where God's provision for the wants of animals is em-
phasized, and Gen., I 29–30; Job, XXXVIII 39, 41; Matt., VI 26; and see Pope's
Il., XV 311n. For the kind of view Pope is opposing, see Nemesius, *Nature of Man*
(tr. Wither, 1636), p. 64, and for the view Pope adopts, compare Topsell, leaf
A 4v: ". . . next unto Man are these Creatures rankt in dignity, and they were
ordained by God to live upon the same earth, and to be Fellow-commoners with
Man; having all the Plants and Vegetables appointed them for their food as
well as Man had . . ." Cf. also King, p. 91n [Warton and Pattison]: "Some
[creatures] manifestly serve for the food and support of others, . . . and may at
the same time be happy in a Consciousness of their own Existence. . . Nay, Man
himself contributes to the Happiness, and betters the Condition of the Brutes in
several respects; by cultivating and improving the Ground, by watching the
Seasons, by protecting and providing for them, when they are unable to protect
and provide for themselves;" and J. Clarke, *Enquiry into the Cause and Origin of
Evil* (1720), in *BLS*, III 207. As his illustrations show, Pope's argument in this
passage is both that man is made for the animals as well as the animals for man,
and that animals are made for themselves as well as for men.
    29–30. "The word *spreads* in the latter verse, as allusive to *table* in the former,
is eminently happy" [Wakefield]. And cf. the equivoque in *flowery lawn*.
    33. "Note the exquisite refinement by which *to pour his note* [the usual
locution] is raised into *pours his throat*" [Pattison].
    35–6. So Prior's "generous horse" (I 204*ff*) submits to "man's inferior force"
because "Pleas'd with his weight, and proud of his command". And cf. I 61–2n,
the passage from Pope's letter to Martha Blount.

Is thine alone the seed that strews the plain?
The birds of heav'n shall vindicate their grain:
Thine the full harvest of the golden year?
Part pays, and justly, the deserving steer: 40
The hog, that plows not nor obeys thy call,
Lives on the labours of this lord of all.

    Know, Nature's children all divide her care;
The fur that warms a monarch, warm'd a bear.
While Man exclaims, "See all things for my use!"   45
"See man for mine!" replies a pamper'd goose;
And just as short of Reason he must fall,

45–6 *Om. quotation marks 1733.*
46 *Between ll. 46–47, 1733–34b have four lines:*
    What care to tend, to lodge, to cram, to treat him,
    All this he knew; but not that 'twas to eat him.
      As far as Goose could judge, he reason'd right,
    But as to Man, mistook the Matter quite;
47 he must] Man will *1733–36.*

    1735a–43a om. the second couplet above and print the first with knows
for knew *and* 'tis *for* 'twas.

    39–40. Cf. Deut., xxv 4; 1 Tim., v 18; and T. Tenison, *Sermon against Self-Love* (1689), p. 19: "There is not . . . a mear Ox that treads out the corn meerly for his own Service . . ." Tenison's application is the reverse of Pope's, but his point is the same, that "God hath disposed all things in mutual subserviency to one another." Cf. also the comment of the horse in Gay, *Council of Horses*, 57–8:
        He sows, he reaps the harvest's gain,
        We share the toil and share the grain.
    39. *golden year*] Dryden's *Aen.*, ii 409: "the yellow year".
    40. *deserving steer*] Cf. Virgil, *Geo.*, ii 515: "meritosque iuvencos" [Wakefield].
    43. Gay, *Council of Horses*, 51: "But doth not [man] divide the care?"
    44. Cf. Lucian, *Demonax*, xli (*Wks.*, tr. Loeb, i 163–4): "On seeing an aristocrat who set great store on the breadth of his purple band, Demonax, taking hold of the garment . . ., said in his ear: 'A sheep wore this before you, and he was but a sheep for all that!' "; and Buchanan's epigram, *In amicum quendam* (*Poemata*, Amsterdam, 1689, pp. 355–6).
    45–6. *Adventurer* cites Charron [1 xl]. EC quotes Montaigne, ii 329: "For why may not a *Goose* say thus, . . . I am the Darling of Nature? Is it not Man that treats, lodges, and serves me?" Carruthers compares Gay's fable *The Man and the Flea*, and Wakefield, Cowley's *Plagues of Aegypt*, st. 1:
        All Creatures the Creator said Were Thine:
        No Creature but might since say, "Man is Mine!"

Who thinks all made for one, not one for all.
   Grant that the pow'rful still the weak controul,
Be Man the Wit and Tyrant of the whole: 50
Nature that Tyrant checks; he only knows,
And helps, another creature's wants and woes.
Say, will the falcon, stooping from above,
Smit with her varying plumage, spare the dove?
Admires the jay the insect's gilded wings?   55
Or hears the hawk when Philomela sings?
Man cares for all: to birds he gives his woods,

52 helps] feels *1733–35a.*

48. The point is made again, with reference to political relationships, at III 241ff.

49–52. Cf. Montaigne, II 164–5: "But when amongst the more moderate Opinions, I meet with Arguments, that endeavour to demonstrate the near resemblance betwixt us and Animals, how much they share in our greatest Priviledges, and with how great probability they compare and couple us together, in earnest, I abate a great deal of our presumption, and willingly let fall the Title of that imaginary Sovereignty, that some attribute to us over other Creatures. But supposing all this were true, there is nevertheless a certain Respect, and a general Duty of Humanity, that ties us not only to Beasts that have Life and Sense, but even to Trees and Plants. We owe Justice to Men, and Grace and Benignity to other Creatures that are capable of it. There is a certain Natural Commerce, and Mutual Obligation betwixt them and us . . ."

50. Cf. *Ess.*, I 231–2. Psa., VIII 6–8.
Wit] The only intellectual being in the terrestrial system.

51–2. For the idea that nature gave compassion to man only, cf. Juvenal, *Sat.*, XV 131ff.

53–6. The traditional belief that man alone has sense of beauty: cf. Cicero, *De off.*, I iv 14; Bossuet, *De la connaissance de Dieu et de Soi-Même* (*Œuvres*, Paris, 1862, I 96).

57–66. Cf. Montaigne, II 206: "To what Solicitude do we not submit for their Convenience. I do not think, that Servants of the most abject Condition would willingly do that for their Masters, that Princes think it an Honor to do for their Beasts. *Diogenes* seeing his Relations solicitous to redeem him from Servitude: *They are Fools*, said he, *'tis that which treats, and nourishes, and that serves me*; and they who make so much of Beasts, ought rather to be said to serve them, than to be served by them."

57. *Man . . . gives*] Gay, *Council of Horses*, 45–6:
           Now grateful man rewards my pains
           And gives me all these wide domains.

To beasts his pastures, and to fish his floods;
For some his Int'rest prompts him to provide,
For more his pleasure, yet for more his pride: 60
All feed on one vain Patron, and enjoy
Th'extensive blessing of his luxury.
That very life his learned hunger craves,
He saves from famine, from the savage saves;
Nay, feasts the animal he dooms his feast,   65
And, 'till he ends the being, makes it blest;
Which sees no more the stroke, or feels the pain,
Than favour'd Man by touch etherial slain.

67–8 *1733 reverses the present order of these lines and reads:* The . . .
slain, Not less foresees . . . Pain.

---

59. Emphasized in G.-B. Gelli's *Circe* (tr T. Brown, 1702), p. 62. Cf. also
Locke, *Civil Govt.*, II vii 93: ". . . every man, who loves his own power, profit, or
greatness, may, and naturally must . . . keep those animals from hurting or
destroying one another, who labour and drudge only for his pleasure and
advantage; and so [they] are taken care of, not out of any love the master has
for them, but love of himself, and the profit they bring him."

63–6. Cf. *Reflexions on Man* (1733), p. 78: ". . . it does not appear unequal
that creatures, who are so much beholden to our care for the comfort of their
life . . ., should sometimes lose it for our subsistence . . ."

63–4. J. Clarke, *Enquiry into the Cause and Origin of Evil* (1720) in *BLS*, III 207:
"Were such Creatures left wholly to themselves, there are innumerable Acci-
dents by which many of them would be destroyed; . . . Whereas in the present
Circumstances, all the Art and Industry of Man is made Use of . . . to give them
Meat in due Season, and to secure them against all those Dangers . . ."

64. *savage*] Cf. III 168*n*.

65–6. King, p. 118: "An Ox, for instance, or a Calf, is bred, nourished, and
protected for some time, in order to become fit Food for Man." Cf. Hill, *The
Happy Man*, 9–10:

> The grateful herds, which his own pastures feed,
> Pay their ask'd lives, and in due tribute bleed.

67. Cf. *Ess.*, I 81*ff*; King, p. 119: ". . . Animals are ignorant of Futurity . . . So
that . . . they rejoyce in the present Good, and are neither tormented with the
Remembrance of what is past, nor the Fear of what is to come; and lastly, are
kill'd with less Pain than they would be by a Distemper or old Age"; and J.
Clarke, *Enquiry into the Cause and Origin of Evil* (1720), in *BLS*, III 207.

68. Several of the Ancients, and many of the Orientals at this day, esteem'd
those who were struck by Lightning as sacred Persons, and the particular

The creature had his feast of life before;
Thou too must perish, when thy feast is o'er! 70
   To each unthinking being, Heav'n a friend,
Gives not the useless knowledge of its end:
To Man imparts it; but with such a view
As, while he dreads it, makes him hope it too:
The hour conceal'd, and so remote the fear, 75
Death still draws nearer, never seeming near.
Great standing miracle! that Heav'n assign'd
Its only thinking thing this turn of mind.
   II. Whether with Reason, or with Instinct blest,

Favourites of Heaven. [P. *1734a–51, but 1735a has* more modern Orientals esteem'd *for* Orientals . . . day, *and 1735b–51 have since for* at this day.]

  See Holyday's Juvenal (1673), *Sat.*, VI, n. 72: ". . . they believ'd that such bodies [of those struck by lightning] did not putrefie; and as foolishly thought such persons to be honour'd by *Jupiter*"; and Pope's epitaph on John Hughes and Sarah Drew (vol. VI).

  touch ethereal] Milton uses the same phrase (*Sams. Agon.*, 549), of waters— "translucent, pure With touch ethereal of Heav'n's fiery rod" [Wakefield].

  70. Cf. Lucret., III 938–9, and Dryden's transl., III 130–1:
     Why dost not thou give thanks as at a plenteous feast,
     Cramm'd to the throat with life, and rise and take thy rest?

  71–8. Cf. I 77*ff.*

  75–8. Cf. Aristotle, *Rhet.*, 1382a; Plutarch, I 309; Hen. Vaughan's transl. of Nierembergius' *Life and Death*, in *Flor. Solitud.* (*Wks.*, ed. L. C. Martin, 1914, I 297): "The certainty of it [death], and the incertainty of the time and manner, . . . deserves to be . . . most pleasing and acceptable; for amongst all the wondrous Ordinances of Divine providence, there is none more Excellent for the Government of man than Death, being so wisely disposed of, that in the height of incertainty, it comprehends and manifests an infallible certainty"; *Guardian*, 18. Pattison cites Bulstrode, *Essays* (1715), p. 384.

  77. "The *miracle* . . . is that while man is the only animal whose faculties enable him to apprehend the certain approach of death, his action is not paralysed by it" [Pattison].

  78. *thinking thing*] Cf. Temple (I 309): "Man is a thinking Thing, whether he will or no . . ." [EC]; Pascal, p. 171: "Man is a Reed . . .; but then he is a thinking Reed."

  79*ff. Reason* or *Instinct* alike operate for the good of each *Individual*, and they operate also to SOCIETY, in *all Animals*. [P. *1735b–43a, but 1739–43a omit* they.]

  79. I.e. whether man or animal.

> Know, all enjoy that pow'r which suits them best;   80
> To bliss alike by that direction tend,
> And find the means proportion'd to their end.
> Say, where full Instinct is th'unerring guide,
> What Pope or Council can they need beside?
> Reason, however able, cool at best,   85
> Cares not for service, or but serves when prest,
> Stays 'till we call, and then not often near;
> But honest Instinct comes a volunteer;

80 them] 'em *1733–43a.*

---

82. Cf. 1 183, and Prior, 1 230: "[Animals] use the means proportion'd to their end."

83–98. Pope throughout adopts the orthodox view of instinct as the direct power of God acting in animals (cf. Aquinas, *Sum. theol.*, 1 ii, q.xiii, a.2), and therefore superior in its accuracy to reason. See the attacks on "theriophily" discussed by G. Boas in *The Happy Beast* (1933), ch. vi; and J. B. Piobetta, *Pierre Chanet* (1937), chs. iii, v. Cf. also Charron (1 282–3), who opposes the orthodox position partly because not to allow the faculty of reason to beasts is impiously to exalt them—it being a "nearer Resemblance to God himself . . . To be led by the Unerring Hand of God, than left to our own imprudent Conduct, and to act Regularly, by an Habitual, and Constant, and Necessary Impulse, than by such a Choise and Liberty, as is subject to Hazard and Rashness"; and cf. Montaigne, ii 195. One advantage of the orthodox doctrine was that it could be used both to elevate man's position (cf. *Ess.*, 1 173–232 and notes) and to point its limitations, as here; and cf. Boileau, *Sat.*, viii; G.-B. Gelli, *Circe, passim*; Swift, *The Logicians Refuted*, 11–18:

> [I] must in spite of them, maintain,
> That man and all his ways are vain;
> And that this boasted lord of nature
> Is both a weak and erring creature;
> That instinct is a surer guide
> Than reason, boasting mortals' pride;
> And that brute beasts are far before 'em.
> *Deus est anima brutorum.*

83. Granville, *Heroick Love*, iii i:

> Instinct of Nature is the only Guide
> Unerring. Vain Light of Reason! Ah how frail!

84. *Council*] "The Roman Catholic council, which claims to be infallible" [EC].

86*ff.* Pattison calls attention to the military metaphor.

Sure never to o'er-shoot, but just to hit,
While still too wide or short is human Wit;   90
Sure by quick Nature happiness to gain,
Which heavier Reason labours at in vain.
This too serves always, Reason never long;
One must go right, the other may go wrong.
See then the acting and comparing pow'rs   95
One in their nature, which are two in ours,
And Reason raise o'er Instinct as you can,
In this 'tis God directs, in that 'tis Man.
  Who· taught the nations of the field and wood
To shun their poison, and to chuse their food?   100

89–92 *Add. 1743b, 1751.*
99 wood] wood *in all editions (and in the MSS.), but corrected to* flood
on the errata slip of 1736.

91–2. To attribute animal acts to instinct, Montaigne argues (II 195), is to suppose "Nature, with a maternal Sweetness, to accompany and lead them, as it were, by the hand, . . . whilst she leaves us to Chance and Fortune, . . . so that their Brutish Stupidity surpasses, in all Conveniences, all that our Divine Intelligence can do." In Boileau's 5th Satire, the ass, "Sans avoir la raison, . . . marche sur sa route", while man, "qu'elle éclaire, en plein jour ne voit goutte".

95. Cf. II 59–60.

96. For the same idea applied to God, cf. Browne, *Relig. Med.*, I xiii: ". . . consultation and election, which are two motions in us, make but one in him."

98. Pattison notes that this is received scholastic opinion: cf. III 83–98n. EC compares *Spectat.*, 121.

99–108. "The effects of animal instinct may be employed as evidence either of a contriving mind, or of a providential care, in the Creator. They are here adduced in neither point of view, but to show the equable distribution of the means by which the great end of the universe is attained; that means being, reason in man, instinct in animals" [Pattison]. The verbs chosen underline the kinship of animal with human activities.
  These and similar instances of animal sagacity form one of the favourite themes of Augustan physico-theology. For the *who* formula specifically, cf. I 31–4n.

100. So Prior says of the lower creatures that they "Abhor the poison and receive the food" (I 226): and cf. Charleton, pp. 41–2; *Spectat.*, 121; John Leng, *Natural Obligations to believe . . . Religion* (1719), in *BLS*, III 65.

Prescient, the tides or tempests to withstand,
Build on the wave, or arch beneath the sand?
Who made the spider parallels design,
Sure as De-moivre, without rule or line?
Who bid the stork, Columbus-like, explore   105
Heav'ns not his own, and worlds unknown before?

101–2. Evidently an allusion, in the first instance, to the supposed nesting habits of the halcyon, "on the wave" (cf. Plutarch, v 211–12, and Montaigne, ii 238), and in the second, to the reported nesting habits, "beneath the sand", of the kingfisher (cf. Willughby's *Ornithology*, 1678, p. 146), with which the halcyon was usually identified.

103–4. Cf. Topsell, p. 785: "Surely Euclides that famous Geometrician . . . need not be ashamed to learn from Spiders the drawing of divers of his figures and Geometricall proportions" (and cf. pp. 779, 1069); and Hill's *The Drone and the Cobweb*, in Savage's Miscellany (1726), p. 123:

> . . . with dextrous Skill
> He drew thin Rafters the cross'd Web to fill;
> All equidistant from their Center hung,
> And, justly rang'd, to the soft Beam-work clung;
> The Fabrick glow'd; intent, he wheel'd exact,
> And thready Joists, in angly Orbits tack'd;
> No juster cou'd the Artist's Compass twine,
> When his nice Hand wou'd sweep some circling Line.

103. *parallels*] *OED* notes that *parallel* as an adjective is sometimes applied to "curved lines . . . continuously equidistant . . . (e.g. concentric circles . . .)". I take this to be the meaning of the substantive here: cf. Hill's "equidistant" concentric circles, above; Bailey, *s.v.*; and *OED*, *s.v.* B 1, 1 and 2.

104. *De-moivre*] Demoivre, *an eminent Mathematician*. [P. *1739–43a*.] Abraham de Moivre (1667–1754), a French Protestant who settled in London after the revocation of the Edict of Nantes, interested himself in mathematics, became a friend of Newton and member of the Royal Society, propounded what is to-day known as "De Moivre's Theorem" in trigonometry, and in his *Doctrine of Chances* (1718) contributed significantly to the theory of probability.

105–8. Cf. Jer., viii 7: "Yea, the stork in the heaven knoweth her appointed times . . ."; Pliny, *Hist. nat.* (tr. Holland, 1601), i 281: "[Cranes] put not themselves in their journey, nor set forward without a counsell called before, and a generall consent. . . a captain they chuse to conduct them, whom the rest follow. In the rereward behind there be certaine of them set and disposed to give signall . . . for to raunge orderly in rankes, and keepe close together in array . . ." Pattison compares *Par. Lost*, vii 425 ff.

106. So in Blackmore's description of the storks (*Prince Arthur*, 1695, p. 146):

Who calls the council, states the certain day,
Who forms the phalanx, and who points the way?
   III. God, in the nature of each being, founds
Its proper bliss, and sets its proper bounds: 110
But as he fram'd a Whole, the Whole to bless,
On mutual Wants built mutual Happiness:
So from the first eternal ORDER ran,
And creature link'd to creature, man to man.
Whate'er of life all-quick'ning æther keeps,   115

... through the Heav'ns their trackless Flight they take,
And for new Worlds, their present Seats forsake.

107. Pluche, *Spectacle de la nat.* (tr. 1760), I 198: "What particular bird takes the charge upon him of assembling their grand council, and fixing the day of their departure?" L. de Beaufort, *Cosmopoea Divina* (Leyden, 1656), 126–7.

108. *phalanx*] In allusion to the compactness and military discipline of the formation rather than its shape, which, as *points* shows, Pope knew to be triangular: cf. Milton's migratory birds (VII 426) "ranged in figure wedge"; Plutarch, V 175: ". . . forming a triangular body, with the sharp angle of that figure they penetrate the wind . . . and preserve their order unbroken"; and Cicero, *De nat. deor.*, II xlix 125. Du Bartas (1st wk, 5th day, 870*ff*) stresses the military discipline of cranes.

109–14. Pattison quotes Hooker, I iii 5: ". . . as [natural agents] . . . have their law, which law directeth them in the means whereby they tend to their own perfection: so likewise another law there is, which toucheth them as they are sociable parts united into one body; a law which bindeth them each to serve unto other's good, and all to prefer the good of the whole before whatsoever their own particular . . ."

109–10. Aristotle, *Eth. Nic.*, 1176a: "Each animal is thought to have a proper pleasure, as it has a proper function; viz. that which corresponds to its activity"; Aquinas, *Sum. c. gent.*, II lxxxii: "In everything that is able to attain to a certain perfection we find a natural desire for that perfection since *good is what all desire*, yet so that *each thing desires the good proper to it*"; *Par. Lost*, v 468–9.

114. *link'd*] Cf. III 7, the "chain" of love.

115*ff.* How far SOCIETY carry'd by INSTINCT. [P. *1735b–43a.*]

115. *æther*]. *OED* defines this as "the element breathed by the Gods", citing this line as the first instance of its use in this sense in English. For some account of the cluster of meanings around the word, see J. W. Beach, *Concept of Nat. in 19th Cent. Engl. Poetry* (1936), pp. 94*ff*, and for its "quickening" associations cf. Lucretius's designation of it (I 250) as *pater Aether*, and Pope's *Il.*, I 514*n*: "The ancient Philosophers supposed the *Aether* to be igneous, and by its kind Influence upon the *Air* to be the Cause of all Vegetation."

N

Or breathes thro' air, or shoots beneath the deeps,
Or pours profuse on earth; one nature feeds
The vital flame, and swells the genial seeds.
Not Man alone, but all that roam the wood,
Or wing the sky, or roll along the flood,   120
Each loves itself, but not itself alone,
Each sex desires alike, 'till two are one.
Nor ends the pleasure with the fierce embrace;

115-18. Cf. Virgil, *Geo.*, IV 219*ff.*, *Aen.*, VI 724*ff*, and the latter psssage in Dryden's version (VI 980*ff*):

> Know, first, that heav'n, and earth's compacted frame,
> And flowing waters, and the starry flame,
> And both the radiant lights, one common soul
> Inspires and feeds, and animates the whole.
> This active mind, infus'd thro' all the space,
> Unites and mingles with the mighty mass.
> Hence men and beasts the breath of life obtain,
> And birds of air, and monsters of the main.
> Th' ethereal vigor is in all the same,
> And every soul is fill'd with equal flame.

116. *shoots . . . deeps*] So in *Par. Lost* (III 585-6), the sun "Shoots invisible virtue even to the Deep."

117. *pours . . . earth*] Cf. *Par. Lost*, IV 242-3: "but nature boon Poured forth profuse on hill and dale and plain."

118. *The . . . flame*] Not merely a figure of speech in Pope's day. Cf. Chambers, art. Flame: "Vital Flame, Flamma or Flammula vitalis, a fine warm, igneous substance, supposed by many . . . to reside in the hearts of animals, as necessary to life, or rather, as that which constitutes life itself. . . Mr. Boyle found the *vital Flame* of animals, if life may be so called, survives or outlasts the *Flame* of spirit of wine, or of a wax or tallow candle"; Charleton, pp. 14-16, 25, 26, 30; Berkeley, *Siris* (1744), p. 205. Milton's Christ, at the Creation (*Par. Lost*, VII 236), "vital virtue infus'd and vital warmth."

genial] Above, I 133*n*.

119*ff.* Cf. Lucret., I 1*ff*; Palingen., V 484*ff.*

119-20. Creatures classified by the element they inhabit, as in I 233. For the phrasing, Pattison compares Boileau, *Sat.*, VIII 1-2:

> De tous les animaux qui s'élèvent dans l'air,
> Qui marchent sur la terre, ou nagent dans la mer.

123. *embrace*] Cf. III 12*n*.

They love themselves, a third time, in their race.
Thus beast and bird their common charge attend,   125
The mothers nurse it, and the sires defend;
The young dismiss'd to wander earth or air,
There stops the Instinct, and there ends the care;
The link dissolves, each seeks a fresh embrace,
Another love succeeds, another race.   130
A longer care Man's helpless kind demands;

124 They] All *1733*.
125 Thus beast and bird] The Beast, the Bird *1733*.

---

124. Cf. Aristotle, *Eth. Nic.*, 1161b: ". . . parents love their children as being a part of themselves . . ."; Aquinas, *Sum. theol.*, II ii, q.xxvi, a.9; Coeffeteau, pp. 286–7: "All men loue themselues, . . . and by consequence . . . are passionate . . . for their children who are (as wee may say) their owne workes"; Dryden, *Abs. and Achit.*, 425–6 [EC]:

> Our fond begetters, who would never die,
> Love but themselves in their posterity;

and A. Campbell, *Enquiry into the Orig. of Moral Virtue* (1728), pp. 240–50.

125–32. Cf. Aristotle, *Eth. Nic.*, 1162a: "Between man and wife friendship seems to exist by nature; for man is naturally inclined to form couples—even more than to form cities, inasmuch as the household is earlier and more necessary than the city, and reproduction is more common to man with the animals. With the other animals the union extends only to this point, but human beings live together not only for the sake of reproduction but also for the various purposes of life; for from the start the functions are divided, and those of man and woman are different; so they help each other by throwing their peculiar gifts into the common stock"; John Maxwell, *Promulg. of the Law of Nat.* (p. 137) in his translation of Cumberland: "Mankind are born in Families, constitute and live in Families, in which there is a constant Cohabitation of both Sexes for their mutual Help and Comfort, for the Propagation of their Species, and to take care of their Off-spring, (which continueth weak and feeble much longer than that of the Brutes, and therefore requireth a constant Cohabitation, and continual Care of the Parents): these Family Societies are plainly by the Order and Design of Nature, Mankind are manifestly design'd to live in Family-Societies, the first elementary Societies . . ."; *Plain Dealer*, 28; and Selby-Bigge, *Brit. Moralists*, II 246. On the currency of this set of ideas in Pope's time, see A. O. Lovejoy, "The Length of Human Infancy in 18th Cent. Thought", *Journ. of Philos.*, XIX (1922) 381–5.

131*ff.* How much farther SOCIETY is carry'd by REASON. [P. *1735b–43a*.]

That longer care contracts more lasting bands:
Reflection, Reason, still the ties improve,
At once extend the int'rest, and the love;
With choice we fix, with sympathy we burn;   135
Each Virtue in each Passion takes its turn;
And still new needs, new helps, new habits rise,
That graft benevolence on charities.

138 *Between ll. 138–139, 1733 has:*
        From private Sparkles raise the gen'ral Flame,
        And bid Self-Love and Social be the same.

132–46. Cf. Burton, p. 57: "And surely no Man can . . . consider the Affection of his Mother, and the Love and Pains of his Nurse, the Provision that his Father made for a supply of his present and future Wants; . . . but he must be constrained to make Returns, and to do to others, as himself hath been done to. . . What he is and hath, he hath received, and shall he not give? He hath been liberally dealt with, and shall he be niggardly to others? He owes himself, and all the Good in him to Love, and shall he not love?"

133. *Reflection*] Cf. I 225*n*; III 143*n*; Wollaston, p. 54, and Butler, *Fifteen Sermons*, I vii, viii: ". . . There is a principle of reflection in men, by which they distinguish between, approve, and disapprove their actions. . . Thus the parent has the affection of love to his children; this leads him to take care of, to educate, to make due provision for them; the natural affection leads to this: but the reflection that it is his proper business, what belongs to him, that it is right and commendable so to do; this added to the affection becomes a much more settled principle, and carries him on through more labour and difficulties for the sake of his children, than he would undergo from that affection alone . . ."

Reason] *Spectat.*, 181: "This instinct [family affection] in man is more general and uncircumscribed than in brutes, as being enlarged by the dictates of reason and duty."

135–46. Pope's point is that marriage ramifies into all the characteristic human relationships, affections, and hence virtues: cf. his *Chor. of Youths and Virgins*, st. 3 (see vol. VI) and Milton's praise of wedded love (IV 754–7), by which
        Founded in reason, loyal, just and pure,
        Relations dear, and all the charities
        Of father, son, and brother, first were known.

136. Cf. II 97–100, 183–4.

138. I.e. a general virtuous habit of mind on concrete natural affections. Cf. Cumberland, pp. 156–7: ". . . because the Offspring of Man continues *longer* weak, and in need of the help of its Parents, it is certain, that, thro' length of Time, and frequent *repeated* Acts of their Love, that Affection grows *stronger* in Parents; . . . and so the very *Difficulty* of forming Men . . . causes Parents to set

Still as one brood, and as another rose,
These nat'ral love maintain'd, habitual those: 140
The last, scarce ripen'd into perfect Man,
Saw helpless him from whom their life began:
Mem'ry and fore-cast just returns engage,
That pointed back to youth, this on to age;
While pleasure, gratitude, and hope, combin'd,   145
Still spread the int'rest, and preserv'd the kind.
    IV. Nor think, in NATURE'S STATE they blindly trod;
The state of Nature was the reign of God:
Self-love and Social at her birth began,

139 Still] Thus *1733*.

---

about it with a greater Earnestness and Industry, and daily to give much
greater Proofs of their natural Affection, than what are any where to be met
with other Animals.
    "All the *Indications*, deduc'd from this Head, are the *more carefully* to be
observ'd, because into it finally is to be resolv'd, both the reciprocal *Love of
Children toward their Parents*, and the *Benevolence of Relations* toward one another,
which will, at length, extend it self to a *Love of all Mankind* . . ."
    143. *Mem'ry and fore-cast*] Cumberland, p. 144, regards "Fancy and Mem-
ory" (with the first of which Pope's *forecast* may have some affinities) as the two
prime aids to prudence, which in turn "disposes to the Practice of *moral
Virtues*". And cf. Pope to Lord Oxford, 7 Nov. 1725: ". . . it is nature that makes
us love, but it is experience that makes us grateful. . . But, in truth, both what
good-natured minds have experienced, and what they expect to experience,
fills them to the brim. The better a man is, the more he expects and hopes from
his friend, his child, his fellow-creature; the more he reflects backwards and
aggrandises every good he has received."
    147*ff*. Of the STATE OF NATURE: That it was SOCIAL. [P. *1735b–43a*.]
    As F. C. Osenburg has noted (*The Ideas of the Golden Age and the Decay of the
World in the Engl. Ren.: Abstract of Thesis, Univ. of Illinois*, 1939, pp. 15*ff*), por-
traits of the golden age have been one of the traditional devices of poetic social
criticism, their artificiality arising from the studied arrangement of motifs to
emphasize the values rather than the plausibility of the imagined world. Pope's
portrait is a case in point.
    147–50. I.e. the state of nature was not a state of war, like Hobbes's, and not
without society and law, like Lucretius's, but much more like Locke's, which, as
Willey says (*17th Cent. Background*, p. 266), "approximates . . . the Golden Age of
the Poets".
    147, 148. *State*] With a play on the political meaning: cf. *reign*.

Union the bond of all things, and of Man.   150
Pride then was not; nor Arts, that Pride to aid;
Man walk'd with beast, joint tenant of the shade;
The same his table, and the same his bed;
No murder cloath'd him, and no murder fed.
In the same temple, the resounding wood,   155
All vocal beings hymn'd their equal God:

150. ". . . what cohesion of particles is in the material world, that, the social instinct is in the moral" [Pattison]. Cf. III 7*ff*, 313–14.

151–60. EC compares Montaigne, II 190: "*Plato*, in his Picture of the Golden Age under *Saturn* [*Politicus*, 271a*ff*] reckons, amongst the chief Advantages that a Man then had, his communication with Beasts, of whom inquiring and informing himself, he knew the true Qualities and differences of them all, by which he acquired a very perfect Intelligence and Prudence, and led his Life more happily, than we could do." Wakefield cites Hall's *Satires*, III i [42–5]:

> Then crept in pride, and peevish covetise,
> And men grew greedy, discordous, and nice.
> Now man, that erst hail-fellow was with beast,
> Woxe on to ween himself a God at least.

Cf. also Sidney's verses in *Arcadia* (*Wks.*, ed. Feuillerat, I 135):

> Thus Man was made; thus Man their Lord became:
> Who at the first, wanting, or hiding pride,
> He did to beastes best use his cunning frame;
> With water drinke, herbes meate, and naked hide,
> And fellow-like let his dominion slide;
> Not in his sayings saying I, but we:
> As if he meant his lordship common be.

For the background of this idea, see A. O. Lovejoy and G. Boas, *Primitivism . . . in Antiquity*, I (1935), pp. 20, 93, 96.

151. *nor . . . aid*] Cowley, *David.* II 347: "But *Arts of Pride* all *Nations* soon are taught."

154–68. For the *locus classicus* of this idea and the remainder of the passage, see Ovid's description of Pythagorean philosophy in *Metam.*, xv 75–142; and cf. Pope, *Guardian*, 61.

154. *No . . . him*] Elwin compares Dryden's *Metam.*, xv: "The warm and woolly fleece, that cloth'd her murderer"; but since it is the point of Pythagoras' argument that men can take fleeces from sheep without killing them, Pope's phrase is better understood as referring to skins.

155. *the resounding wood*] Wakefield compares Virgil's "*lucos sonantes*" (*Ecl.*, x 58) and Dryden's transl. (85), "sounding woods".

156. Pattison: "Perhaps suggested by Milton, *Par. Lost*, IV 675–6: 'nor think,

The shrine with gore unstain'd, with gold undrest,
Unbrib'd, unbloody, stood the blameless priest:
Heav'n's attribute was Universal Care,
And Man's prerogative to rule, but spare.   160
Ah! how unlike the man of times to come!
Of half that live the butcher and the tomb;
Who, foe to Nature, hears the gen'ral groan,
Murders their species, and betrays his own.
But just disease to luxury succeeds,   165
And ev'ry death its own avenger breeds;

---

though men were none That Heaven would want spectators, God want praise.' " Cf. Psa., CXLVIII 16. And cf. *Par. Lost*, IV 720-2.

equal] Cf. I 87*n*.

160. Cf. Dryden's *Metam.*, XV 153-4, 705-8:

> Take not away the life you cannot give;
> For all things have an equal right to live.
> Kill noxious creatures, where 'tis sin to save;
> This only just prerogative we have;

and Pope, *Guardian*, 61: "The more entirely the inferior creation is submitted to our Power, the more answerable we should seem for our mismanagement of it..."

161. Cf. the contrast between Gen., I 29-30 and IX 1-6; and the comment on this in A. S. Peake, *Commentary on the Bible* (1929), pp. 138 and 144.

162. Cf Lucret., V 993: "viva videns vivo sepeliri viscera busto"; Ovid's *Metam.*, XV 88: "heu quantum scelus est in viscera viscera condi"; Longinus, *On the Sublime*, III 4; Donne, *Progresse of the Soule*, st. 40; Sprat, *Plague of Athens*, st. 12: "As if the stomach were a tomb"; and *Imit. Hor., Sat.*, II ii 70.

163. *the . . . groan*] Perhaps reversed from Lucret., V 992-3, where the man whose living entrails are being enclosed in the living entrails of an animal "nemora ac montis gemitu silvas replebat."

164. *betrays . . . own*] Cf. Juvenal, *Sat.*, XV 163*ff*; and Rochester, *Satire Against Mankind*, 129-30:

> Birds feed on Birds, Beasts on each other prey;
> But savage Man, alone, does Man betray.

165-6. Cf. Pope, *Guardian*, 61: "Those who . . . divide their lives betwixt an anxious conscience and a nauseated stomach, have a just reward of their gluttony in the diseases it brings with it; for human savages, like other wild beasts, find snares and poisons in the provisions of life, and are allured by their appetite to their destruction."

The Fury-passions from that blood began,
And turn'd on Man a fiercer savage, Man.
    See him from Nature rising slow to Art!
To copy Instinct then was Reason's part;   170
Thus then to Man the voice of Nature spake—
"Go, from the Creatures thy instructions take:
"Learn from the birds what food the thickets yield;
"Learn from the beasts the physic of the field;

167-8. Wakefield cites Dryden's *Metam.* [xv 143-6]:
                Whoever was the Wretch (and curst be he)
                That envied first our food's simplicity,
                Th' essay of bloody feasts on brutes began,
                And after forg'd the sword to murther man.
Cf. also, Plutarch, v 158; Aquinas, *Sum. c. gent.*, III cxii; Montaigne, II 161-2;
Hume's note on *Par. Lost*, XII 30 (1695): ". . . Hunting being a preparatory
Exercise, . . . a *Preliminary* to the Slaughter of Mankind, by that of wild
Beasts . . ."
    168. Cf. Boileau, *Sat.*, VIII; Denham, *Friendship and Single Life*, 34-6; Rich.
Baxter, *Man*, 233-4 (*Additions to the Poet. Frag. of Rich. Baxter*, 1700, p. 145):
                But of all Beast, the *Man-Beast* is the worst,
                To others, and himself, the cruelst Foe.
As J. B. Mayor noted (*Contemp. Rev.*, XIV 122), *savage* here means wild animal,
as in III 64.
    169ff. *Reason* instructed by *Instinct* in the Invention of ARTS, and in the
FORMS of *Society*. [P. *1735b-43a*.]
    A most firmly rooted tradition concerning the rise of arts. Pattison cites Hip-
pocrates (ed. Littré), VI 486, and Bacon, *De augm.*, v ii; EC compares Montaigne, II xii; and cf. also Plutarch's *De sollert. animal.*; G.-B. Gelli's *Circe*, Dial. VIII.
    169-70. Cf. Cicero, *De leg.*, I viii [26]: "Artes vero innumerabiles repertae
sunt docente natura: quam imitata ratio res ad vitam necessarias sollerter
consecuta est" [Wakefield].
    173-4. Thus in Blackmore's *Creation* (VII 157) the lower orders "Their Food
distinguish and their Physic know."
    173. Cf. *Spectat.*, 121: "Dampier, in his Travels [ed. Masefield, 1906, I 70],
tells us, that when Seamen are thrown upon any of the unknown coasts of
America, they never venture upon the fruit of any tree, how tempting soever it
may appear, unless they observe that it is marked with the pecking of birds; but
fall on without any fear or apprehension where the birds have been before
them."
    174. Warburton compares Pliny, *Hist. nat.*, VIII [xl-xli]. Cf. Aristotle, *Hist.
animal.*, 612a; Cicero, *De nat. deor.*, II 1; G.-B. Gelli, *Circe*, Dial. II; W. Derham,
Physico-Theology (1714), p. 58n.

"Thy arts of building from the bee receive;   175
"Learn of the mole to plow, the worm to weave;
"Learn of the little Nautilus to sail,
"Spread the thin oar, and catch the driving gale.
"Here too all forms of social union find,
"And hence let Reason, late, instruct Mankind: 180
"Here subterranean works and cities see;
"There towns aerial on the waving tree.
"Learn each small People's genius, policies,

---

175. A subject lovingly expatiated on by Augustan physico-theologians, who usually paraphrase the comments of the Alexandrian mathematician Pappus. Thus the scientist John Ray (*Wisdom of God in the Creation*, 1714, p. 133) extols the hexagonal form of the bee's cell as being exceptionally strong, capacious, and suitable to the bee's shape, and moreover, "the Cells on each side the Partition are so order'd, that the Angles on one side insist upon the Centres of the bottoms of the Cells on the other side, and not Angle upon, or against Angle; which also must needs contribute to the strength and firmness of the work": cf. also W. Derham, *Physico-Theology* (1714), p. 233 and *n*.; Boyle, v 430. After a description still more glowing than Ray's, Blackmore concludes (*Creation*, VII 174): "Can *Euclid* more, can more *Palladio* teach!"

176. *Learn . . . plow*] Fénelon, *Demonstration of the Existence . . . of God* (tr. Boyer, 2nd ed., 1720), p. 36, observes that the mole was compensated for its defective vision with a snout "so pointed and so sharp . . . that in one Moment, he pierces through the hardest Ground"; and cf. G.-B. Gelli's *Circe* (tr. T. Brown, 1702, p. 22), where the mole before his metamorphosis "was a Prosecutor of my Mother Earth, *alias* a *Plough-man*".

177-8. *Vide* Oppian Halieut. *Lib.* I. [P. *1733*.] Oppian, Halieut. Lib. I. describes this Fish in the following manner. They swim on the surface of the Sea, on the back of their Shells, which exactly resemble the Hulk of a Ship; they raise two Feet like Masts, and extend a Membrane between which serves as a Sail; the other two Feet they employ as Oars at the side. They are usually seen in the Mediterranean. [P. *1734ab, 1735b-43b, but 1735c and 1736 have* bulk *for* hulk; *1739-43b put the second sentence between quotation marks, 1735b-36 italicize it. 1735a varies as follows*: It swims, the Shell, resembles, it raises, extends, are employ'd.] Cf. also G.-B. Gelli, *Circe* (tr. T. Brown, 1702), p. 210. Wakefield compares Dryden, *Ann. Mirab.*, st. 155.

181-2. Referring especially to ant-hills and bee-hives.

183. Cf. Virgil, *Geo.*, IV 149*ff*; Pliny, *Hist. nat.*, XI iv-xxii; Montaigne, II 194: "Is there a Polity better ordered, the Offices better distributed, and more

"The Ant's republic, and the realm of Bees;
"How those in common all their wealth bestow,   185
"And Anarchy without confusion know;
"And these for ever, tho' a Monarch reign,
"Their sep'rate cells and properties maintain.
"Mark what unvary'd laws preserve each state,
"Laws wise as Nature, and as fix'd as Fate.   190
"In vain thy Reason finer webs shall draw,

185 wealth] Stores *1733-43a.*
189 each] their *1733-43a.*

inviolably observed and maintained, than that of Bees?"; Browne, *Relig. Med.,*
I xv: "the civility of these little Citizens [ants, bees, spiders]"; Shadwell,
Virtuoso, III i: "Did you not observe the Wisdom, Policies, and Customs of that
ingenious people [spiders]?"; Shaks., *Hen. V,* I ii 187*ff.*

184. *republic, realm*] The received distinction: cf. the epist. dedic. to *Theatre of
Insects,* in Topsell, leaf Ffff 4r: "the Monarchial government of Bees, the
Democratical of Ants"; and *ibid.,* pp. 639, 1077, 1079. The ants' "republican-
ism" is mentioned by Shadwell (*Virtuoso,* III i) and Milton (*Par. Lost.,* VII 484-8).

185-8. EC compares *Guardian,* 157: "Bees . . . have each of them a hole in
their hives; their honey is their own; every bee minds her own concerns. . . It is
not so with Ants: They have nothing of their own: A grain of corn which an Ant
carries home, is deposited in a common stock: It is not designed for her own use,
but for the whole community . . ." And cf. Tindal, *Christianity as old as the Creation*
(1730), p. 165.

186. Cf. Topsell, p. 1075: ". . . [ants] need no King to govern them, for each
of them can regulate his own passions . . ."; and *Guardian,* 157.

189-80. So Du Bartas says of bees (1st wk, 5th day, 932-5):
          . . . bright *Phoebus,* whose eternall Race
          Once every Day about the World doth pace,
          Sees here no citie, that in Rites and Laws
          (For Equitie) neer to their Justice draws;
and cf. III 183*n* (Montaigne); Topsell, p. 1078: ". . . there is none amongst man
that doth govern better than the pismire . . ."

191-4. Cf. the remark attributed to Anacharsis in Plutarch's *Life of Solon,*
and to Solon by Diog. Laert., I lviii, and Stanley, p. 26: "Laws are like Cob-
webs which intangle the lesser sort, the greater break through." The remark is
also quoted by Esprit, p. 47, and adapted by Swift, I 295. Cf. also Dekker, *Match
Me in London,* IV i; Webster, *Duch. of Malfi,* I i 198-201; Greville, *Mustapha,* 1st
chor. 59-60; Dryden, *Don Seb.,* V i; Denham, *Of Justice,* 103*ff.*

"Entangle Justice in her net of Law,
"And right, too rigid, harden into wrong; ⎤
"Still for the strong too weak, the weak too strong.
"Yet go! and thus o'er all the creatures sway,   195
"Thus let the wiser make the rest obey,
"And for those Arts mere Instinct could afford,
"Be crown'd as Monarchs, or as Gods ador'd."
      v. Great Nature spoke; observant Men obey'd;
Cities were built, Societies were made: 200
Here rose one little state; another near
Grew by like means, and join'd, thro' love or fear.
Did here the trees with ruddier burdens bend,
And there the streams in purer rills descend?
What War could ravish, Commerce could bestow,   205
And he return'd a friend, who came a foe.

197–8 *1733–34b read:*
      "Who for those Arts they learn'd of Brutes before,
      As *Kings* shall crown them, or as *Gods* adore."
199 Men] Man *1743a (probably a misprint).*

192–3. Wakefield cites the maxim "Summum jus summa iniuria" [Cicero, *De off.*, I x; also found in Terence's *Heaut. tim.*, IV v 48, as EC notes] and compares Horace, *Ep.*, I vi 15–16.

194. Pattison cites John of Salisbury, *Entheticus* [i.e. *De dogm. philos.*], 1527–8 [*Opera Omnia* (ed. Giles, 1848), v]:
      Sic, Anacharsis ait, cohibent civilia jura
         Invalidos, magnis quolibet ire licet.
And cf. Shaks., *K. Lear*, IV vi 169–72.

198. *or . . . ador'd*] The traditional account of the origin of the Greek deities. Cf. Pattison's references at this place; Horace, *Ep.*, II i 5*ff*; Waller, *To Zelinda*. 23–30; and Temple, I 192: "Among the simpler Ages or Generations of Men, in several Countries, those who were the first Inventors of Arts generally received and applauded as most necessary or useful to Human Life, were honoured Alive, and after Death worshipped as Gods."

199*ff*. Origine of POLITICAL SOCIETIES. [P. *1735b–43a*.]

200. Cf. Horace, *Ars. poet.* (tr. Roscommon), 399; "Cities were built, and useful laws were made" [Wakefield]; Lucret., v 1109–10.

201–2. Cf. Lucret., v 1019–25.

Converse and Love mankind might strongly draw,
When Love was Liberty, and Nature Law.
Thus States were form'd; the name of King unknown,
'Till common int'rest plac'd the sway in one.   210
'Twas VIRTUE ONLY (or in arts or arms,
Diffusing blessings, or averting harms)
The same which in a Sire the Sons obey'd,
A Prince the Father of a People made.
    VI. 'Till then, by Nature crown'd, each Patriarch sate,
King, priest, and parent of his growing state;   216
On him, their second Providence, they hung,
Their law his eye, their oracle his tongue.

207–8 *Om. 1733.*
211 'Twas] Then *1733–35a.*

---

207. *Love . . . draw*] Lucret., v 1112: "nam facies multum valuit . . ."
208. Adapted from *El. to Abel.*, 82 [Wakefield].
210*ff.* Origine of MONARCHY. [P. *1735b–43a.*]
211–14. In the infancy of the world, says Boileau (*Sat.*, v 92), "Le mérite y faisoit la noblesse et les rois"; and cf. Dryden, *Sigism. and Guisc.*, 510–13:

> Thus born alike, from virtue first began
> The diff'rence that distinguish'd man from man:
> He claim'd no title from descent of blood,
> But that which made him noble made him good.

214. Cf. Locke, *Civil Govt.*, II vi 74: ". . . it is obvious . . . how easy it was in the first ages of the world . . . for the father of the family to become the prince of it . . ." [EC].
215*ff.* [Origin] of PATRIARCHIAL GOVERNMENT. [P. *1735b–43a.*]
The usual description of the origins of government. See Aristotle, *Politics*, I ii; Hooker, I x 4–5; Ralegh, *Hist. of the World*, I ix; *Par. Lost*, XII 23–5; Temple, I 100*ff*; Locke, *Civil Govt.*, II vi 75*ff*. P. Hume's note on *Par. Lost* (1695), XII 26 is a typical rendering: "That all *Primitive* and *Natural Power* was *Paternal*, that is the Authority Fathers of Families had over their Descendants, is undoubted; whence the Head of every Tribe was its Patriarch, governing all its Particulars for their common Peace and mutual Support, according to the Dictate of right Reason, the Law of Nature, under whom all the Easie Subjects were of the same common size, and equal condition, as being Brethren . . ."
217–24. Like the writers cited above, especially Locke and Temple, Pope finds the origins of patriarchal authority in filial habit and the natural veneration of the offspring for their instructor and provider.

He from the wond'ring furrow call'd the food,
Taught to command the fire, controul the flood,   220
Draw forth the monsters of th'abyss profound,
Or fetch th'aerial eagle to the ground.
'Till drooping, sick'ning, dying, they began
Whom they rever'd as God to mourn as Man:
Then, looking up from sire to sire, explor'd   225
One great first father, and that first ador'd.
Or plain tradition that this All begun,
Convey'd unbroken faith from sire to son,
The worker from the work distinct was known,
And simple Reason never sought but one: 230
Ere Wit oblique had broke that steddy light,

219 the food] their Food *1733–43a.*
229 worker] Workman *1733–35a.*

219–22. "The manner in which the four elements were subdued is comprised in these four lines . . ." [Warton].

225–8. Cf. W. Dawes, *Anat. of Atheism* (1693), p. 17:

> Or thirdly we from Reason's sacred Law,
> This Inference most evidently draw,
> And with St. Paul, from Things created prove
> The Being of that God, who sits above:
> Or lastly, this was from Tradition brought,
> And by our Fathers to their Children taught.

Spectat., 201: ". . . the universal concurrence of all the nations under heaven in the great article of adoration, plainly shew that devotion or religious worship must be the effect of tradition from some first founder of mankind, or that it is conformable to the natural light of reason . . ."

225–6. With reference to the familiar chain of causes, ending in God: cf. G.-B. Gelli, *Circe* (tr. T. Brown, 1702), p. 247: ". . . reason . . wou'd instruct you to trace out a first cause, or mover, by running from one cause to another, till at last you came to the supreme . . ."; Dryden, *Relig. Laici*, 12–14; Thomson, *Summer* (1727), 1091–4.

228. The Hind in Dryden, *Hind and Panther*, II 217, speaking for the Roman Catholic point of view, observes that traditions are "deriv'd from sire to son".

231. For the image, Ward translates from Bacon [*Nov. org.*: *Distributis operis* par. 14]: ". . . like an irregular glass, it [the mind] alters the rays of things by its figure and different intersections." The prism figure was a favourite with Pope: cf. *E. on C.*, 311, *Mor. Ess.*, I 34*ff.*

Man, like his Maker, saw that all was right,
To Virtue, in the paths of Pleasure, trod,
And own'd a Father when he own'd a God.
LOVE all the faith, and all th'allegiance then;   235
For Nature knew no right divine in Men,
No ill could fear in God; and understood
A sov'reign being but a sov'reign good.
True faith, true policy, united ran,
That was but love of God, and this of Man.   240
Who first taught souls enslav'd, and realms undone,

---

232. Cf. 1 294 and Gen., 1 31.

233. As described above, III 135ff.

235ff. Origine of TRUE RELIGION and GOVERNMENT from the Principle of LOVE: and of SUPERSTITION and TYRANNY, from that of FEAR. [P. 1735b–43a.]

235. In Stoic political theory, tyranny was said to operate on the principle of fear, proper rule on the principle of confidence and love: cf. Cicero, De off., II vii. Also, J. T. Desaguliers, Newt. Syst. of the World (1728), p. 4:

> When Kings were not ambitious yet to gain
> Other's Dominions, but their own maintain;
> When, to protect, they only bore the Sway,
> And Love, not Fear, taught Subjects to obey.

236. Locke's thesis throughout his Civil Govt., and cf. Par. Lost, XII 24–8.

241–82. The usual account of the corruption of the state of nature, which finally drove men to formal government and laws. Cf. Locke, Civil Govt., II viii 111: "But the golden age . . . had more virtue, and consequently better governors, as well as less vicious subjects; and there was then no stretching prerogative on the one side to oppress the people, nor consequently, on the other, any dispute about privilege, to lessen or restrain the power of the magistrate; and so no contest betwixt rulers and people about governors or government. Yet, when ambition and luxury, in future ages, would retain and increase the power, without doing the business for which it was given, and aided by flattery, taught princes to have distinct and separate interests from their people, men found it necessary to examine more carefully the original and rights of government, and to find out ways to restrain the exorbitances and prevent the abuses of that power, which they having entrusted in another's hands, only for their own good, they found was made use of to hurt them"; and Hooker, I x 5.

241–2. "In this Aristotle placeth the difference between a King and a Tyrant, that the first supposeth himself made for the People; the other that the People are made for him . . . Pol. lib. v. cap. 10" [Warburton]. Cf. Hooker, I x 5; Locke, II viii; and Thomson, Liberty, IV 972 [Pattison]; Greville, Treat. of Monarchy, st. 66, where it is said that tyranny, "transcendent, grows secure

Th' enormous faith of many made for one;
That proud exception to all Nature's laws,
T'invert the world, and counter-work its Cause?
Force first made Conquest, and that conquest, Law;   245
'Till Superstition taught the tyrant awe,
Then shar'd the Tyranny, then lent it aid,
And Gods of Conqu'rors, Slaves of Subjects made:
She, 'midst the light'ning's blaze, and thunder's sound,

247 then lent] and lent *1733–34b, 1736*.

Flattering it self that all is made for one;" and Dryden, *Abs. and Achit.*, 945,
speaking of the Whigs and opponents of Charles: "That one was made for
many, they contend".

242. *enormous*] "Deviating from ordinary rule or type; . . . monstrous",
OED. Cf. IV 307.

243. Cf. Locke, *Civil Govt.*, II xv 172: ". . . despotical power . . . is a power
which neither Nature gives, for it has made no such distinction between one
·man and another, nor compact can convey"; Denham, *Sophy*, IV i 26–9.

244. Bacon, *Adv. of Learning*, II xxi 1, speaks of "That gigantic state of mind
which possesseth the troublers of the world, . . . who . . . would give form to the
world according to their own humours (which is the true Theomachy) . . ."

245–6. Cf. Ch. Blount, *Great is Diana of the Ephesians* (1695), p. 7: "The
primitive Institution of Idolatry receiv'd its Birth from Princes, at whose charge
it was afterward Educated by Ecclesiasticks; the one made the Idol, and the
other ordain'd the worship of it"; and Lord Herbert, *Anc. Relig. of the Gentiles*,
esp. chs. XI, XII, XIV.

245. *Force . . . Conquest*] Cf. Habington, *Queene of Arragon* (1640), III i:
            Kinde heav'n made us all equall, till rude strength
            Or wicked pollice usurp'd a power.

246. Cf. Crowne, *Caligula*, II i: "Priests, by false Gods, keep all the World in
awe."

247. Cf. *E. on C.*, 687–8:
            With tyranny, then superstition joined,
            As that the body, this enslaved the mind.

248. Cf. Greville, *Treat. of Monarchy*, st. 68: "Hence thrones grew Idols, Man
their Sacrifice."

249–62. With Pope's interpretation of superstition, cf. Plutarch's essay on the
subject (I 172*ff*), of which Pope digests the substance in a letter to Caryll,
3 Sept. [1718].

249–52. Cf. Lucret., v 1218*ff*; Plutarch, I 170: "he that dreads divine power
dreads every thing, the land, the sea, the air, the sky, the dark, the light."

When rock'd the mountains, and when groan'd the ground,
She taught the weak to bend, the proud to pray,   251
To Pow'r unseen, and mightier far than they:
She, from the rending earth and bursting skies,
Saw Gods descend, and fiends infernal rise:
Here fix'd the dreadful, there the blest abodes;   255
Fear made her Devils, and weak Hope her Gods;
Gods partial, changeful, passionate, unjust,
Whose attributes were Rage, Revenge, or Lust;
Such as the souls of cowards might conceive,
And, form'd like tyrants, tyrants would believe.   260

250. Cf. Dryden, *Theod. and Hon.*, 266: "Air blacken'd, roll'd the thunder, groan'd the ground."

253–6. Cf. Pope's *Il.*, VI 117n: "This is conformable to the whole System of *Pagan* Superstition, the Worship whereof being grounded not on Love but Fear, seems directed rather to avert the Malice and Anger of a wrathful and mischievous Daemon, than to implore the Assistance and Protection of a benevolent Being."

256. A significant reversal of Statius (*Thebaid*, III 661): "Primus in orbe deos fecit timor."

257ff. Cf. Pope's letter (III 249–62n): ". . . the superstitious man looks on the great Father of all as a tyrant. . . Accordingly he serves his Maker but as slaves do their tyrants, with a gloomy savage zeal against his fellow-creatures, whom he insults and persecutes with all barbarity, whenever they seem never so little deficient in their duty, though at the same time he trembles with the dread of being ill-used himself, notwithstanding all his endeavours of service to their common Lord"; and John Smith, *Select Discourses* (1660), p. 26: ". . . the true Cause and Rise of Superstition is indeed nothing else but a false opinion of the Deity, that renders him dreadfull and terrible, as being rigorous and imperious; that which represents him as austere and apt to be angry . . ."

257–60. Cf. Plutarch, I 174, 181; and Chambers, art. God: "To authorize their own crimes, and justify their vices and debaucheries, men constituted criminal, vicious, and licentious *Gods*, unjust, rapacious, and tyrannical *Gods*, covetous and thievish *Gods*, drunken *Gods*, impudent *Gods*, cruel and bloody *Gods*."

259. Cf. Plutarch, I 178: ". . . God is the brave man's hope, and not the coward's excuse."

260. Cf. Greville, *Treat. of Monarchy*, st. 56, where despotism
      Takes not God as He is, but makes him new
      Like to his ends, large, narrow, false, or true;
Burton, p. 104: ". . . Men will think God to be as they are: And hence is it, That

Zeal then, not charity, became the guide,
And hell was built on spite, and heav'n on pride.
Then sacred seem'd th'etherial vault no more;
Altars grew marble then, and reek'd with gore:
Then first the Flamen tasted living food;   265
Next his grim idol smear'd with human blood;
With Heav'n's own thunders shook the world below,

so many Men who are in their Temper peevish and revengeful . . . translate
their own Humours into their Theology. . . Hence . . . the Heathens . . . in their
Divinity transferr'd all the Evil Passions of Men to their Gods."

261-2. Thos. Chubb makes the point (*Tracts*, 1730, p. 276) that if men conceive God to be vicious they will conceive their duties to him to be sectarian
hatred, religious persecution, etc. For Pope's contemporaries these lines were
capable of reference to the enthusiastic sects.

261. *Zeal . . . charity*] Cf. Richard Corbet, *R. C.*, 1-2:
            When too much zeal doth fire devotion,
            Love is not love, but superstition;

262. *hell . . . spite*] Tindal (*Christianity as Old as the Creation*, 1730, p. 101)
criticizes modern "*Creeds* made out of spite".

263-4. *Then . . . then*] Cf. III 155-6. Chudleigh, *Ess.*, p. 207: ". . . In the
Heathen World, a Blind Zeal, a bigotted Devotion, and a superstitious Dread of
Hell, enrich'd their Temples, adorn'd their shrines, and made their Altars vie
with the glittering Canopy of Heaven."

and . . . gore] A traditional view of the origin of blood-sacrifice. Cf. the fragments from Theophrastus cited by E. Bevan, *Later Greek Religion* (1927), p. 49:
"Then as the practice of men in regard to sacrifice departed farther and farther
from the true norm, they began to resort to sacrifices of the most horrible kind,
full of cruelty, so that the curses long ago pronounced on the human race might
seem now to have had their fulfilment: men began to slaughter, to redden the
altars with carnage, from the time when under the stress of famine and war they
first tasted blood . . ."

265-6. Cf. Tindal, *Christianity as old as the Creation* (1730), p. 93: "The *Pagans*
sacrificing of Beasts was not so bad in itself, as what it soon occasion'd, human
Sacrifices . . ."

266. Bowles notes the parallel with *Par. Lost*, I 392-3: "First Moloch, horrid
king, besmear'd with blood Of human sacrifice".

267-8. Cf. Pope to Caryll, 19 July 1711: "Nothing has been so much a scare-
crow to them as the too peremptory and seemingly uncharitable assertion of an
utter impossibility of salvation to all but ourselves, invincible ignorance
excepted, which indeed some people define under so great limitations and with
such exclusions, that it seems as if that word were rather invented as a salvo or
expedient, not to be thought too bold with the thunderbolts of God (which are

O

And play'd the God an engine on his foe.
    So drives Self-love, thro' just and thro' unjust,
To one Man's pow'r, ambition, lucre, lust: 270
The same Self-love, in all, becomes the cause
Of what restrains him, Government and Laws.
For, what one likes if others like as well,
What serves one will, when many wills rebel?
How shall he keep, what, sleeping or awake,   275
A weaker may surprise, a stronger take?
His safety must his liberty restrain:

---

hurled about so freely almost on all mankind by the hands of the ecclesiastics)
than as a real exceptive to almost universal damnation."

268. EC notes the image from engines of war, e.g. the catapult.

269 ff. The Influence of SELF-LOVE operating to the SOCIAL and *Public Good*. [P. *1735b–43a*.]

269. *thro' . . . unjust*] As described in III 121 ff and 241 ff.

269–72. Warton cites Hooker [I x 5]: "At the first, when some certain kind of regiment was once approved, it may be that nothing was then further thought upon for the manner of governing, but all permitted unto their wisdom and discretion which were to rule; till by experience they found this for all parts very inconvenient. . . They saw that to live by one man's will became the cause of all men's misery. This constrained them to come unto laws, wherein all men might see their duties beforehand, and know the penalties of transgressing them." Cf. also, Greville, *Treat. of Monarchy*, st. 72; Locke, *Civil Govt.*, II vii 94.

271–86. Lucret., v 1139–53 (tr. Loeb): ". . . men are eager to tread under foot what they have once too much feared. So things came to the uttermost dregs of confusion, when each man for himself sought dominion and exaltation. Then there were some who taught them to create magistrates, and established law. . . For mankind, tired of living in violence, . . . were readier of their own will to submit to . . . rules of law . . . , for violence and injury enclose in their net all who do such things, and generally return upon him who began . . ."

273–4. Warton again compares Hooker [I viii 7]: ". . . if I cannot but wish to receive all good, even as much at every man's hand as any man can wish unto his own soul, how should I look to have any part of my desire herein satisfied, unless myself be careful to satisfy the like desire . . . in other men, we all being of one and the same nature." And cf. Greville, *Treat. of Monarchy*, st. 131:

        . . . weak Thrones shall find
    The wit of time, and selfness in men's hearts,
    Will teach how one man, many men may bind,
    And raise the head by counterpoize of parts.

All join to guard what each desires to gain.
Forc'd into virtue thus by Self-defence,
Ev'n Kings learn'd justice and benevolence: 280
Self-love forsook the path it first pursu'd,
And found the private in the public good.
    'Twas then, the studious head or gen'rous mind,
Follow'r of God or friend of human-kind,
Poet or Patriot, rose but to restore   285
The Faith and Moral, Nature gave before;
Re-lum'd her ancient light, not kindled new;
If not God's image, yet his shadow drew:
Taught Pow'r's due use to People and to Kings,
Taught nor to slack, nor strain its tender strings,   290

290 nor to] not to *1733–35b*.

---

278. E. Young (*Imper. Pelagi*, str. IV, st. 14) speaks of "those guards of gain,
the Laws"; and cf. La Rochefoucauld, II cxviii; *Civil Polity* (1703), p. 5: ". . .
having reason and foresight, they [men] have invented Methods by speech or
otherwise to consent to Orders or Rules by which the Weaker are protected
from the Insults of the Stronger; the whole Community having agreed upon
such *Terms* as may preserve every individual Member . . ."
    282. Cf. Greville, *Treat. of Monarchy*, st. 34, where the right kind of throne,
based on reverence, reason, and affection, is said to "wear the publick in the
private good".
    283*ff*. Restoration of *True Religion* and *Government* on their first Principle.
Mixt Governments; with the various Forms of each, and the TRUE USE OF
ALL. [P. *1735b–43a, but 1739–43a add as a second paragraph*]: The Deduction and
Application of the foregoing Principles, with the *Use* or *Abuse* of *Civil* and
Ecclesiastical Policy, was intended for the subject of the third book.
    Cf. Thomson, *Winter* (1726), 258*ff*.
    285–6. W. Jaeger, *Paideia* (tr. Highet), I (1939) 107: ". . . it is typical of Greek
ideas that the law-giver is . . . named beside the poet, and the formulas which
define the law beside the wise utterances of the poet." Pope is here expressing
the classical and neo-classical conception of the poet's function; cf. Johnson,
Rasselas, ch. x.
    286. *Faith and Moral*] Above, III 235–40. *Moral* here is equivalent to "ethical
principles".
    289–96. Compare the stanza added to *Ode for Music* in 1730 (vol. VI).
    290. Bacon, *Of Empire*: "To speake now of the true Temper of *Empire*: it is a
Thing rare, & hard to keep; for both Temper & Distemper consist of Con-

The less, or greater, set so justly true,
That touching one must strike the other too;
'Till jarring int'rests of themselves create
Th'according music of a well-mix'd State.
Such is the World's great harmony, that springs   295

291 or] and *1733–43a*.   293 'Till] And *1733–35a*.

---

traries. . . The Answer of *Apollonius* to *Vespasian*, is full of Excellent Instruction, *Vespasian* asked him; *What was Neroes overthrow?* He answered; *Nero could touch and tune the Harpe well; But in Government, sometimes he used to winde the pins too high, sometimes to let them downe too low.*"

290–4. A musical figure traditional in political contexts. Warton cites Cicero, *De republ.* [II xlii] [tr. Sabine and Smith (1929), p. 192]: "For, as in the music of lyre and flute and as even in singing and spoken discourse there is a certain melody which must be preserved in the different sounds—and if this is altered or discordant it becomes intolerable to the ears of a connoisseur—and as this melody is made concordant and harmonious in spite of the dissimilar sounds of which it is composed, so the state achieves harmony by the agreement of unlike individuals, when there is a wise blending of the highest, the lowest, and the intervening middle classes in the manner of tones. And what musicians call harmony in song is concord in a state." The latter third of this passage is preserved only by Augustine's quotation of it in *De civ. dei*, II xxi (which Pattison cites). Cf. also Shaks., *Hen. V*, II i 180ff; *Troil. and Cress.*, I iii 109–10: Greville, *Treat. of Monarchy*, sts. 329ff; Marvell, *First Anniv. of the Govt. under O. C.*, 67ff.

291–2. Cf. Shaks., *Sonn.*, VIII; Drayton, *Edward . . . to Alice Ctess. of Salisbury*, 21–2:

　　　　One well-tunde string, set truely to his like,
　　　　Strooke nere at hand doth make another strike;

Browne, *Pseud. Epid.*, VII xviii; Marvell, *Fleckno*, 37–40; Cowley, *David.*, I 479–80; Oldham, *To . . . Ch. Morwent*, st. 13; Rowe, *Tamerlane*, I i; J. Sheffield, *On Mr. Hobbs*; Swift, *Tale of a Tub* (ed. Smith and Guthkelch, 1920), p. 167: "For, there is a peculiar *String* in the Harmony of Human Understanding, which in several individuals is exactly of the same Tuning. This, if you can dexterously screw up to its right Key, and then strike gently upon it; Whenever you have the Good Fortune to light among those of the same Pitch, they will by a secret necessary Sympathy, strike exactly at the same time."

292. *strike*] I.e. cause to sound.

295–302. Cf. Introd., pp. xxxivf, lviii, lxii.

295–6. Hurd compares Denham, *Cooper's Hill*, 203–4. Cf. Marvell, *First Anniv. of the Govt. under O.C.*, 67–8:

　　　　Such was that wondrous Order and Consent
　　　　When Cromwell tun'd the ruling Instrument.

From Order, Union, full Consent of things!
Where small and great, where weak and mighty, made
To serve, not suffer, strengthen, not invade,
More pow'rful each as needful to the rest,
And, in proportion as it blesses, blest,   300
Draw to one point, and to one centre bring
Beast, Man, or Angel, Servant, Lord, or King.
For Forms of Government let fools contest;

296 Order, Union] Union, Order *1733–43a*.

297–300. A common theme in moral and sermon literature, often with
implied or stated reference to 1 Cor., XII. Cf. Bellarmine, p. 214; Geo. Hickes,
Sermon Preached . . . April 1, 1684 (1684), p. 7; Thos. Clutterbuck, *Spittle-Sermon
Preached . . . March 30, 1687* (1687), p. 19; Chudleigh, *Ess.*, pp. 98–9; Swift, IV
112–14, 117; Cumberland, p. 121; John Fell, *Sermon Preach'd . . . Dec. 22, 1680*
(1680), pp. 2–3: "We are all born naked and unarmed, needing the assistance of
each other; but wanting strength or weapons to enforce it: but the divine Wisdom has so suited things, that the strong depends upon the weak, as much as the
weak do's on the strong: the rich is assisted by the poor, as the poor is by the
rich: the wise is aided by the ignorant, as the ignorant is by the wise. The
Scepter rests upon the mattock and the spade, and the Throne upon the plough.
The great animal of a Republic has as much consent of parts, as much dependence of them on each other, as any living creature has. St. Paul at the 12. of the
first to the Corinthians excellently describes it."

301–2. Cf. J. Norden, *Viciss. Rerum* (1600), st. 94:

> *Lord* and *slaue, master* and *seruant* wee find
> To liue unlike, yet in good harmonie,
> If true concording *discord* beautifie.

301. *Draw . . . point*] Perhaps an application of Bacon's pyramidal figure in
De sap. vet., VI: ". . . omnis rerum natura instar pyramidis acuta sit: . . . natura
tanquam in unum coire videatur."

one centre] Cf. III 14. Denham, *Cooper's Hill*, 331–3:

> Tyrant and slave, those names of hate and fear,
> The happier stile of king and subject bear:
> Happy when both to the same centre move.

303–6. Cf. Pope to Lady M. W. Montagu [20 Aug. 1716]: "One is ignorant,
or at best doubtful, of the merits of differing religions and governments: but
private virtue one can be sure of."

303–4. Essentially the doctrine of Aristotle in the *Politics*, where he argues
that forms of government are to be judged according to their effectiveness in
procuring the aim of every good state, which is that the inhabitants of it should
be happy. Cf. Temple, 1 105 and 259: "Now were the Constitution of any

Whate'er is best administer'd is best:
For Modes of Faith, let graceless zealots fight; 305
His can't be wrong whose life is in the right:

Government never so perfect, . . . if the Administration be ill, . . . there will be more just Occasions given of Discontent and Complaint, than from any Weakness or Fault in the original Conception or Institution of Government . . .; those are generally the best Governments where the best Men govern; and let the Sort or Scheme be what it will, those are ill Governments where ill Men govern. . ."

Warburton notes (1751) that the lines were misinterpreted in a contemporary pamphlet (as they were later by Warton and others), with the consequence that Pope jotted down in the offending book: "The author of these lines [Pope] was far from meaning that no one Form of Government is, in itself, better yn another . . . but that no form of Government, however excellent or preferable in itself, can be sufficient to make a People happy, unless it be administerd with Integrity. On ye contrary, the Best sort of Governmt, when ye Form of it is preserved, and ye *administration* corrupt, is most dangerous." I quote from a photograph of Brit. Mus. Egerton MS. 1950, f. 9r, supplied me by Mr George Sherburn. For a fuller MS. version of this note, see App. B.

305–10. The position of the Cambridge Platonists, and other "Latitude men"; cf. J. Glanvill, *Ess. upon Sev. Import. Subj.* (1676), p. 31; E. Fowler, *The Princ. and Pract. of Certain Moderate Divines* (1671), pp. 18, 120; J. Tillotson, *Wks.* (1728), II 167; R. Cudworth, *Sermon Preached . . . March 31, 1647*, p. 14: "He that endeavours really to mortifie his lusts, and to comply with that truth in his life, which his Conscience is convinced of; is neerer a Christian, though he never heard of Christ; than he that believes all the vulgar Articles of the Christian faith, and plainly denyeth Christ in his life"; J. Smith, *Select Discourses* (1660), p. 9; B. Whichcote, *Wks.* (Aberdeen, 1751), II 20: "*Nothing is desperate in the condition of good men*; they will not live and die in any dangerous error." See also Temple, I 56; Chudleigh, *Poems*, leaf K 7v.

305–6. Hurd compares Cowley, *On the Death of Mr. Crashaw* [45–50, 55–6]:
For even in *Error* sure no *Danger* is
When joyn'd with so much *Piety* as *His* . . .
His Faith perhaps in some nice Tenents might
Be wrong; his *Life*, I'm sure, was *in the right*.
Warton cites what seems to be a misremembered version of the following verses of Lord Herbert [*Haered. ac Nepot. suis Praecepta*, 97–8]:
Ne crucient animum quae circa Religionem
Vexantur Lites, sit modo vita proba.

305. *Modes of Faith*] Cf. *E. on C.*, 446: ". . . faith itself has different dresses worn."

graceless] An equivoque.

In Faith and Hope the world will disagree,
But all Mankind's concern is Charity:
All must be false that thwart this One great End,
And all of God, that bless Mankind or mend.   310
   Man, like the gen'rous vine, supported lives;

307–8 *Add. 1743b, 1751.*

307–8. Cf. Augustine, *Conf.*, XII xxv; B. Whichcote, *Moral and Relig. Aphorisms* (1753), p. 118: "For I am persuaded; that Christian love and affection . . . is a point of such importance . . . that it is not to be prejudiced, by *supposals* of differences, in points of religion anie wayes disputable; . . . which . . . have indeed enlarged Divinitie; but have lessened Charitie . . . For maintenance of truth, is rather God's charge (John, XVI 13); and the continuance of charitie ours (Heb., XIII 1)"; Pope to Blount, 10 Feb. 1716: "I think it was a generous thought, and one that flowed from an exalted mind, that it was not improbable but God might be delighted with the various methods of worshipping him which divided the whole world . . . I as little fear God will damn a man who has charity, as I hope that any priest can save him without it"; to Caryll, 19 July 1711: "For besides the small number of the truly faithful in our church, we must again subdivide, and the Jansenist is damned by the Jesuit, the Jesuit by the Jansenist, the strict Scotist by the Thomist, &c. There may be errors, I grant, but I cannot think them of such consequence as to destroy utterly the charity of mankind—the very greatest bond in which we are engaged by God to one another as Christians."

308. Cf. 1 Cor., XIII 13; and Jas., II 20. For the phrasing, compare Dryden, *Relig. La.*, 449–50:

> For points obscure are of small use to learn;
> But common quiet is mankind's concern.

309–10. Cf. Greville, *Treat. of Hum. Learning*, st. 143:

> The chiefe Vse then in man of that he knowes,
> Is his paines taking for the good of all,
> Not fleshly weeping for our owne made woes,
> Not laughing from a Melancholy gall,
> Not hating from a soule that ouerflowes
> With bitternesse, breath'd out from inward thrall:
>   But sweetly rather to ease, loose, or binde,
>   As need requires, this fraile fall'n humane kinde.

311. *gen'rous vine*] An old phrase (cf. *OED, s.v. generous*) quickened with a new context.

311–16. Pope closes the epistle (cf. its beginning) with two figures relating to the love that binds the universe. The love of the vine and elm was often cited in this connection (e.g. by Burton, *Anat. of Mel.*, Part 3, sect. 1, memb. 1, subs. 2), and Newton's principle of attractive force holding the planets in their orbits was

The strength he gains is from th'embrace he gives.
On their own Axis as the Planets run,
Yet make at once their circle round the Sun:
So two consistent motions act the Soul;   315
And one regards Itself, and one the Whole.
    Thus God and Nature link'd the gen'ral frame,
And bade Self-love and Social be the same.

---

assimilated in Pope's time to older ideas of the diffusive love of God, e.g. by Thomson in *Liberty*, III (1735) 45*ff*:

> . . . the secret Band of Love,
> The kind Attraction that to central Suns
> Binds circling earths . . .

See A. D. McKillop, *Background of Thomson's Seasons*, 1942, pp. 31*ff*, esp. 35–6. As always in the *Essay* (cf. II 111*ff* n), the ideal described for man is an image of the divine unity that obtains in the macrocosmos.

312. *embrace*] A charged word in this epistle: cf. above, 12 and 123.

313–16. Warton cites *Spectat.*, 588: "Is it [benevolence] inconsistent with self-love? Are their Motions contrary? No more than the diurnal rotation of the earth is opposed to its annual; or its motion round its own center, which might be improved as an illustration of self-love, to that which whirls it about the common center of the world, answering to universal benevolence." And cf. Burton, *A Second Vol. of Discourses* (1685), pp. 515–16: "So then notwithstanding this Exception from Self-love, we may love universally, and do Good to all: for, these are two natural Principles, that agree well together; which seems to be well represented in the natural World. For (as the Astronomers tell us) the Earth at the same time moves round its own Axis, and yet makes a Progression in the Ecliptick Circle, in which it always keeps the same steady Position, in reference to all the circumambient Bodies. This doth represent the Man of a regular Self-love, and an universal Charity: He moves about his own Center, but yet retains his Relation to the rest of Mankind, and keeps his Parallelism to the Axe of the Universe, as I may say."

318. The central theme of much ethical writing in Pope's time and before. E.g., Cumberland, p. 16: "The Endeavour, to the utmost of our power, of promoting the common Good of the whole System of rational Agents, conduces . . . to the Good of every Part, in which our own Happiness, as that of a Part, is contain'd"; Butler, *Fifteen Sermons* (1726), I iii: "These ends do indeed perfectly coincide: and to aim at public and private good are so far from being inconsistent, that they mutually promote each other. . ."

ARGUMENT of the FOURTH EPISTLE[1]

Of the Nature and State of Man, *with respect to* Happiness.

I. FALSE *Notions of Happiness, Philosophical and Popular, answered from* VER. 19 to 76. II. *It is the End of all Men, and attainable by all,* VER. 29. *God intends Happiness to be* equal; *and to be so, it must be* social, *since all particular Happiness depends on general, and since he governs by* general, *not* particular Laws, VER. 35. *As it is necessary* 5 *for* Order, *and the peace and welfare of* Society, *that* external goods *should be* unequal, *Happiness is not made to consist in these,* VER. 49. *But, notwithstanding that inequality, the* balance *of Happiness among Mankind is kept even by Providence, by the two Passions of* Hope *and* Fear, VER. 67. III. *What the Happiness of* Individuals *is, as far as* 10 *is consistent with the constitution of this world; and that the* good Man *has here the advantage,* VER. 77. *The error of imputing to* Virtue *what are only the calamities of* Nature, *or of* Fortune, VER. 93. IV. *The folly of expecting that God should alter his general Laws in favour of particulars,* VER. 111. V. *That we are not judges who are* 15 *good; but that whoever they are, they must be happiest,* VER. 131, &c. VI. *That* external goods *are not the proper rewards, but often inconsistent with, or destructive of Virtue,* VER. 167. *That even these can make no Man happy without Virtue: Instanced in* Riches, VER. 185. Honours, VER. 193. Nobility, VER. 205. Greatness, VER. 217. 20 Fame, VER. 237. Superior Talents, VER. 259. *With pictures of human Infelicity in Men possest of them all,* VER. 269, &c. VII. *That* Virtue *only constitutes a Happiness, whose object is* universal, *and whose prospect* eternal, VER. 309, &c. *That the* perfection *of* Virtue *and* Happiness *consists in a* conformity *to the* 25 ORDER *of* PROVIDENCE *here, and a* Resignation *to it here and hereafter,* VER. 325, &c.[2]

---

1. See the note on the "Argument" of Epistle 1.
2. *1734-34b* add a final sentence: Or (in other words) in *Love of God,* and *Charity* to *all men.*

EPISTLE IV

OH HAPPINESS! our being's end and aim!
    Good, Pleasure, Ease, Content! whate'er thy name:
    That something still which prompts th'eternal sigh,
For which we bear to live, or dare to die,
Which still so near us, yet beyond us lies,   5
O'er-look'd, seen double, by the fool, and wise.
Plant of celestial seed! if dropt below,
Say, in what mortal soil thou deign'st to grow?
Fair op'ning to some Court's propitious shine,

4 or dare] nor fear *1734–35a*; or] and *1735c–43a*.

Epistle IV. Of the NATURE and STATE of MAN, with respect to HAPPINESS.
[P. *1735b–43a*.]

1*ff.* "He begins his address to Happiness after the manner of the ancient
hymns, by enumerating the titles and various places of abode of his goddess"
[Warton]. Geo. Herbert's *The Pulley* contains in miniature the theme that Pope
works out, in somewhat different terms, in this epistle.

1. Cf. Aristotle, *Eth. Nic.*, 1097 a*f.* Pattison compares Prior, I 14*ff.*

3. *That . . . still*] So in Prior, *The Ladle*, 162–4: "Amidst our plenty something
still . . . Is wanting"; and cf. *Ess.*, I 96.

4. Cf. IV 309*ff*, 345*ff.*

6. "Overlooked in the things which would yield it, and in other things magnified by the imagination" [EC].

7–8. For the image, cf. R. Gould (*To the . . . Beaux Esprits*, st. 15), who com-
pares happiness to a plant that is "not the Growth of the Terrestrial Soil";
Milton, *Lycidas*, 78: "Fame is no plant that grows on mortal soil"; and Marvell,
The Garden, 13–14.

7. *Plant . . . seed*] Dryden, *Abs. and Achit.*, 305–6:

        Desire of pow'r, on earth a vicious weed
        Yet, sprung from high, is of celestial seed.

Aristotle, *Eth. Nic.*, 1099b: "Now if there is *any* gift of the gods to men, it is
reasonable that happiness should be god-given . . ."

8. *mortal*] "The epithet is important. Where amongst human beings?"—
Morris. Cf. the quotation from *Lycidas*, above.

Or deep with di'monds in the flaming mine?   10
Twin'd with the wreaths Parnassian lawrels yield,
Or reap'd in iron harvests of the field?
Where grows?—where grows it not?—If vain our toil,
We ought to blame the culture, not the soil:
Fix'd to no spot is Happiness sincere,   15
'Tis no where to be found, or ev'ry where;
'Tis never to be bought, but always free,
And fled from Monarchs, ST. JOHN! dwells with thee.
    Ask of the Learn'd the way, the Learn'd are blind,
This bids to serve, and that to shun mankind;   20
Some place the bliss in action, some in ease,
Those call it Pleasure, and Contentment these;

18 ST. JOHN] *Lelius 1734.*

10. Appropriate to the plant figure, on the old belief that minerals were
organisms ripened by the sun's rays: cf. *Par. Lost*, III 608–12; Thomson, *Summer*
(1727), 125*ff*.

11–12. Cf. Marvell, *The Garden*, 1–6.

12. Wakefield cites Pope's Statius, 10, where Cadmus "reaped an iron
harvest of his toil"; Dryden's *Aen.*, XII 964, and *All for Love*, I i; and Virgil, *Aen.*,
III 45–6.

13–16. Cf. Boileau, *Ep.*, v 51*ff*; and Sir John Beaumont, *Of True Liberty*, 5–8:
    We need not travaile, seeking wayes to blisse;
    He that desires contentment, cannot miss:
    No garden walles this precious flowre embrace,
    It common grows in ev'ry desart place.

15–16. Cf. Horace, *Ep.*, I xi 22*ff*; and Crowne, *Darius*, II ii:
    There is no State, in which the bounteous gods
    Have not plac'd Joy, if Man would seek it out.

15. *sincere*] Unmixed, pure, as perhaps at II 255. Pope uses the phrase
"happiness sincere" in his *Il.*, XXIV 671.

18. Morris supposes an allusion to the phrase "happy as a king".

19–28. In allusion to the disagreement of the ancient schools about the
summum bonum; cf., for example, Montaigne, II 406; Temple, I 173; Milton,
Par. Reg., IV 272–330.

From Pope's draft of a revised version of these lines in his letter to Warburton
of 18 January 1743, it is clear that the antithesis is between the Stoics and
Epicureans, as elsewhere in the Essay, with a reference to the Sceptics at 25–6.

20. *that . . . mankind*] This is the criticism levelled at Cato's Stoicism in
Cicero, *De fin.*, IV xxv 68.

21. Cf. *Ess.*, II 7.

> Some sunk to Beasts, find pleasure end in pain;
> Some swell'd to Gods, confess ev'n Virtue vain;
> Or indolent, to each extreme they fall,   25
> To trust in ev'ry thing, or doubt of all.
>   Who thus define it, say they more or less
> Than this, that Happiness is Happiness?
>   II. Take Nature's path, and mad Opinion's leave,
> All states can reach it, and all heads conceive;   30
> Obvious her goods, in no extreme they dwell,

23–6 *Add. 1743b, 1751; but cf. textual note, l. 28n.*
28 *Between ll. 28–29, 1734–43a have:*
>   One grants his Pleasure is but Rest from pain,
>   One doubts of All, one owns ev'n Virtue vain.

23–4. *Beasts, Gods*] Cf. *Ess.*, II 8.

23. *pleasure . . . pain*] As in Young, *Love of Fame*, III 105: ". . . love of pleasure into pain betrays."

24. Cf. *Mor. Ess.*, III 333–4. The allusion, as Pattison notes, is to Brutus's dying words in Dio Cass., XLVII 49. Bacon quotes them in *Adv. of Learning*, II xxiii 46; Oldham in *A Satyr Against Virtue*, 73; and Cowley in *Brutus*, st. 5.

swell'd . . . Gods] The usual indictment of the Stoics. For typical statements, cf. Milton, *Par. Reg.*, IV 300ff; Dryden, Dedication of *Don. Seb.*: ". . . the ruggedness of a stoic is only a silly affectation of being a god."

confess . . . vain] Cf. Sprat, *Plague of Athens*, st. 31: "Virtue was now esteem'd an empty name."

25–6. Cf. *Ess.*, II 5.

26. *doubt . . . all*] Milton, *Par. Reg.*, IV 296: "A third sort doubted all things, though plain sense."

29ff. HAPPINESS the END of all Men, and attainable by all. [P. *1735b–43a.*]
The accepted view, in traditional ethics. Cf. Aristotle, *Eth. Nic.*, 1099b: "It [happiness] will also on this view be very generally shared; for all who are not maimed as regards their potentiality for virtue may win it by a certain kind of study and care"; Seneca, *Ep.*, IV 8; Milton, *Par. Reg.*, IV 466–8:
>   Yet he who reigns within himself, and rules
>   Passions, desires, and fears, is more a king—
>   Which every wise and virtuous man attains;

Hutcheson, pp. 202–3: "How clearly does the *Order of our Nature* point out to us our true *Happiness* and *Perfection*, and lead us to it as naturally as the several *Powers* of the *Earth*, the *Sun*, and *Air*, bring *Plants* to their Growth, and the Perfection of their Kinds."

Nature's path] Cf. II 161.

31. *Obvious*] The Latin sense assimilates this to the "path" figure.

There needs but thinking right, and meaning well;
And mourn our various portions as we please,
Equal is Common Sense, and Common Ease.
    Remember, Man, "the Universal Cause   35
"Acts not by partial, but by gen'ral laws;"
And makes what Happiness we justly call
Subsist not in the good of one, but all.
There's not a blessing Individuals find,
But some way leans and hearkens to the kind.   40
No Bandit fierce, no Tyrant mad with pride,

---

32. Ideas expanded below, 309–72.

34. Near-axioms of traditional thought. On the former, Pattison quotes Descartes, *De la methode*, I [tr. Veitch]: "Good sense is, of all things among men, the most equally distributed . . ."; and cf. Charleton, p. 64. On the latter, cf. *Guardian*, 54; and *Applebee's Original Weekly*, 3 Feb. 1733: "All the things in the World reduce themselves to a *certain* kind of *Balance*. The *good* and *bad* Fortune of several *Conditions* is so even poised, that almost *equal* Proportions of *both* are to be found in *all*."

Pope writes to Allen, in a letter apparently describing one of his last illnesses (EC, IX 200–1) "I am in no pain, my case is not curable, and must in course of time, as it does not diminish, become painful at first, and then fatal. And what of all this? Without any distemper at all, life itself does so, and is itself a pain, if continued long enough. So that Providence is equal, even between what seem so wide extremes as health and infirmity."

35*ff*. GOD governs by *general* not *particular* Laws: intends Happiness to be *equal*, and to be so, it must be *social*, since all perfect Happiness *depends on general*. [P. *1735b–43a, but 1736–43a* have particular *for* perfect.]

35–8. Cf. II 249*ff*; III 1–2, 111–14, and *passim*.

39–40. So in Young, *Love of Fame*, VII 155–8: "What we prize As our chief blessing, must from others rise."

40. *leans . . . hearkens*] EC notes the adaptation of the phrase from Donne's *Valediction, Forbidding Mourning* [31], and Wakefield paraphrases: "Man waits, as it were, all ear! for the approbation of another's feelings, before he can decide upon the reality of his own happiness from a present enjoyment."

41–4. For the general argument, instancing both bandit and tyrant, cf. Augustine, *De civ. dei*, XIX xii. Cicero observes (*De. amicit.*, XXIII) that even a Timon requires some one to lash at, no man being capable of happiness in total isolation: "Sic natura solitarium nihil amat semperque ad aliquod tamquam adminiculum annititur. . ."; and cf. *Civil Polity* (1703), p. 3; Swift, IV 118: "The wickedest man upon earth taketh a pleasure in doing good to those he loveth . . ."; and *Ess.*, IV 363*n* (*Guardian*).

No cavern'd Hermit, rests self-satisfy'd.
Who most to shun or hate Mankind pretend,
Seek an admirer, or would fix a friend.
Abstract what others feel, what others think,   45
All pleasures sicken, and all glories sink;
Each has his share; and who would more obtain,
Shall find, the pleasure pays not half the pain.
    ORDER is Heav'n's first law; and this confest,

42 rests] rest *1734–43a*.   49 first] great *1735c–43a*.

45–6. Cf. Seneca, *Ep.*, VI 4: "Nullius boni, sine socio, iucunda possessio est."
47–8. Pattison compares Southwell, *Times go by Turns*, 22–4:
        Few all they neede, but none have all they wish;
        Unmedled [unmingled] joys here to no man befall,
        Who least hath some, who most hath never all.
    48. Horace, *Ep.*, I ii 55: ". . . nocet empta dolore voluptas"; Shaks., *Love's Labour's Lost*, I i 72–3; Sheffield, *Ess. on Satire*, 174–5:
        Each pleasure hath its price, and when we pay
        Too much of pain, we squander life away;
Mor. Ess., II 99. Pattison cites Ralegh, *The Lye*, and Jer. Taylor, *Sermon* XV [*Wks.* (1844), I 694]: ". . . if we go beyond what is needful, . . . we disorder the certainty of our felicity. . ."
    49. *ORDER . . . law*] Cf. I 129–30; Swift, IV 187: "All government is from God, Who is the God of order . . ."
    49*ff.* It is necessary for ORDER and the common Peace, that *External Goods* be *unequal*, therefore Happiness is not constituted in these. [P. *1735b–43a*.]
    Cf. above, I 233*ff*, and J. Balguy, *Divine Rectitude* (1730), pp. 58–60: "Nothing is more evident, than that if Mankind were reduced to an Equality, . . . the Affairs of the World would either stand still, or run into the utmost Confusion. But supposing it a Matter indifferent to Society, . . . there is good Reason to believe that the present Inequality would still have prevailed upon other Accounts. As the *Order* and the Harmony of the World require a Variety and Subordination of *Kinds*, so the same may be said in respect of Individuals. . . [Subordination] promotes likewise *Moral Good*, by affording such Occasions of Exercising Men's Virtues and improving their Minds, as could not have been had without it. Moderation, Contentment, Humility, and the like Virtues depend in a great Measure on these Inequalities . . . a regular Subordination being right, fit, and amiable in itself, may well be considered as God's Ordinance; who has made evident Provision for it in the Diversity of Talents and Natural Endowments which appears throughout our whole Species [cf. *Ess.*, II 161*ff*, 247*ff*]. The original Disparities of their Minds naturally tend to produce

Some are, and must be, greater than the rest, 50
More rich, more wise; but who infers from hence
That such are happier, shocks all common sense.
Heav'n to Mankind impartial we confess,
If all are equal in their Happiness:
But mutual wants this Happiness increase, 55
All Nature's diff'rence keeps all Nature's peace.

50 greater] mightier *1735c–43a*.

---

different Circumstances and Conditions of Life. But it may not be improper to add, that these Distinctions are far less material than is commonly imagined. In respect of the most valuable Enjoyments, and the principal Blessings of Life, Men are nearly equal."

49–51. A favourite subject of sermon literature. Cf. J. Hales, *Golden Remains* (1659), pp. 157–8; G. Hickes, *Sermon Preached . . . April 1, 1684* (1684), p. 7; R. Moss, *The Providential Division of Men into Rich and Poor* (1708), in *Twenty-five Sermons preached at the Anniv. Meetings of the Children educ. in the Charity Schools . . . , by several . . . Dignitaries* (1729), p. 110. Also, *Spectat.*, 219, and La Bruyère, II 241.

53–4. Swift, IV 202: ". . . I lay it down as a certain truth, that God Almighty hath placed all men upon an equal foot, with respect to their happiness in this world, and the capacity of attaining their salvation in the next; or, at least, if there be any difference, it is not to the advantage of the rich and mighty."

55–6. Cf. I 169*ff*, 233*ff*, II 249*ff*, III 111*ff*, 295*ff*. A traditional doctrine, capable (as here) of political, social, and economic applications (cf. Cumberland pp. 322–3; La Bruyère, II 139–41; Swift, IV 114–16; *Civil Polity* (1703), p. 52) but resting ultimately on the cosmological concept of *concordia discors* postulated throughout Pope's poem. For an interesting illustration, see T. Clutterbuck's *Spittle Sermon Preached . . . March 30, 1687* (1687), p. 10: "It is by this *Communication*, that all things in the *World* . . . do subsist. And every thing having an Office, or excellency of its own, different from that which is anothers, by this mutual Vicissitude, in giving a supply to each others wants, the whole comes to be preserv'd and remain entire. Thus if the Water is beholding to the Earth for bearing and supporting it, the Earth is beholding to the Water for moistening it, and making it fruitful. If the Flowers adorn . . . the Ground, the Ground gives strength and nourishment to the Flowers. The Fountain that comes from the Sea, empties it self into its bosom again. . . And this *Communication* is in all Civil Societies too. Those several ranks and degrees of Men, that Inequality and seeming Discord makes up the greater Harmony in the whole, and unites and consolidates the parts the better together. Thus does the Wise man direct the Strong, and the Strong protect the Wise. The Rich supplies the Poor, and the Poor . . . labours for the Rich."

Condition, circumstance is not the thing;
Bliss is the same in subject or in king,
In who obtain defence, or who defend,
In him who is, or him who finds a friend: 60
Heav'n breaths thro' ev'ry member of the whole
One common blessing, as one common soul.
But Fortune's gifts if each alike possest,
And each were equal, must not all contest?
If then to all Men Happiness was meant,   65
God in Externals could not place Content.
Fortune her gifts may variously dispose,

57–62. J. Hales, *Golden Remains* (1659), p. 73: "Now . . . what is the main end of our life? . . . It is, or should be, nothing else but *virtue* and *happiness*: Now these are alike purchasable in all estates; Poverty, *disease*, distress, contumely, contempt, these are as well the object of *virtue*, as *wealth*, liberty, honor, reputation . . .: *Happiness* therefore may as well dwell with the poor, miserable, and distressed persons, as with persons of *better fortune*, since it is confest by all, that *happiness* is nothing else but *Actio secundum virtutem, a leading of our life according to virtue*. As great art may be exprest in the *cutting* of a *flint*, as in the cutting of a diamond. . ."; and cf. La Bruyère, I 210: "There is . . . a kind of charm inherent in each different condition . . . : the Great please themselves in excess, their inferiors in moderation; those delight in lording and commanding, these take a pleasure, and even a pride, in serving and obeying . . ."

58. Pattison compares Horace, *Ep.*, I xii 5–6.

62. *as . . . soul*] I 267*ff*, II 237*ff*, III 21*ff*.

63–4. Specific political application of the principle discussed above, 55–6*n*. Cf. Cumberland, pp. 65–6; La Bruyère, II 140; Jer. Collier, *Ess. upon Sev. Moral Subjects*, IV (1725), 270–1.

67*ff*. The balance of human happiness kept equal (notwithstanding *Externals*) by HOPE and FEAR. [*P. 1735b–43a, but 1739–43a add as a second paragraph*] The Exemplification of this Truth, by a view of the *Equality* of *Happiness* in the several particular *Stations* of Life, were [was] design'd for the subject of a future Epistle.
Cf. Temple [I 305]: "Whether a good Condition, with Fear of being ill, or an ill, with Hope of being well, pleases or displeases most" [EC]; *ibid.*, 306, 309; Horace, *Odes*, II x 21–4, and *Sats. and Odes of Hor.* (1715), p. 62:
An Even Well-pois'd Mind, an Evil State
With Hope, a Good with Fear does moderate;
and Burton, p. 93: "For he that lives not in a due regard to God, nor acts agreeable to his . . . best considered Thoughts, cannot be happy, because he's unquiet

And these be happy call'd, unhappy those;
But Heav'n's just balance equal will appear,
While those are plac'd in Hope, and these in Fear: 70
Not present good or ill, the joy or curse,
But future views of better, or of worse.
    Oh sons of earth! attempt ye still to rise,
By mountains pil'd on mountains, to the skies?
Heav'n still with laughter the vain toil surveys,   75
And buries madmen in the heaps they raise.
    III. Know, all the good that individuals find,
Or God and Nature meant to mere Mankind;

68 happy call'd, unhappy those] call'd unhappy, happy those
    1734–35a.
70 If while th'Unhappy hope, the Happy fear *1735a.*

and disturb'd with Thoughts that contradict and condemn his Actions. Whereas the religious, vertuous, honest Man hath a peaceable Mind, and a quiet
Conscience, and he that hath this, whatever his other Circumstances are, his
Condition cannot be very ill."
    73–6. Cf. Introd., pp. lix–lx.
    73–4. Cf. Boethius, *De cons. phil.*, II pr. vi (tr. H. R. James): "What now shall
I say of rank and power, whereby, because you know not true power and dignity, ye hope to reach the sky?" Pope to Blount, 13 Sept. 1725: "Discharge the
load of earth that lies on you like one of the mountains under which, the poets
say, the giants, the men of the earth, are whelmed. Leave earth to the sons of
earth; your conversation is in heaven . . ." EC compares for the phrasing
Dryden's Virgil, *Geo.*, I 374–6:
        . . . arm'd, against the skies, the sons of earth.
        With mountains pil'd on mountains, thrice they strove
        To scale the steepy battlements of Jove.
    75. Wakefield cites Psa., II 4. Cf. Milton's account of the frustration of Babel,
Par. Lost, XII 59: ". . . Great laughter was in Heaven"; and Pope's *Il.*, V 517*n*.
    76. Pope to Atterbury, 23 Sept. 1720: "Methinks God has punished the
avaricious as he often punishes sinners, in their own way, in the very sin itself;
the thirst of gain was their crime; that thirst continued became their punishment and ruin."
    77ff. In what the Happiness of *Individuals* consists, and that the GOOD MAN
has the advantage, even in this world. [P. *1735b–43a.*]
    78. *mere Mankind*] "I.e. mankind as such" [Pattison]. But the force of the
phrase is also to diminish man.

P

Reason's whole pleasure, all the joys of Sense,
Lie in three words, Health, Peace, and Competence.   80
But Health consists with Temperance alone,
And Peace, oh Virtue! Peace is all thy own.
The good or bad the gifts of Fortune gain,
But these less taste them, as they worse obtain.
Say, in pursuit of profit or delight,   85
Who risk the most, that take wrong means, or right?
Of Vice or Virtue, whether blest or curst,
Which meets contempt, or which compassion first?
Count all th'advantage prosp'rous Vice attains,
'Tis but what Virtue flies from and disdains: 90
And grant the bad what happiness they wou'd,

79 Reason's whole] All Reason's *1735a*; pleasure] pleasures
1734–43a.
82 oh] fair *1734–35a*; O *1735b–43a*.
83 The gifts of Fortune good or bad may gain *1734–35a*.

80. Three requisites usually stressed in Pope's day, though often in varying
combinations: cf. Pope to Lord Oxford, 15 Sept. 1729; Bez. Morrice, "The
Request", in his *Miscell, or Amusements* (1712), p. 43; Pomfret, *Upon the Divine
Attributes: Goodness; The Weekly Oracle*, 18 Jan. 1735: "Whoever considers the
Happiness of human Life, must view it in three Respects: First, in regard to the
principal Part thereof, to wit his Soul or Mind; Secondly in respect of his Body,
or the Cloathing of his Soul; Thirdly, in respect to a Competency of Externals . . ."

83–4. Cf. Seneca, *Ep.*, xxvii, xlii; J. Balguy, *Divine Rectitude* (1730), pp.
53–4; Swift, iv 206; J. Norris, *Poems and Discourses* (1684), p. 30 (quoting
Hierocles): ". . . *all Pleasure is the Companion of Action, it has no Subsistence of its
own, but accompanies us in our doing such and such things. Hence 'tis that the worser
Actions are accompanied with the meaner Pleasures. So that the good Man does not only
excell the wicked Man in what is good, but has also the advantage of him even in Pleasure,
for whose sake alone he is wicked.*"

84. *worse*] Adverbial.

85–6, 89–90. Wollaston, pp. 408–9: "For if the soul be *mortal*, and all perception perishes for ever at our death, what in this case does a good man *lose* by
his virtue? . . . On the other hand, what does a vitious man gain? Only such
injoyments, as a virtuous man *leaves* . . ."

91–2. Jonson observes (*Discoveries, Works*, ed. Herford-Simpson, viii 566)
that "reputation of *Honesty*" cannot be had "but by living well". Cf. Cumber-

One they must want, which is, to pass for good.

    Oh blind to truth, and God's whole scheme below,

Who fancy Bliss to Vice, to Virtue Woe!

Who sees and follows that great scheme the best,   95

Best knows the blessing, and will most be blest.

But fools the Good alone unhappy call,

For ills or accidents that chance to all.

See FALKLAND dies, the virtuous and the just!

See god-like TURENNE prostrate on the dust!   100

95 sees . . . follows] see . . . follow *1735a*.
96 the] his *1734–34b*; knows the] know their *1735a*.
99 dies] falls *1734–35a*.

---

land, p. 72; Burton, p. 142: "Not all the Riches of the Earth, possesst by one man, if he be covetous, proud, if unjust, or uncharitable, can purchase him a good Name. He may . . . applaud and hug himself; but Men will not speak, or (I am sure) not think well of him."

    93*ff*. That no man is unhappy thro' VIRTUE. [P. *1735b–43a*.]

    93. *Oh . . . truth*] Cf. *Rape of the Lock*, I 104.

    95–6. Cf. I 283*ff*, IV 327*ff*.

    97–8. Cumberland, p. 23: "In comparing the Effects of good and evil Actions, those good or evil Things, which can neither be procur'd, nor avoided, by *human Industry*, are not to be taken into the Account. Such are those which happen by natural *Necessity*, or by mere *Chance*, from external Causes: for these both may, and do, happen alike both to good and bad"; J. Balguy, *Divine Rectitude* (1730), p. 56.

    98. Eccles., IX 11: "I returned, and saw . . . that the race is not to the swift, nor the battle to the strong, neither yet bread to the wise, nor yet riches to men of understanding, nor yet favour to men of skill; but time and chance happeneth to them all."

    99. Falkland was killed at the battle of Newbury, 20 Sept. 1643. Clarendon calls him (*Hist. of the Rebellion*, ed. Macray, 1888, III vii 217) a person "of such prodigious parts", such "inimitable sweetness and delight", such a "flowing and obliging . . . goodness to mankind", and such "simplicity and integrity of life", that his loss alone will make the Civil Wars "execrable to all posterity".

    100. Turenne was slain 27 July 1675 at Sassbach in Baden. For the epithet "godlike", see the early accounts in C.-G. Picavet, *Documents biogr. sur Turenne* (1611–75), Lille, 1914; and cf. the dedication by Pope's friend Ramsay of his *History of Turenne*, 1735, where Turenne is called "the Support of the Throne, the Father of his Soldiers, the Delight of his Countrymen, and An Honour to Human Kind".

See SIDNEY bleeds amid the martial strife!
Was this their Virtue, or Contempt of Life?
Say, was it Virtue, more tho' Heav'n ne'er gave,
Lamented DIGBY! sunk thee to the grave?
Tell me, if Virtue made the Son expire,   105
Why, full of days and honour, lives the Sire?
Why drew Marseille's good bishop purer breath,
When Nature sicken'd, and each gale was death?
Or why so long (in life if long can be)
Lent Heav'n a parent to the poor and me?   110
    IV. What makes all physical or moral ill?
There deviates Nature, and here wanders Will.

---

101. Sidney was fatally wounded at Zutphen, 22 Sept. 1586.

102. "The general conception of this whole passage seems derived from Lansdowne's verses [in his poem entitled *Occasioned by the Foregoing Verses*, 29 *ff*]" [Wakefield]. Though Lansdowne's terminology conflicts with Pope's his point is the same: that the virtuous man does not perish *because* he is virtuous.

103-6. "The Hon. Robert Digby, who died, aged 40, April 19, 1726 . . . [His father] William, fifth Lord Digby, was 74 when this fourth epistle was published . . ." [EC]. For Pope's epitaph on the son see vol. VI.

107-8. For a description of this plague and the conduct of Belsunce, the bishop referred to, see R. Crawfurd, *Plague and Pestilence in Lit. and Art* (1914), pp. 200-8; also, *A Brief Journal of what passed in the City of Marseilles, While it was Afflicted with the Plague, In the Year 1720* (1721). Though most of the doctors and clergy who did not flee fell victim to the disease, Belsunce survived: "Wherever the poorest lay, there he went confessing, consoling, and exhorting them to patience. To the dying he carried the Sacrament, to the destitute the whole of his money in alms. Though plague invaded his palace and carried off those about him, it spared him" (Crawfurd, p. 204).

108. Cf. the *Brief Journal* (cited above), p. 53, where it is said that the rotting bodies furnish "Exhalations which must poison the Air". For the phrasing, Wakefield compares a couplet from an anonymous poem [*A Midnight Thought*, 7-8] in Dryden's sixth *Miscellany*:
> When Nature sickens, and with fainting Breath
> Struggles beneath the bitter Pangs of Death.

109. (*in . . . be*)] Wakefield cites Virgil, *Aen.*, x 861: ". . . diu, res si qua diu mortalibus ulla est"; and cf. Cicero, *Tusc. disp.*, I xxxix 94: "Quae vero aetas longa est aut quid omnino homini longum?"

110. Pope's mother died, aged 91, 7 June 1733.

112. Cf. above, I 149*ff*.

God sends not ill; if rightly understood,
Or partial Ill is universal Good,
Or Change admits, or Nature lets it fall,   115
Short and but rare, 'till Man improv'd it all.
We just as wisely might of Heav'n complain,
That righteous Abel was destroy'd by Cain;
As that the virtuous son is ill at ease,
When his lewd father gave the dire disease.   120
Think we, like some weak Prince, th'Eternal Cause,
Prone for his fav'rites to reverse his laws?
    Shall burning Ætna, if a sage requires,
Forget to thunder, and recall her fires?
On air or sea new motions be imprest,   125

113 *Instead of ll. 113–116, 1734–34b have:*
        God sends not Ill, 'tis Nature lets it fall
        Or Chance escape, and Man improves it all.

---

115. *Or . . . admits*] Cf. I 147 and note. The earlier reading, "chance" (cf. textual notes), was not necessarily in conflict with the doctrine of Providence summarized in I 290: cf. Aquinas's discussion entitled "That Divine Providence Does Not Exclude Chance or Luck", (*Sum. c. gent.*, III lxiv) and the application of the word in Eccles., and Cumberland, above, IV 97–8n.

116. *Short . . . rare*] Cf. N. Grew, *Cosmologia Sacra* (1701), III ii 28, 34; Hutcheson, p. 185: "The Pains of the *external Senses* are pretty frequent, but how short in comparison of the long Tracts of Health, ease, and Pleasure? How rare is the Instance of a Life spent in violent Pain?"

'till . . . all] E.g. in his fall and its consequences.

119–20. Cf. Exod., XX 5; Lipsius, *De constantia*, II xvii (tr. J. Stradling) "What marueill is it then if he punish in the posteritie those faultes which be not properlie diuers, but by certen communication of seede made ioynt . . ."

123–4. Empedocles was variously reported to have fallen into the crater of Aetna while trying to conceal himself, to have been the victim of an eruption which he was seeking to observe scientifically, or to have thrown himself into the volcano to confirm reports that he had become a God. (See Diog. Laert., VIII 69, 74, and J. Bidez, *La Biographie d'Empédocle* (1894), pp. 35ff, 67ff, 90ff.) Pope's lines fit best the second version.

125–30. *Adventurer* compares Wollaston, pp. 178–9: ". . . as to the *course of nature*, if a *good* man be passing by an infirm building, just in the article of falling, can it be expected, that God should *suspend* the force of gravitation till he is gone by, in order to his deliverance; or can we think it would be increased, and the

Oh blameless Bethel! to relieve thy breast?
When the loose mountain trembles from on high,
Shall gravitation cease, if you go by?
Or some old temple, nodding to its fall,
For Chartres' head reserve the hanging wall?   130
    v. But still this world (so fitted for the knave)
Contents us not. A better shall we have?
A kingdom of the Just then let it be:
But first consider how those Just agree.
The good must merit God's peculiar care;   135
But who, but God, can tell us who they are?

128 if] as *1739–43a.*

---

fall hastened, if a *bad* man was there, only that he might be caught, crushed, and
made an example? If a man's safety or prosperity should depend upon winds or
rains, must *new* motions be imprest upon the atmosphere, and *new* directions
given to the floating parts of it, by some *extra-ordinary* and *new* influence of
God?" In a note to this passage, Wollaston (quoting Plotinus) asks, like Pope,
whether it is "not more likely . . . that when a house falls, he that it falls upon
should be killed, what sort of a man soever he be . . ."

125-6. For some account of Hugh Bethel (d. 1748), one of Pope's oldest and
firmest friends, see vol. IV, Biog. App. Croker supposes (EC, II 438, *n.* 5) from a
letter of Pope's to Bethel, "then in Italy" (Ruffhead, *Life of Pope,* 1769, p. 315*n*),
that this couplet alludes to some discomforts undergone in the voyage, Bethel
being troubled with asthma (EC, IX 298). On his blamelessness, see Pope to
Swift, 3 Sept. 1726, to Allen, 20 Jan. 1744; and to Bethel himself, 9 Aug. 1733,
where he calls this couplet "all a poor poet can do, to bear testimony to the
virtue he cannot reach".

129-30. Wakefield compares Cicero, *De fato,* III, where Cicero says, speaking
of the stone that fell and injured the bandit Icadius, that even if Icadius had not
been there "saxum tamen illud casurum fuisse".

130. Francis Chartres or Charteris (1675-1732), a notorious scoundrel,
lately dead. Cf. Biog. App., vol. IV; and Pope's note to *Mor. Ess.,* III 20.

133. *kingdom . . . Just*] I.e. of the righteous in the sight of God. Cf. Pope to
Swift, 15 Oct. 1725: ". . . . I have fancied . . . that we should meet [after death]
like the righteous in the millenium, . . . content to enjoy the kingdom of the just
in tranquillity."

135. Cf. Ovid, *Metam.,* VIII 724: "Cura pii diis sunt"; Dryden's translation
(VIII 198): " 'The good,' said I, 'are God's peculiar care' "; and his *Ess.* (ed.
Ker), I 273.

136. A favourite theme of Lipsius: cf. *De constantia,* II xvi. Warton cites Wol-

One thinks on Calvin Heav'n's own spirit fell,
Another deems him instrument of hell;
If Calvin feel Heav'n's blessing, or its rod,
This cries there is, and that, there is no God.   140
What shocks one part will edify the rest,
Nor with one system can they all be blest.
The very best will variously incline,
And what rewards your Virtue, punish mine.
"Whatever IS, is RIGHT."—This world, 'tis true,   145

---

142 *Between ll. 142–143, 1734–34b have:*
    Give each a System, all must be at strife;
    What diff'rent Systems for a man and wife?

---

laston, pp. 200*ff.* P. 201: "We are not always certain, who are *good,* who *wicked.*" P. 204: ". . . the true characters of men must chiefly depend upon the *unseen* part of their lives . . ." See also J. Balguy, *Divine Rectitude* (1730), p. 53.

137–41. For the general thesis, compare *Spectat.,* 257: ". . . the same actions may represent a man as hypocritical and designing to one, which make him appear a saint or hero to another. . . [God] is the only proper judge of our perfections . . ." The violent clash of opinion about Calvin is abundantly illustrated in Bayle, Dict., art. Calvin, remarques M, N, Q, R, X, and *passim.*

141–4. I.e. (as in the Calvin illustration) the very best men will differ in their judgement, with the result that what you take to be a reward of what you call virtue will seem to me a punishment of what I call virtue. Cf. Robt. Howard *Vestal Virgin,* IV i:
    None beg the same, the Pray'rs of all the best,
    Are little more than Curses for the rest;
Wollaston, p. 179.

144. Pope to Atterbury, 8 Sept. 1718: "It is pleasant enough to consider that people who imagine themselves good Christians, should be so absurd as to think the same misfortunes, when they befal others, a punishment of vice, when they happen to themselves, an exercise of virtue."

145–6. *This . . . Caesar*] "He alludes to the complaint of Cato in Addison's tragedy, IV iv [23–4]:
    Justice gives way to force: the conquer'd world
    Is *Caesar's: Cato* has no business in it"—
[EC]. Cf. Pope to Swift, 23 March 1728: "This world is made for Caesar, as Cato said . . ."; and Dryden, *Aureng-Zebe,* II i: "The world is made for the bold impious man."

145. Cf. *Ess.,* I 294 and notes.

Was made for Caesar—but for Titus too:
And which more blest? who chain'd his country, say,
Or he whose Virtue sigh'd to lose a day?
  "But sometimes Virtue starves, while Vice is fed."
What then? Is the reward of Virtue bread?   150
That, Vice may merit; 'tis the price of toil;
The knave deserves it, when he tills the soil,
The knave deserves it when he tempts the main,
Where Folly fights for kings, or dives for gain.
The good man may be weak, be indolent,   155
Nor is his claim to plenty, but content.
But grant him Riches, your demand is o'er?

154 Folly] Madness *1734–34b*; kings, or dives] Tyrants, or *1734–34b, 1735b–36*; dives] drowns *1739–43a*.

---

146. Cf. *Ess.*, II 198.

148. Alluding to the anecdote told of Titus by Suetonius, VIII viii. Cf. Boileau on the same subject, *Ep.*, I 113–14, and the translation in the English version of his *Wks.*, II (1711) 19: "And when he lost a day, he sighed at night."

150ff. Plotinian arguments: cf. Introd., pp. xxxii–xxxiii.

150. *Is . . . bread?*] See IV 97–8n (Eccles.).

151–4. Wm. Talbot, *Sermon Preached . . . the 26th of Febr. 1691/2* (1692), p. 15: ". . . there is hardly any man so bad but has something of good in him, at least some natural or moral good, some good quality, by which he is useful and serviceable to the World: Now for God to reward the natural or moral goodness of otherwise very bad men, with outward temporal blessings, seems very agreeable to that rule by which he governs himself in the distributions of recompences, (*viz.*) to reward every one according to his works; and is so far from being a reasonable objection against his Justice or Goodness, that no doubt the Atheist would more violently, and . . . more plausibly object against both, if God should suffer that, whether natural or moral goodness, to be altogether unrewarded: Besides, bad men are many times instruments in the hands of God for the execution of his purposes, . . . and their serving the ends of Providence . . . God looks upon himself . . . obliged to reward with outward recompences . . ."

151. *That*] I.e. bread.

154. *Folly*] As in Erasmus, p. 100: "Another for a small and incertain gain exposes his life to the casualties of Seas and Winds, which yet no money can restore. Another had rather get Riches by War than live peaceably at home."

156. Cf. Blackmore, *Prince Arthur* (1695), IV 777–8, 781–4:
    Content alone can all their Wrongs redress;
    Content, that other Name for *Happiness* . . .

"No—shall the good want Health, the good want Pow'r?"
Add Health and Pow'r, and ev'ry earthly thing;
"Why bounded Pow'r? why private? why no king?"   160
Nay, why external for internal giv'n?
Why is not Man a God, and Earth a Heav'n?
Who ask and reason thus, will scarce conceive
God gives enough, while he has more to give:
Immense that pow'r, immense were the demand;   165
Say, at what part of nature will they stand?
    VI. What nothing earthly gives, or can destroy,
The soul's calm sun-shine, and the heart-felt joy,
Is Virtue's prize: A better would you fix?
Then give Humility a coach and six,   170
Justice a Conq'ror's sword, or Truth a gown,

162 a God, and] an Angel, *1735a.*
169–72 *1734–34b read* And *for* Then *in 170, and close 169 with a comma, 170 and 172 with interrogation points; 1735a keeps the interrogation point after 172.*

        'Tis equal, if our Fortunes should augment,
        And stretch themselves to the same vast Extent
        With our Desires, or those Desires abate,
        Shrink, and Contract themselves, to fit our State.

160. I.e., why a private citizen?

167–9. Aristotle, *Eth. Nic.*, 1100b: "Success or failure in life does not depend on these [externals], but . . . virtuous activities or their opposites are what constitute happiness or the reverse"; Seneca, *Ep.*, LXXVIII 15: ". . . praemium non corona, nec palma est . . .: sed virtus, et firmitas animi, et pax . . ."

168. *The . . . sun-shine*] For the image, cf. Seneca, *Ep.*, XXVII 3: "Sola virtus praestat gaudium perpetuum, securum: etiam si quid obstat, nubium modo intervenit, quae infra feruntur, nec unquam diem vincunt"; Chudleigh, *On the Vanities of this Life*, 5–7:

        As th' upper Region is serene and clear,
        No Winds, no Clouds are there,
        So with perpetual Calms the virtuous Soul is blest;

Young, *Imper. Pelagi*, str. IV, st. 16: "True joy, the sunshine of the soul"; *El. to Abel.*, 209: "Eternal sun-shine of the spotless mind!"

169ff. That *External Goods* are not the proper rewards of *Virtue*, often inconsistent with, or destructive of it; but that all these can make no man happy without *Virtue*. Instanced in each of them. [P. *1735b–43a.*]

Or Public Spirit its great cure, a Crown.
Weak, foolish man! will Heav'n reward us there
With the same trash mad mortals wish for here?
The Boy and Man an individual makes,   175
Yet sigh'st thou now for apples and for cakes?
Go, like the Indian, in another life
Expect thy dog, thy bottle, and thy wife:
As well as dream such trifles are assign'd,
As toys and empires, for a god-like mind.   180
Rewards, that either would to Virtue bring
No joy, or be destructive of the thing:
How oft by these at sixty are undone
The virtues of a saint at twenty-one!
To whom can Riches give Repute, or Trust,   185

173–180 *Add. 1743b, 1751.*
185–6 *1734–43a read:*

        For *Riches*, can they give but to the Just,
        His own Contentment, or another's Trust?

---

171. *a . . . sword*] Cf. IV 219*ff.*

gown] "This may refer to the gown of a University degree, or, as in 197, to the preacher's gown" [Morris].

172. *cure*] Perhaps used with ironic overtones from the word's other senses: "care", "spiritual charge", etc.

174. Dryden, *Pal. and Arc.*, I 420–3:

        But why, alas! do mortal men in vain,
        Of Fortune, Fate, or Providence complain?
        God gives us what he knows our wants require,
        And better things than those which we desire.

175. "I.e. the conjunction of boy and man; hence the verb is properly in the singular" [Ward].

177–8. Contrast I 99*ff.*

181–4. Cf. Milton, *Par. Reg.*, II 453–6:

        Extol not riches, then, the toil of fools,
        The wise man's cumbrance, if not snare; more apt
        To slacken virtue and abate her edge
        Than prompt her to do aught may merit praise;

Bellarmine, p. 214: "I question not but a great many poor Men are now Inheritors of the Kingdom of Heaven, who, if a large share of this world's Goods had befallen them, would have been ruin'd for ever."

185*ff.* I. RICHES. [P. *1735b–43a.*] Cf. Milton, *Par. Reg.*, II 432*ff.*

Content, or Pleasure, but the Good and Just?
Judges and Senates have been bought for gold,
Esteem and Love were never to be sold.
Oh fool! to think God hates the worthy mind,
The lover and the love of human-kind,   190
Whose life is healthful, and whose conscience clear;
Because he wants a thousand pounds a year.

    Honour and shame from no Condition rise;
Act well your part, there all the honour lies.
Fortune in Men has some small diff'rence made,   195
One flaunts in rags, one flutters in brocade,
The cobler apron'd, and the parson gown'd,
The friar hooded, and the monarch crown'd.
"What differ more (you cry) than crown and cowl?"
I'll tell you, friend! a Wise man and a Fool.   200

185–6. Swift, IV 118: "Thus, for example, great riches are no blessing in themselves. . . . How then do they become blessings? No otherwise, than by being employed in feeding the hungry, clothing the naked, rewarding worthy men, and in short, doing acts of charity and generosity."

190. *the . . . human-kind*] Pattison compares Suetonius' phrase (VIII i), used of Titus: "amor ac deliciae generis humani".

193ff. 2. HONOURS. [P. *1735b–43a*.]

194. The central maxim (along with that which opens Epistle II) of traditional ethics: cf. Introd., p. xxxv; Seneca, *Ep.*, LXXVII 17: "Quomodo fabula, sic vita; non quam diu, sed quam bene acta sit, refert"; *Spectat.*, 219, 406; *Plain Dealer*, 28; Pope to Cromwell, 18 March 1708; Wycherley, *To a Vain Young Courtier* (*Posthum. Wks.*, 1728, p. 217):

        . . . who can act his ill Part well,
        Does him, who acts a good one ill, excell.
        Since it is not so much his Praise, whose Part
        Is best, but His, who acts it with most Art.

195–6. For the type of opinion Pope is opposing, cf. La Rochefoucauld, IV xvi: ". . . it is not the Qualities, but the Fortunes of Men, that makes the difference between them."

196. The surprise in the verbs, as Warburton noted, helps stress Pope's point that fortunes do not change the men.

200. Cf. Terence, *Eunuch.*, II ii 1–2: "Di immortales, homini homo quid praestat? Stulto intellegens Quid interest?"; and Bacon, *Apophthegms*, 255: "One of the philosophers was asked: *What a wise man differed from a fool?* He answered: *Send them both naked to those that know them not, and you shall perceive.*"

Fool] For the pronunciation, EC calls attention to Shaks., *3 Hen. VI*, v vi [18–20].

You'll find, if once the monarch acts the monk,
Or, cobler-like, the parson will be drunk,
Worth makes the man, and want of it, the fellow;
The rest is all but leather or prunella.
    Stuck o'er with titles and hung round with strings,
That thou may'st be by kings, or whores of kings.   206
Boast the pure blood of an illustrious race,
In quiet flow from Lucrece to Lucrece;

207–208   1734–43a read:
        Thy boasted Blood, a thousand years or so,
        May from Lucretia to Lucretia flow.

---

201. EC sees an allusion to "Philip V of Spain, who resigned his crown to his son, Jan. 10 1724, and retired to a monastery", reascending the throne after his son's death the succeeding August.

203–4. C. Forbes (*N & Q*, 1st ser., 1 246) compares Petronius, LXXV: "Consilium est quod homines facit, caetera quisquilia omnia"; and cf. the further correspondence, *ibid.*, pp. 362, 414, 452. La Rochefoucauld, III ii: "True Worth does not depend upon Times nor Fashions. They that have only the Advantage of a *Court Air*, any where else are no better than their Neighbours. But good *Sence*, *Learning*, and *Wisdom*, are Qualifications that recommend a Man, and make him *Valued* every where, and at all times."

204. I.e. dress: the cobbler's apron of leather, the clergyman's gown of prunella.

205–6. 3. TITLES. [P. *1735b–43a.*]

205. A contemptuous image of carcasses dressed for the table (or for sacrifice) may be relevant here.

hung . . . strings] Burnet, *Hist. of His Own Time* (ed. Airy, 1897), 1 485: ". . . when he [Halifax] talked to me . . . of his contempt of the world, I asked him what he meant to be getting so many new titles, which I called the hanging himself about with bells and tinsel." Cf. *Imit. Hor., Ep.*, 1 vi 15 and note.

206. A distinction, which like many others in the poem (e.g. IV 180), ostensibly sets apart two realms of value in order to identify them. Pope says in a letter to Allen (EC, IX 200), "though they call Kings the fountains of honour, I think them only the bestowers of titles."

207ff. 4. BIRTH. [P. *1735b–43a.*]

Cf. Juvenal, *Sat.*, VIII 1*ff*; Charron, 1 lix; Boileau, *Sat.*, v; Dryden, *Wife of Bath, Her Tale*, 378*ff*; *Plain Dealer*, 39.

207–8. Wakefield cites Boileau, *Sat.*, v 85–6:
        Et si leur sang tout pur, ainsi que leur noblesse
        Est passé jusqu'à nous de Lucrèce en Lucrèce?

But by your father's worth if yours you rate,
Count me those only who were good and great.   210
Go! if your ancient, but ignoble blood
Has crept thro' scoundrels ever since the flood,
Go! and pretend your family is young;
Nor own, your fathers have been fools so long.
What can ennoble sots, or slaves, or cowards?   215
Alas! not all the blood of all the HOWARDS.
       Look next on Greatness; say where Greatness lies?
"Where, but among the Heroes and the Wise?"
Heroes are much the same, the point's agreed,

214 Nor] Not *1734–43a*.

211–12. Wakefield compares Jos. Hall, *Sat.*, [IV] iii [5–6]:
              Or tedious bead-rolls of descended blood,
              From father Japhet since Deucalion's flood.
Cf. also Dryden, *Abs. and Achit.*, 301–2:
              . . . a successive title, long and dark,
              Drawn from the moldy rolls of Noah's ark;
and Young, *Love of Fame*, I 141–2.
     214. Pattison quotes Rochester's verses on the great family [*Artemisia in the Town to Chloe in the Country*, 213–14]:
              Who with strong beer and beef the country rules,
              And ever since the Conquest have been fools.
     217ff. 5. GREATNESS. [P. *1735b–43a*.]
     219–24. Juvenal, *Sat.*, X 133ff [Pattison]. Cf. also Augustine, *De civ. dei*, IV iv; Milton, *Par. Reg.*, III 71ff; *Par. Lost*, XI 689ff:
              For in those days might only shall be admired,
              And valour, and heroick virtue call'd.
              To overcome in battle, and subdue
              Nations, and bring home spoils with infinite
              Manslaughter, shall be held the highest pitch
              Of human glory, and, for glory done,
              Of triumph, to be styl'd great conquerors,
              Patrons of mankind, gods, and sons of gods—
              Destroyers rightlier called, and Plagues of men;
Daniel, *To the Ladie Margaret*, 20ff; Boileau, *Sat.*, XI 77ff; Esprit, p. 333; Swift, *Tale of a Tub* (ed. Smith and Guthkelch, 1920), p. 94; Young, *Love of Fame*, VII 31ff; Dryden, *Ess.* (ed. Ker), II 13: ". . . those ungodly man-killers whom we poets, when we flatter them, call heroes; a race of men who can never enjoy quiet in themselves, till they have taken it from all the world".

From Macedonia's madman to the Swede;   220
The whole strange purpose of their lives, to find
Or make, an enemy of all mankind!
Not one looks backward, onward still he goes,
Yet ne'er looks forward farther than his nose.
No less alike the Politic and Wise,   225
All sly slow things, with circumspective eyes:
Men in their loose unguarded hours they take,
Not that themselves are wise, but others weak.
But grant that those can conquer, these can cheat,
'Tis phrase absurd to call a Villain Great: 230
Who wickedly is wise, or madly brave,
Is but the more a fool, the more a knave.
Who noble ends by noble means obtains,
Or failing, smiles in exile or in chains,
Like good Aurelius let him reign, or bleed   235
Like Socrates, that Man is great indeed.

224 farther] further *1734–35a*.   228 Not] Nor *1734–43a*.

---

220. *Macedonia's madman*] For this view of Alexander, see Seneca, *De benef.*,
I xiii; Spenser, *F.Q.*, I v 48 [Pattison]; Boileau, *Sat.*, VIII 99: "cet écervelé, qui
mit l'Asie en cendre" [Warton]; Swift, *Tale of a Tub* (ed. Smith and Guthkelch,
1920), p. 170, where the activities of Alexander, Jack of Leyden, and Descartes
are all attributed to the same vapour of madness; and John Hughes, *House of
Nassau* (1718), st. 18, which refers to Alexander as "the madman".

   the Swede] Charles XII (1682–1718), whom Thomson later called in *Winter*
(1744), 980, "the frantic Alexander of the North". Cf. *Gent. Mag.*, II (1732) 644:
"The Life of Charles XII, of Sweden, as written by Voltaire [publ. 1730], is a
Series of Imprudence and Temerity, Revenge and Folly. His behavior at *Bender*
shews him rather fitted for Bedlam than to govern a Nation."

   223. Jonson, *Catiline*, III iv 247: "Ambition, like a torrent, ne'er looks back."
   225–6. Cf. *Rape of the Lock*, III 117–18. L. 226 suggests a comparison of the
politic to Milton's Satan (*Par. Lost*, IV 536–7): "his proud step he scornful
turned, But with sly circumspection".
   227. Cf. *Macbeth*, I vii 69–70.
   229–32. La Rochefoucauld, IV xiv: "No Man can be perfectly Just and Good
without a great Measure of Sense and Right Reason, which will always carry
[him] to Choose the juster side in every Action of his Life. And it is a Foolish
thing to extol wicked Men, and Knaves, as the World commonly do, for
Persons of Wit and Understanding." Young, *Love of Fame*, I 143–7.

What's Fame? a fancy'd life in others breath,
237 a] that *1734–43a.*

233–6. Cf. Aristotle, *Eth. Nich.*, 1100b; Milton, *Par. Reg.*, III 88–92, 96–9:
>But, if there be in glory aught of good,
>It may by means far different be attained,
>Without ambition, war, or violence—
>By deeds of peace, by wisdom eminent,
>By patience, temperance. . .
>Poor Socrates, . . .
>By what he taught and suffered for so doing,
>For truth's sake suffering death unjust, lives now
>Equal in fame to proudest conquerors.

R. Gould, *Epist. Dedic.* to *The Playhouse*, in *Poems* (1689), p. 158.

235. *bleed*] The word has been rightly censured as unsuited to the manner of Socrates' death. It ought to be observed, however, that the syntactic arrangement shows Pope to have been at pains to juxtapose terms of equal generality and heroic connotation in order to define the character of his antithesis—which is not between the fates of Aurelius and Socrates as individuals, but between the good man reigning and the good man martyred. For this purpose, *bleed* is suggestive.

237*ff.* 6. FAME [P. *1735b–43a.*]
Warton compares Wollaston, pp. 215–6: "Thirst after Glory . . . is but a dream, . . . the *effect* of it . . . is but *what must cease* when the man dies: and, after all, . . . it lives but in the *breath* of the people. . . Men . . . fancy a perpetuity of fame . . .: but alas! it is a stupid delusion, when they imagine themselves *present*, and *injoying* that fame at the reading of their story after their death. And, beside, *in reality*, the man is not known ever the more to posterity, because his name is transmitted to them . . . When it is said, *J. Caesar* . . . beat *Pompey*, . . . it is the same thing, as to say, the conqueror of *Pompey* etc. was *Caesar* . . . The amount then is only this: that the Conqueror of *Pompey* conquerd *Pompey*; or some body conquerd *Pompey*; or rather, since *Pompey* is as little known now as *Caesar, some body* conquerd *some body*. Such a *poor business* is this boasted immortality . . ." See also Milton, *Par. Reg.*, III 100–4:
>Yet, if for fame and glory aught be done,
>Aught suffered—if young African for fame
>His wasted country freed from Punic rage—
>The deed becomes unpraised, the man at least,
>And loses, though but verbal, his reward;

and Cicero, *Somn. Scip.*, VI–VII.

237. *What's Fame?*] Cf. *Imit. Hor., Ep.*, I vi 46.

a . . . breath] For the image, cf. Thos. May, *Reign of Henry the Second* (1633), bk II, 284–5: "fame, which still depends On others breath"; Cowley, *Life and Fame*, st. 3; Milton, *Par. Reg.*, III 54–5; Pope, *Temple of Fame*, 505.

A thing beyond us, ev'n before our death.
Just what you hear, you have, and what's unknown
The same (my Lord) if Tully's or your own.   240
All that we feel of it begins and ends
In the small circle of our foes or friends;
To all beside as much an empty shade,
An Eugene living, as a Cæsar dead,
Alike or when, or where, they shone, or shine,   245

237–40. Cf. Montaigne, II 485: "It should seem, that to be known, is in some sort to have a Man's Life and its duration in another's keeping. I for my part hold, that I am not but in my self, and of that other Life of mine which lies in the Knowledge of my Friends, . . . I know very well that I am sensible of no Fruit nor Enjoyment, but by the Vanity of a fantastick Opinion; and when I shall be dead, I shall be much less sensible of it; . . ."

239–40. *Spectat.*, 467: "Others have sacrificed themselves for a name which was not to begin till they were dead, giving away themselves to purchase a sound which was not to commence till they were out of hearing"; Blackmore, "On Fame" (*Poems on Various Subjects*, 1718, p. 307):

> Do's *Maro* smile, when we extol his Lays?
> Or *Tully* listen in his Urn to Praise?
> Do Shouts of Triumph soothe great *Caesar's* Ear?
> Or Fame, young *Ammon*, thy cold Ashes cheer?

241–4. Cf. La Rochefoucauld, IV vi: "All this Honour and Reputation which [seekers of fame] look upon as boundless, is yet confined within a little room in their own Imagination. For this crowds all Posterity into one Age, by setting those Men before their Eyes as if they were all present together, which they shall never live to see nor enjoy." Pope to Allen, 24 Nov. 1737: "The only pleasure which any one, either of high or low rank, must depend upon receiving, is in the candour or partiality of friends, and that small circle we are conversant in . . ."

243–4. *as much . . . dead*] I.e. a Eugene living is as much an empty shade as a Caesar dead.

243. *an . . . shade*] Oldham, *Counterpart to the Sat. Against Virtue*, st. 7:

> What art thou, Fame, for which so eagerly we strive?
> What art thou, but an empty shade,
> By the reflection of our actions made?

244. *Eugene*] "Prince Eugene of Savoy [1663–1736], the commander of the Imperial armies in the War of the Spanish Succession and the joint hero with Marlborough of Blenheim and Malplaquet" [Ward]. When this epistle was published, he was, as Morris notes, still commanding in the field, though over seventy.

Or on the Rubicon, or on the Rhine.
A Wit's a feather, and a Chief a rod;
An honest Man's the noblest work of God.
Fame but from death a villain's name can save,
As Justice tears his body from the grave,   250
When what t'oblivion better were resign'd,
Is hung on high, to poison half mankind.

247. "Alluding to the pen with which the wit writes, and the baton or trun-
cheon . . . of the general" [Pattison]. Cf. Sheffield, *Ess. upon Poetry*, l. 40:
"Fancy is but the Feather of the Pen"; Pope to Craggs, 15 July 1715: ". . . these
idle fellows of the feather" [wits].

248. Hurd compares the passage [in the pseudo-Platonic *Minos*, 319a],
where Socrates insists that the good man is the most sacred of all creatures. I am
indebted to my colleague, C. M. Dawson, for helping me to trace this reference.
Ward cites John Fletcher's *An Honest Man's Fortune* [93-4]:

> Man is his own star; and that soul that can
> Be honest is the only perfect man.

Cf. also, La Bruyère, 1 55: "The hero seems only to be a soldier, while the great
man is of all professions, scholar, soldier, statesman, and courtier; put them together, they are not both worth one honest man"; R. Gould, *Satyr upon Man*
(*Poems*, 1689, p. 211).

honest Man] On the concept of *l'honnête homme* in French thought, see H. A.
Grubbs, *Damien Mitton* (1932), ch. VI. The meaning of the phrase in Pope's
context is probably still more comprehensive: cf. Geo. Herbert's definition of the
word in his poem, *Constancie*; W. Charleton's preface to *Epicurus's Morals* (1656):
"Honesty, which comprehends all the Virtues . . ."; Temple, 1 98: "Goodness, is
that which makes Men prefer their Duty and their Promise, before their
Passions, or their Interest; and is properly the Object of Trust: in our Language,
it goes rather by the Name of Honesty; though what we call an Honest Man, the
Romans called a Good Man"; Cumberland, p. 22.

249-52. EC sees an allusion to the exhumation of the Caroline regicides on
30 Jan. 1661, when "their putrid corpses were hung for the day upon a gibbet at
Tyburn." Cf. also, Jonson, *A Little Shrub Growing By*, 1-4:

> Ask not to know this Man. If fame should speak
> His name in any metal, it would break.
> Two letters were enough the plague to tear
> Out of his grave, and poison every ear;

Wm. Dawes, *Of the Right Use, and Abuse, of the Things of this World* (1712), p. 11:
"How *inconsiderable* a *figure* do *such* men generally make, how are they *despis'd*,
or, at best, *hated* and *fear'd*, while they *live*, how *unpity'd* do they *dye*, how do their
name and *memorial*, either *rot* and *perish*, or, which is worse, *stink*, after their
death."

Q

All fame is foreign, but of true desert,
Plays round the head, but comes not to the heart:
One self-approving hour whole years out-weighs   255
Of stupid starers, and of loud huzzas;
And more true joy Marcellus exil'd feels,
Than Cæsar with a senate at his heels.
      In Parts superior what advantage lies?
Tell (for You can) what is it to be wise?   260

254. Cf. J. Sheffield, *Ess. upon Poetry*, l. 18; and Vida's *De arte poet.* in Pitt's translation (1725), III 436–7:

> Unmeaning terms will crowd in every part,
> Play round the ear, but never reach the heart.

Plays . . . head] A twist of Persius' phrase, *Sat.*, I 117: "circum praecordia ludet."

255–6. Aristotle, *Eth. Nic.*, 1169a: "[The good] man would prefer a short period of intense pleasure to a long one of mild enjoyment, a twelve-month of noble life to many years of humdrum existence, and one great and noble action to many trivial ones"; Oldham, *Counterpart to the Sat. against Virtue*, st. 9; *Spectat.*, 172: "Triumph, applause, acclamation, are dear to the mind of man; but it is still a more exquisite delight to say to yourself, you have done well, than to hear the whole human race pronounce you glorious, except you yourself can join with them in your own reflections."

For the phrasing, cf. J. Sheffield, *To a Coquet Beauty*, 21–2:

> One hour of love's delight outweighs
> Whole years of universal praise.

257. "Marcus Marcellus (died B.C. 46) may be ranked with M. Cato as the best and most public spirited of the Pompeian party. After Pharsalus, he withdrew to Mytilene, where he devoted himself to literature and philosophy" [Pattison]. Following a remark of Warton's, of uncertain authority, editors have regularly applied the allusion to the Duke of Ormond, a Jacobite leader, who fled at the death of Anne to the Pretender's court and spent the rest of his life in exile. Thompson, on the other hand, applies the allusion to Bolingbroke. There seems no cogent reason for either application.

258. Cf. Shaks., *Jul. Caes.*, II iv 35–6: "The throng that follows Caesar at the heels, Of senators, of praetors".

259ff. 7. SUPERIOR PARTS. [P. *1735b–43a*.]
Prior, III 343–6:

> Avails it then, O reason, to be wise?
> To see this cruel scene with quicker eyes?
> To know with more distinction to complain
> And have superior sense in feeling pain?

260. *You*] I.e. Bolingbroke.

'Tis but to know how little can be known;
To see all others faults, and feel our own:
Condemn'd in bus'ness or in arts to drudge
Without a second, or without a judge:
Truths would you teach, or save a sinking land?   265
All fear, none aid you, and few understand.
Painful preheminence! yourself to view
Above life's weakness, and its comforts too.

Bring then these blessings to a strict account,
Make fair deductions, see to what they mount.   270
How much of other each is sure to cost;
How each for other oft is wholly lost;
How inconsistent greater goods with these;

---

261. Cf. II 43ff.

263. *drudge*] Applicable to Pope's career as translator and editor, 1715-25.

264. Compare Pope's remark (Spence, p. 170): "When a man is much above the rank of men, who can he have to converse with?" Spence adds that Pope had been speaking of Bacon and Bolingbroke.

265-6. EC applies the lines to Bolingbroke's labours on behalf of the Opposition.

266. Pattison notes that this is the constant complaint of Marcus Aurelius [cf. VIII xlii-xlv, xlix, li, liii, etc.].

267-8. Cf. Thos. Southerne, *The Loyal Brother*, III ii:
                    What is't to be a Prince?
          To have a keener sense of our misfortunes:
          That's all our wretched gain.

267. *Painful preheminence*] Cf. Addison, *Cato*, III v 23 [Carruthers].

269-70. Cowley, *The Complaint*, st. 3:
                    Go, Renegado, cast up thy Account,
                    And see to what Amount
                    Thy foolish gains . . .;
Pope to Cromwell, 27 Apr. 1708: "But perhaps you will say, the whole world has something to do, something to talk of, something to wish for, something to be employed about: but pray, sir, cast up the account, put all these somethings together, and what is the sum total but just nothing?"

271. Jer. Collier, "Of Religious Temper", in his *Ess. upon Sev. Moral Subjects*, IV (1709) 98: "The Possession of an Object does not make it Eligible, if any ill Consequence hangs upon it. Before we determine our Choice we should look forward to the Issue, and compute upon the Profit and Loss."

273-6. La Bruyère, I 135: "Let us not envy some men their accumulated

How sometimes life is risq'd, and always ease:
Think, and if still the things thy envy call,   275
Say, would'st thou be the Man to whom they fall?
To sigh for ribbands if thou art so silly,
Mark how they grace Lord Umbra, or Sir Billy:
Is yellow dirt the passion of thy life?
Look but on Gripus, or on Gripus' wife: 280
If Parts allure thee, think how Bacon shin'd,
The wisest, brightest, meanest of mankind:

281 Bacon] Wh** *1734a*.
282 The wisest, brightest, meanest] Wh**, the Shame and
    Scandal *1734a*.

---

riches . . .; we could not sacrifice, as they do, health, quiet, honour, and conscience to obtain them: it is to pay so dear for them that the bargain is a loss";
Thos. Chubb, *Tracts* (1730), p. 446; Swift, IV 207–8: "Would any of you, who
are in health and strength of body, with moderate food and raiment earned by
your own labour, rather choose to be in the rich man's bed, under the torture of
the gout, unable to take your natural rest, or natural nourishment, with the
additional load of a guilty conscience, reproaching you for injustice, oppres-
sions, covetousness, and fraud?"

277. *ribbands*] Cf. IV 205.

278. *Lord Umbra*] Cf. the "empty shade" of IV 243.

Sir Billy] Elwin applies the name to Sir William Yonge (d. 1755; see vol. IV,
Biog. App.), of whom Lord Hervey wrote (*Memoirs*, ed. Sidgwick, 1931, I 36):
"Without having done anything that I know of remarkably profligate . . . his
name was proverbially used to express everything pitiful, corrupt, and contemptible." Pope uses the same sobriquet in the *Epilogue to the Satires* (Dial.
I 13), probably with Yonge in mind, but in the present context there seems no
need to particularize the reference.

279. *yellow dirt*] Shaks., *Cymbeline*, III vi 54:
                    All gold and silver rather turn to dirt!
                    As 'tis no better reckon'd, but of those
                    Who worship dirty gods;
Jonson, *The Case Is Altered*, IV ix: "Gold is but mucke."

280. "The name Gripus translated that [more correctly, parallels the sense]
of Harpagon, the hero of Molière's *L'Avare*. Gripe is a character in Vanbrugh's
Confederacy, whose wife spends his money" [Ward].

281–2. *Wh*** (cf. textual notes)] Philip, Duke of Wharton (1698–1731),
whose scandalous career is the subject of *Mor. Ess.*, I 180ff.

282. *meanest*] H. K. Baker argues in *Pope and Bacon: The Meaning of "Meanest"*
(repr. from *Baconiana*, Jan. 1937), that "meanest" is not to be taken pejora-

Or ravish'd with the whistling of a Name,
See Cromwell, damn'd to everlasting fame!
If all, united, thy ambition call,   285
From ancient story learn to scorn them all.
There, in the rich, the honour'd, fam'd and great,
See the false scale of Happiness complete!
In hearts of Kings, or arms of Queens who lay,
How happy! those to ruin, these betray,   290
Mark by what wretched steps their glory grows,
From dirt and sea-weed as proud Venice rose;
In each how guilt and greatness equal ran,
And all that rais'd the Hero, sunk the Man.

---

tively. But cf. the leader in *The London Journal*, 1 July 1732 (repr. in *Gent. Mag.*, II, 1732, 833): "What is call'd Learning . . . is not at all necessary to form a *Great Man*: He may be *Great* without any of [the arts and sciences], and *Mean* with them all. Lord Bacon, tho' *cover'd with Learning*, so cover'd that his *Sense* could not many times be seen thro' it, was one of the *meanest* Men in the World; *vicious* in Prosperity, and an *abject Coward* in Adversity."

283. Hurd compares Cowley's line [72] in his translation of Virgil's *O fortunatos nimium* [*Geo.*, II 458*ff*]: "Charm'd with the foolish whistlings of a Name".

284. *damn'd . . . fame*] By the praise received during his ascendancy, as well as by his after-reputation in Pope's day: cf. R. Gould, *Prologue* (*Poems*, 1689, p. 133):

> If to be prais'd does give a man pretence
> To Glory, Honour, Honesty and Sense,
> Cromwell had much to say in his defence.

Wakefield compares the phrase used of the bad poet in Roscommon's *Ess. on Trans. Verse* [78]: "Condemn'd to Live to all succeeding Times", and the phrase applied to Perrault in a MS. variant of *E. on C.* (EC, II 40 *n.* 5): "damned to fame".

285. *all*] The worldly goods dealt with separately above, 185*ff*, 275*ff*.

288. *scale*] Ladder: cf. *steps* in 291.

290. "I.e. what a form their happiness took, consisting in ruining the kings who trusted and [betraying] the queens who loved them" [Thompson].

291-308. For a MS. revision and expansion of these lines, applying them to Marlborough, see EC, III 87-8 and frontispiece. The printed leaf on which Pope has entered these alterations is now in the possession of the Yale University library.

293-4. The general figure seems to be that of a pulley-well, the elements of the life of grandeur being compared first to its contents and next to its mechanism (of ascending and descending receptacles).

Now Europe's laurels on their brows behold,   295
But stain'd with blood, or ill exchang'd for gold,
Then see them broke with toils, or sunk in ease,
Or infamous for plunder'd provinces.
Oh wealth ill-fated! which no act of fame
E'er taught to shine, or sanctify'd from shame!   300
What greater bliss attends their close of life?
Some greedy minion, or imperious wife,
The trophy'd arches, story'd halls invade,
And haunt their slumbers in the pompous shade.
Alas! not dazzled with their noon-tide ray,   305
Compute the morn and ev'ning to the day;
The whole amount of that enormous fame,

---

297 sunk] lost *1734–35a*.

297–300. Cf. Pope to Martha Blount, 22 June [1722]: "When I have been describing his agreeable seat [Digby's: cf. IV 103–6], I cannot make the reflection I have often done upon contemplating the beautiful villas of other noblemen, raised upon the spoils of plundered nations, or aggrandized by the wealth of the public. I cannot ask myself the question, 'What else has this man to be liked? What else has he cultivated or improved? What good, or what desirable thing appears of him, without these walls?'"

299–300. Cf. Dryden, *To my . . . kinsman, John Driden*, 38–9:
> For God, who gave the riches, gave the heart
> To sanctify the whole, by giving part.

which . . . shine] Wakefield compares Horace, *Od.*, II ii 1*ff*:
> Nullus argento color est . . .
>   nisi temperato
> Splendeat usu.

304. Wakefield compares Horace, *Od.*, II xvi 9–12. For the image, compare the prince's words in Southerne's *The Loyal Brother*, III ii:
> The vulgar think us happy; and, at a distance,
> Like some fam'd ruinous pile, we seem to flourish:
> But we, who live at home, alone can tell
> The sad disquiets and decays of peace,
> That always haunt the dwelling.

pompous shade] Wakefield notes that the phrase appears in Addison's [?] *The Play-House*, 4.

307. *enormous*] Cf. III 242.

A Tale, that blends their glory with their shame!
   VII. Know then this truth (enough for Man to know)
"Virtue alone is Happiness below."   310
The only point where human bliss stands still,
And tastes the good without the fall to ill;

---

310 *1735b–51 emphasize the line with quotation marks.*

---

308. *Tale*] "Tally", as well as "story": cf. "compute" in 306.

309*ff.* That VIRTUE only constitutes a Happiness, whose Object is *Universal*, and whose Prospect *Eternal*. [P. *1735b–43a.*]

310. Cf. IV 168*n* (Seneca); Juvenal, *Sat.*, x 364, in Henry Vaughan's translation, 549: "Virtue alone can make a happy life"; and cf. Claudian's panegyric of Manlius Theodorus, 1–6 (*Ipsa quidem Virtus pretium sibi*, etc.).

Virtue] What Pope (and many writers of his time) mean by "virtue" in this kind of context can be gathered from Burton, pp. 101–2: ". . . an universal Benevolence, that's Vertue; and a Benevolence to Mankind, that's Charity: So that as it is the same water that washes on the *English* and *Spanish* shores, and from them receives different Names; so it is the same Vertue that makes us love other Men, which makes us love our selves, and God, and all his Creatures. . ." R. S. Crane has shown in an important article ("Suggestions toward a Genealogy of the 'Man of Feeling'," *ELH* I (1934) 205*ff*) that in the sermons of the later seventeenth and early eighteenth centuries virtue is regularly identified with benevolence.

311–12. I Cor., XIII 8: "Charity never faileth: but whether there be prophecies, they shall fail; whether there be tongues they shall cease; whether there be knowledge, it shall vanish away"; Prior, *Charity*, 27*ff*:

> Each other gift, which God on man bestows,
> Its proper bounds, and due restriction knows;
> To one fixt purpose dedicates its power;
> And, finishing its act, exists no more.
> Thus, in obedience to what Heaven decrees,
> Knowledge shall fail, and prophecy shall cease;
> But lasting Charity's more ample sway,
> Nor bound by time, nor subject to decay,
> In happy triumph shall for ever live,
> And endless good diffuse, and endless praise receive.

311. "The allusion here seems to be to the pole, or central point, of a spherical body: which, during the rotatory motion of every other part, continues immovable and at rest" [Wakefield]. If Wakefield is right, the "spherical body" is perhaps the wheel of fortune. But cf. 312*n.*

312. A reference to Eden may hover in the background here: cf. *taste* and *fall*, and the quotation from Bacon at 317*n.*

Where only Merit constant pay receives,
Is blest in what it takes, and what it gives;
The joy unequal'd, if its end it gain,   315
And if it lose, attended with no pain:
Without satiety, tho' e'er so blest,
And but more relish'd as the more distress'd:
The broadest mirth unfeeling Folly wears,

313–14. I.e. the only point where merit uninterruptedly receives its reward, in the recipient bringing the happiness of receiving, in the giver the happiness of giving. On the role of merit in the recipient, see Wm. Fleetwood, *Sermon Preached . . . the 25th of March, 1689* (1689), pp. 7–8: ". . . the works of Charity are . . . acceptable both to God and Man, when exercis'd on those that *only want*. . . But when both Want and Merit meet, the Practice of the Grace is . . . more agreeable to God and Man. It is a complicated act of Goodness then, it is approving and rewarding Virtue, encouraging the merits of the Receiver, as well as pitying and relieving his Distress."

314. EC compares Shakespeare on mercy in *Merch. of Ven.*, IV i [184–5]. Cf. also, Pope's description of Arete, queen of the Phaeacians, in his *Odyssey*, VII 96: "In virtue rich; in blessing others, blest"; Prior's description of charity in *Charity*, 61: "For ever blessing, for ever blest"; and Chudleigh, *Ess.*, p. 99.

315–16. Essentially the argument of the *pari* or wager emphasized by Pascal: cf. L. Blanchet, "L'attitude religieuse des jésuites et les sources du pari de Pascal", *Revue de métaphysique et de morale*, XXVI (1919), 477ff, 617ff. Adaptations and variations of it may be found in Denham, *Of Old Age*, 699–704; Dryden, *Don Sebast.*, I i; Wm. Dawes, *Anat. of Atheism* (1693), p. 21; *Spectat.*, 143.

317. Cf. Bacon, *Adv. of Learning*, II xxii 15: ". . . all other excellencies, though they advance nature, yet they are subject to excess; only charity admitteth no excess: for so we see, aspiring to be like God in power, the angels transgressed and fell; . . . by aspiring to be like God in knowledge, man transgressed and fell; . . . but by aspiring to a similitude of God in goodness or love, neither man nor angel ever transgressed or shall transgress" (and cf. his essay, *Of Goodness and Goodness of Nature*). In directing man's energies from knowledge and power to love, Bacon states a theme analogous to Pope's: cf. I 125ff and IV 73–6.

318. Seneca, *De benef.*, IV 21 (*Wks.*, tr. Lodge, 1614, p. 78): "And albeit she [virtue] perceiue, that her faithfulnesse beare the punishment of perfidiousnes, yet she abateth no whit of her courage, neither is abashed thereat, but standeth still aloft aboue her punishment"; La Bruyère, II 49: "Virtue has that happiness in it, to be its own reward and support . . .; the want of assistance and applause, so far from injuring it, strengthens, purifies, and renders it more perfect; whether in or out of Fashion it is still virtue."

319–20. Cf. Cicero, *De fin.*, II xx 65: "Non enim hilaritate, nec lascivia, nec visu aut ioco, comite levitatis, saepe etiam tristes firmitate et constantia sunt

Less pleasing far than Virtue's very tears.   320
Good, from each object, from each place acquir'd,
For ever exercis'd, yet never tir'd;
Never elated, while one man's oppress'd;
Never dejected, while another's bless'd;
And where no wants, no wishes can remain,   325

---

beati"; Pope to Bethel, 24 June 1727: "[Offices of benevolence] often afford the
highest pleasure; . . . At the same time it must be owned, one meets with cruel
disappointments in seeing so often the best endeavours ineffectual to make
others happy. . . But still, I affirm, those very disappointments of a virtuous
man are greater pleasures than the utmost gratifications and successes of a mere
self-lover."

321. Cf. Pope to Bethel, 9 Aug. 1726; *Misc. Thoughts* (EC, x 556): "A good-
natur'd man has the whole world to be happy out of: whatever good befals his
species, a well-deserving person promoted, a modest man advanc'd, an indigent
one relieved, all this he looks upon but as a remoter blessing of Providence on
himself; which then seems to make him amends for the narrowness of his own
fortune, when it does the same thing he would have done had it been in his
power. . ."; Geo. Lyttelton, *To my Lord Hervey. In the Year 1730*, 44–53; E. Young,
Vindic. of Prov. (2nd ed., 1728), p. 44.

322. So of "virtue" in Orrery's *Black Prince*, v i 135–6:
        'Tis onely Sin not suffering that it fears,
        It grows the stronger, the more weight it bears;
and cf. R. Grove, *Profitable Charity* (1695), p. 15: ". . . Charity shut up within our
own Breasts, languishes and decays and comes to nothing; but when we give it
Vent by frequent exercise, it feeds it self by being spent . . ."

323–4. Cf. 1 Cor., xii 26: "And whether one member suffer, all the members
suffer with it; or one member be honoured, all the members rejoice with it";
Thos. Whincoop, *Spittle Sermon Preached . . . April 23, 1701* (1701), p. 6: "According to this Description then [of charity], we are obliged to all mutual Offices of
tender concern for another's good, and endeavouring to promote it always, in
being heartily compassionate towards all the Evils another suffers, and rejoycing
in the good things He is partaker of . . ."

324. Cf. 1 Cor., xiii 4: ". . . charity envieth not . . ."; Burton, p. 139:
"Again, The Charitable Man, he that hath Universal good Will, accounts that
Good which is so to others, though he himself hath no share in it; and so can be
pleas'd with another Man's Welfare, which an uncharitable and envious Soul
is tormented with."

325–6. Seneca, *Ep.*, lxxxix 8: ". . . ad virtutem venitur per ipsam"; Wm.
Fleetwood, *Sermon Preached . . . the 25th of March, 1689* (1689), p. 5: "There is that
sweetness and complacency in doing good, that even the bare desires and

Since but to wish more Virtue, is to gain.
See! the sole bliss Heav'n could on all bestow;
Which who but feels can taste, but thinks can know:
Yet poor with fortune, and with learning blind,
The bad must miss; the good, untaught, will find;   330
Slave to no sect, who takes no private road,
But looks thro' Nature, up to Nature's God;

wishes of it, when it is beyond our power to do it, give us a good degree of peace and quiet and content within . . ."

326. Cf. Robt. Baron, "Fortune's Tennis-Ball", st. 145 (in his *Pocula Castalia* (1650)):

> What though he nor rewards nor knows my pain?
> In vertuous Acts the very doing's gain.

327ff. That the *Perfection* of *Happiness* consists in a *Conformity* to the *Order* of *Providence* here, and a *Resignation* to it, here and hereafter. [P. *1735b–43a*.]

On the general thesis of this verse paragraph and its relation to the next, cf. Burton, p. 137: "But all Goods will not give this Pleasure, but rather disquiet us after they are gone; only the good use of our selves, vertuous Resolves and Performances, and especially the Acts of Charity and Benevolence; these are not only pleasant whilst they are, but afterwards the remembrance of them is full of Delight.

"Nor yet is this all the Pleasure we have from them, for they fill us with lively and good Hopes. The loving Soul feels it self in so excellent a State, that it knows certainly this must be the State of God himself, that he must love, and then he must love those that are so like him. Besides, he knows that Love to men is the most effectual way to engage their Love to Him. No Man can lightly hate him that loves him; and by this means he's filled with the joys of Hope: the probable expectation that it shall go well with him amongst Men, and in this World, is pleasant to him; But the Perswasion he hath of the Love of God, and the Happiness of Heaven, this is Joy unspeakable."

327. Cf. iv 61ff.

328. Cf. iv 32. Aristotle, *Eth. Nic.*, 1120b: "There is . . . nothing to prevent the man who gives less from being the more liberal man, if he has less to give"; Charleton, p. 174; Pope to Trumbull, 12 March 1713: "As in the next world, so in this, the only solid blessings are owing to the goodness of the mind, not the extent of the capacity . . ."; to Broome, 10 Nov. 1725 and 4 Dec. 1724; *Guardian*, 166: "The poor man who has this excellent frame of mind, is no less intitled to the reward of this virtue than the man who founds a college."

331. Cf. iii 305ff.

332–4. Cf. Spenser, *Hymn to Heavenly Beauty*, 22ff; Bacon, *Adv. of Learning*, 1 i 3; Prior, 1 407–13, 625–46; Chudleigh, *Ess.*, p. 9: ". . . by contemplating the Effects, we shall rise to the Cause, and by considering that wonderful, that

Pursues that Chain which links th'immense design,
Joins heav'n and earth, and mortal and divine;
Sees, that no being any bliss can know,   335
But touches some above, and some below;
Learns, from this union of the rising Whole,
The first, last purpose of the human soul;
And knows where Faith, Law, Morals, all began,
All end, in LOVE of GOD, and LOVE of MAN.   340
    For him alone, Hope leads from goal to goal,
And opens still, and opens on his soul,
'Till lengthen'd on to Faith, and unconfin'd,

amazing Power, that inimitable Wisdom, that admirable Beauty, that trans-
porting Harmony, and that immutable Order, which at first discover'd themselves in the formation of the Universe, and are still every where visible in it, we
shall be led to their Divine Original ..."

339–40. Cf. III 157–318; Matt., XXII 37–40; Tyrrell, *A brief Disquisition of the
Law of Nat.* (1701), p. 24: ". . . under this general Rule of endeavouring the
common Good of Rational Beings, or Universal Benevolence, is contained Piety
towards God, and the highest Goodwill or Charity towards Men, and is the
Summ both of the Moral Law of *Moses*, and of the Gospel of our Saviour
Jesus Christ"; Pope to Atterbury, 20 Nov. 1717.

340–1. The connection of ideas in the two paragraphs is perhaps the theological principle that "by charity man is strengthened in hope" (Aquinas, *Sum.
c. gent.*, III cliii).

341–52. "On the present occasion, the poet unites the deductions of philosophy with the promises of revelation. Faith in bliss unknown alludes to 1 Cor.,
II 9: 'Eye hath not seen, nor ear heard, neither have entered into the heart of
man, the things which God hath prepared for them that love him'" [Roscoe].
But it would be more exact to say that Pope chose his language to *remind* his
reader of Revelation. The only faith he could explicitly acknowledge within the
terms of his poem (cf. I 73–4n) was one that "nature plants" (345). An analogous argument, like Pope's not based on Revelation but cognizant of it, is made
by Burton, pp. 105–6: "And when this good Man's Soul goes out into the
heartiest desires and endeavours for the greatest Good of Men; and he wishes
far more than he can do for them; this lays a firm Foundation of Hope in God . . .
    "He knows that Love which makes him weep over a dying Man, if it was in
conjunction with Power would give him his life again; and he believes that
God's love is not less than his; and therefore he hath hopes of a Resurrection."

341. I.e. from such objectives as are represented in Ep. II and III (through the
extension of self-love into *caritas*) to those represented here: cf. II 274, 285, III 145,
with I 91*ff* and this passage.

It pours the bliss that fills up all the mind.
He sees, why Nature plants in Man alone   345
Hope of known bliss, and Faith in bliss unknown:
(Nature, whose dictates to no other kind
Are giv'n in vain, but what they seek they find)
Wise is her present; she connects in this
His greatest Virtue with his greatest Bliss,   350
At once his own bright prospect to be blest,
And strongest motive to assist the rest.
    Self-love thus push'd to social, to divine,
Gives thee to make thy neighbour's blessing thine.
Is this too little for the boundless heart?   355

349 her] the *1734–34b, 1735b–43a*.

347–8. A traditional argument for immortality based ultimately on the axiom, *Natura nihil facit frustra*. For typical expressions of it, cf. Charron, *De la sagesse*, I vii; F. Gastrell, *Cert. and Necess. of Relig. in General* (1697), p. 143: "... 't would be more agreeable to all the Notions we have of God, and all the Observations we have made upon his other Works, to suppose that, had *this Life* been the Extent of Mans *Being* and *Happiness*, God would not have given him a sense or prospect of *any other* . . ."; *Guardian*, 27; *Spectat.*, 210.

349–52. Cf. III 315–8. Pope to Trumbull, 12 Mar. 1713: "... friendship here is an emanation from the same source as beatitude is there: the same benevolence and grateful disposition that qualifies us for the one, if extended farther, makes us partakers of the other"; Z. Isham, *Sermon Preached . . . on Wednesday in Easter Week*, MDCC (1700), p. 24: "... But in *giving* to the poor, and calamitous, there is a much better Prospect. For both the Action it self is highly vertuous, . . . And there is moreover a great Reward grounded upon the Promises of God, to excite us to Works of Mercy"; *London Journal*, 29 Jan. 1732.

350. *His . . . Virtue*] Pope to Caryll, 18 June 1711: "To relieve the injured— if you will pardon a poetical expression in prose—is no less than to take the work of God himself off his hands, and an easing Providence of its care. It is the noblest act that human nature is capable of . . ."

353*ff.* Cf. Seneca, *Ep.*, VI 6: "Qui sibi amicus est, scito hunc amicum omnibus esse"; Aquinas, *Sum. c. gent.*, III cliii: ". . . a man through having an affection for his own good, is led to have an affection for another's good"; Burton, p. 51: "This Self-love, tho' occasionally and by accident it may hinder Love to others, as it's excessive, and too much confines our Thoughts to one thing; yet the genuine and more natural Off-spring of it, is Love to others; for he that loves one Man, how can he but love another that's like him? If the Objects are alike, the Acts that are about them must be so too."

Extend it, let thy enemies have part:
Grasp the whole worlds of Reason, Life, and Sense,
In one close system of Benevolence:
Happier as kinder, in whate'er degree,
And height of Bliss but height of Charity.   360
    God loves from Whole to Parts: but human soul
Must rise from Individual to the Whole.
Self-love but serves the virtuous mind to wake,

---

356. Cf. Matt., v 43–4.

357–8. Cf. Dryden, *1 Conq. of Granada*, i i: "charity Should even to birds and beasts extended be;" John Maxwell's notes to his translation of Cumberland, p. 302: Pope, *Guardian*, 61 (quoting Plutarch's Life of Cato): "It is no more than the obligation of our very birth to practise equity to our own kind; but humanity may be extended through the whole order of creatures, even to the meanest."

357. I.e. creatures with life only; creatures with feeling or "sense"—as animals; and creatures with reason—as men and angels. Cf. *Par. Lost*, ix 112–13: "creatures animate with gradual life Of growth, sense, reason, all summed up in Man."

359–60. Cf. Wm. Fleetwood, *Sermon Preached . . . at . . . Christ-Church Hospital* (1691), pp. 5–6, *Sermon Preached . . . March 25, 1689* (1689), p. 2; J. Lambe, *Sermon Preached . . . Apr. 22, 1701* (1701), p. 22: "We are not . . . more obliged to Liberality by *Duty* than by *Interest*. We are not more excited thereunto by *Gratitude* than by *Pleasure*, by the most *Exquisite Pleasure* that we are capable of, or can conceive."

361–2. Cumberland, p. 210: "Nay, we seem *first* to know and love *Man*, before the Mind raises it-self to the knowledge and love of *God*, whose *Being*, and amiable Goodness are *discovered* from his *Works*, and chiefly from *Man*"; Pope to Martha Blount [20 Aug. 1716]; and to Swift, 15 Oct. 1725: ". . . I think the way to have a public spirit is first to have a private one; for who can believe . . . that any man can care for a hundred thousand people who never cared for one?"

363. Cf. Cumberland, p. 215: ". . . to study, and *endeavour after the Common Good* of all Rational Beings, superadds to the attempts of an Innocent Self-love, many noble Actions in favour of Objects like our-selves, and thereby begets and compleats a *Habit of Love towards Mankind*, of which Philanthropy the Love of our-selves is but a small Portion"; *Guardian*, 83: "There is hardly a spirit upon earth so mean and contracted, as to centre all regards on its own interest, exclusive of the rest of mankind (cf. *Ess.*, iv 39ff]. Even the selfish man has some share of love, which he bestows on his family and his friends. A nobler mind hath at heart the common interest of society or country of which he makes a part. And there is still a more diffusive spirit, whose being or intentions reach the whole mass of mankind, and are continued beyond the present age, to a succession of future generations."

As the small pebble stirs the peaceful lake;
The centre mov'd, a circle strait succeeds,   365
Another still, and still another spreads,
Friend, parent, neighbour, first it will embrace,
His country next, and next all human race,
Wide and more wide, th'o'erflowings of the mind
Take ev'ry creature in, of ev'ry kind;   370
Earth smiles around, with boundless bounty blest,
And Heav'n beholds its image in his breast.
    Come then, my Friend, my Genius, come along,
Oh master of the poet, and the song!
And while the Muse now stoops, or now ascends,   375
To Man's low passions, or their glorious ends,

364-6. The image (though not the application to self-love) occurs in Chaucer, *House of Fame*, II 280*ff*; Shaks., *1 Hen. VI* I ii 133-5; Marvell, *First Anniv. of the Govt. under O.C.*, 1*ff*; and Pope, *Temple of Fame*, 436*ff*, *Dunc.* A, II 373*ff*. In Donne's *Love's Growth*, 21*ff*, it is used in a context suggestive of Pope's:

> If, as in water stir'd more circles bee
> Produced by one, love such additions take,
> Those like so many spheares, but one heaven make,
> For, they are all concentrique unto thee.

367-8. Wakefield compares Waller, *Of Divine Love* [249-52]:

> Love as He loved! A love so unconfin'd
> With arms extended, would embrace mankind.
> Self-love would cease, or be dilated, when
> We should behold as many selfs as men.

Cf. also, Jos. Hall, *Solil.*, XXVII (in his *Wks.*, III, 1662, 432); and the extract from one of Pope's letters to Allen (EC,IX 199-200): "I can pray for no greater blessing for a friend, than that he may love his own home, his own family, and next his neighbour; . . . yet consider the *whole world* as his relations, though more distant."

369-70. Cf. the passage quoted from *Guardian*, 61, above, 357-8*n*. The next sentence of that passage runs: "Such actions of charity are the overflowings of a mild good-nature on all below us."

372. Cf. Introd., pp. lxii-lxiii. Also, Burton, p. 155; Wm. Fleetwood, *Sermon Preached . . . Mar. 25, 1689* (1689), p. 3; R. Grove, *Profitable Charity* (1695), p. 5: "This extensive and universal Charity is the very Temper of Heaven, the Image of the Divinity."

376. *Man's . . . passions*] E.g. II 217*ff*; III 241*ff*; IV 173*ff*.
    their . . . ends] E.g., II 249*ff*; III 119*ff*; 269*ff*; IV 309*ff*.

Teach me, like thee, in various nature wise,
To fall with dignity, with temper rise;
Form'd by thy converse, happily to steer
From grave to gay, from lively to severe;   380
Correct with spirit, eloquent with ease,
Intent to reason, or polite to please.
Oh! while along the stream of Time thy name
Expanded flies, and gathers all its fame,
Say, shall my little bark attendant sail,   385
Pursue the triumph, and partake the gale?
When statesmen, heroes, kings, in dust repose,
Whose sons shall blush their fathers were thy foes,
Shall then this verse to future age pretend

387–88 *Om.* (*cf. Griffith, p. 281*) *1734–34a, 1735a.*
389 Shall then] And shall *1734–34a, 1735a.*

379–80. *Adventurer* compares Boileau [*Art poet.*, I 75–6]; and Wakefield, the Dryden and Soames translation:

> Happy, who in his verse can gently steer
> From grave to light, from pleasant to severe!

And cf. Quintilian's characterization of Homer, quoted by Pope in his *Il.*, I 59*n*: "Idem laetus et pressus, jucundus et gravis"; and Mallet's *Of Verbal Criticism* (1733), p. 9: "Grave with Agrippa, with Maecenas gay".

379*ff*. Modelled on Horace, *Sat.*, I x 9–14, the motto subsequently chosen for the title page of *Epistles to Several Persons*, 1744, *q.v.*, vol. III, pt. ii. I owe the observation to Mr Bateson.

381. Mallet, *Of Verbal Criticism* (1733), p. 9:

> Horace, who form'd in palaces to please,
> Mix'd mirth with morals; eloquence with ease.

383–6. A blending of two images from Statius, *Silvae*, I iv 120–2 [Hurd]:

> ... immensae veluti conexa carinae
> cumba minor, cum saevit hiems, pro parte furentis
> parva receptat aquas et eodem volvitur austro;

and v i 242–6:

> sic, ubi magna novum Phario de litore puppis
> solvit iter ...
> lataque veliferi porrexit brachia mali
> invasitque vias, it eodem angusta phaselos
> aequore et immensi partem sibi vindicat austri.

389. *pretend*] In the Latin sense: stretch out before, i.e. proclaim.

Thou wert my guide, philosopher, and friend?   390
That urg'd by thee, I turn'd the tuneful art
From sounds to things, from fancy to the heart;
For Wit's false mirror held up Nature's light;
Shew'd erring Pride, WHATEVER IS, IS RIGHT;
That REASON, PASSION, answer one great aim;   395
That true SELF-LOVE and SOCIAL are the same;
That VIRTUE only makes our Bliss below;
And all our Knowledge is, OURSELVES TO KNOW.

393. Cf. III 231.

394–8. Summaries of I–IV, the final line echoing the opening of the argument (I 17ff) and the principle of religious humility on which the whole is based: "Be lowly wise: Think only what concerns thee and thy being." (*Par. Lost*, VIII 173–4).

APPENDIXES

APPENDIX A

THE *ESSAY ON MAN* AND BOLINGBROKE'S *FRAGMENTS*

The internal evidence for believing that Bolingbroke's *Fragments or Minutes of Essays* were composed later than the *Essay on Man*—the evidence is confirmatory, not conclusive—may be summed up as follows:

1. The *Fragments* contain several references to works published after 1731. One may argue that such allusions were inserted at a later time, but the *Fragments* show few signs of having been reworked.

2. The *Fragments* are pretty clearly (with perhaps an exception here and there) printed in the order of composition, each discussion growing out of and referring to the one before. The subject of the first is Cudworth's *Treatise of Eternal and Immutable Morality*, not published till December 1730 (*Monthly Chronicle*, III 248), which Bolingbroke says Pope sent him "long ago". Considering this phrase, and allowing time for Pope to learn of the treatise, to read it himself, and to send it on to his friend, one can hardly suppose that Bolingbroke is writing much earlier than summer of 1731, or about the time when Pope had nearly finished. (Pope had been working on the *Essay* since November 1729: see above, p. xiii.)

3. In the same fragment, Bolingbroke speaks of having already written to Pope on the subject of human knowledge. Unless this is a reference to a writing now unknown, the work meant must be the first of Bolingbroke's four long essays, entitled "On Human Knowledge", which from internal evidence cannot be dated earlier than 1732.

4. A large number of the parallels usually cited from Bolingbroke are concentrated in fragments XLII–LVII. The concatenation of the argument here is close, and though certainty is impossible, one would say that all these fragments were written at a blow. Since fragment LIV alludes to Pope's character of the Man of Ross (in *Moral Essay* III), about whose life the poet was first inquiring of Jacob Tonson in the autumn of 1731 (EC IX 550), the probability is that this whole series of fragments is later than the near-completion of the *Essay on Man* in August, 1731.

APPENDIX B

POPE'S MS. NOTE ON *ESSAY ON MAN*,
III 303-4

An apparently earlier and rejected draft of the note given above (p. 124) is contained in Brit. Mus. Egerton MS. 1950, fol. 8. I transcribe below (again from a photographic reproduction lent me by Mr Sherburn) the final text of the draft, omitting a few phrasal variants that Pope has crossed out.

"I do not say *that Form*, but *that Government*; the *Form* may be better, but the *Government* is not, of that which is worse administred. To force it therefore to mean what I did not mean you must destroy ye Grammatical construction, which w^d be, in that sense, *Those* [i.e. *Forms*] w^{ch} *are* best administred, *are* best. My meaning is, that it is to no more purpose to wrangle in ye Speculation what *Form* of Government is best, unless it be well & uprightly administred, than to dispute what mode of Faith is so, unless we practise w^t it teaches. No Form & no mode whatever but prescribes enough to render people moral & happy, if duly executed & practised; & the Best Form of ye one, or mode of ye other, is not sufficient to those Ends, if ill executed or practised.

"There is a passage in Sir W. Temple's Essay on Government, very much of ye same nature: his words are, (pag 83. 8°)." For Temple's words, see the notes at *Essay*, III 303-4.

INDEX